DEADLY PATHS

A BRUTAL **MURDER.**

A COP ON THE **EDGE.**

DEADLY PATHS

A BRUTAL **MURDER.**

A COP ON THE **EDGE.**

BIG SKY PUBLISHING

www.bigskypublishing.com.au

PETER SEYMOUR WITH JASON K. FOSTER

Big Sky Publishing Pty Ltd
PO Box 303, Newport, NSW 2106, Australia
Phone: 1300 364 611
Fax: (61 2) 9918 2396
Email: info@bigskypublishing.com.au
Web: www.bigskypublishing.com.au

Cover design and typesetting: Think Productions
Printed in China by Asia Pacific Offset Ltd.

National Library of Australia Cataloguing-in-Publication entry (pbk)
Title: Deadly paths : a brutal murder. A cop on the edge / Peter Seymour with Jason K. Foster.
ISBN: 9781922132406 (paperback)
Subjects: Hanes, Nick.
          Seymour, Peter
          Murder--New South Wales--Sydney--Case studies.
          Murder--Investigation--New South Wales--Sydney.
          Post-traumatic stress disorder.
Other Authors/Contributors: Foster, Jason K., author.
Dewey Number: 364.152309944

National Library of Australia Cataloguing-in-Publication entry (ebook)
Title: Deadly paths : a brutal murder. A cop on the edge / Peter Seymour with Jason K. Foster.
ISBN: 9781922132413 (ebook)
Subjects: Hanes, Nick.
          Seymour, Peter
          Murder--New South Wales--Sydney--Case studies.
          Murder--Investigation--New South Wales--Sydney.
          Post-traumatic stress disorder.
Other Authors/Contributors: Foster, Jason K., author.
Dewey Number: 364.152309944

This is dedicated to my dad, John Seymour –
a tremendous father, a great mate, my mentor, my inspiration.

And to my father-in-law, Ted Kneale –
a dedicated family man, a mate and an inspiration
to his children and grandchildren.

The following story is based on actual events; however, certain names have been changed to protect the innocent and shield the guilty.

CONTENTS

Chapter 1:
The Hardest Part

March 2000

The hardest part of being a policeman was seeing someone you were sure was guilty walk free, to see the victims distraught because of a complete and utter travesty of justice. That was why I did my job; to be the guy who did the right thing by good people, to try to bring some balance to the world when evil seemed to be taking over.

Thomas Andrew Keir had walked free after allegedly killing his second wife, Rosalina Canonizado. She'd died in rather suspicious circumstances, and it left a sour taste in the mouths of everyone who had worked so tirelessly to gain a conviction. However, I wasn't worried about myself; most of all, I felt for my mate, Mick Lyons. He'd worked harder than any other copper I had seen to put Keir behind bars, and all his efforts had come to nought.

We had a second shot at it though, and Keir was eventually sentenced to twenty-two years imprisonment for murdering his first wife, Jean Strachan, with a non-parole period of sixteen years. While seeing distraught victims was the hardest part of the job, seeing a victim or a family when that moment of justice finally arrived was the most pleasing. The look on Jean's mother Christine's face when the guilty verdict was delivered was, without a doubt, the pinnacle of my police career.

It was done. I had fought for a conviction for over a decade, and now we finally had it. I could return to my job at the Coroner's Court and, more importantly, I could devote myself to my family again. However, gaining our conviction had come at a cost.

I'd begun spending more and more time away from my family, which was bad enough, but to compound this I'd started having nightmares. Throughout the Keir investigation, my dreams were filled with the colour red, and the evidence from the case, but mostly with visions of Jean's body stuffed inside a drum.

Policemen have nightmares, it comes with the job, and I dealt with them like most cops; I bottled it all up and pushed everything into the darkest recesses of my mind – until my nightmares started to be about my family.

They rocked me to the core. They were more vivid and more intense than anything I'd ever dreamt about before. I started to wake up of a morning feeling like I was coming apart at the seams. I'd gone through my whole career with a sense of being on top of things, of being in control of everything, but now it was slipping away, which was very unnerving. I knew who I was, and yet at the same time I didn't. I'd often look into the mirror, and while sometimes I recognised the man staring back at me, at other times I was confronted with a complete stranger.

I wanted to talk to someone, to share my troubles, but old-school coppers were expected to keep this kind of stuff to themselves. Some things I discussed with my wife, others I didn't. Some things I talked over with my mates, others I didn't. Mostly, I locked everything away in the depths of my mind, in that place every copper has where he keeps things that will always just be for him or her to remember. Unfortunately, it didn't work. My nightmares not only continued, they worsened.

It was towards the end of March. I'd been tossing and turning all night, waking up on the hour every hour, and I was dreading the buzz of my alarm clock. The temperature had been hovering around the high thirties the previous day, and nightfall had only reduced the heat by a few degrees. Summer was over, but the weather was still muggy, made worse by the fact that my bedroom was upstairs, where the heat had settled.

I woke up, rolled over and checked my alarm clock: 3 am.

'Pete, are you okay?' my wife Sue asked me as she rolled over and cuddled me.

'Yeah, darl, I am. You go back to sleep.' I closed my eyes and tried to sleep. Many things I'd seen throughout my career played over again and again in my mind, until I finally drifted off.

My youngest daughter and I were walking along a bitumen road that led to a railway overpass. There were deep-red bricks forming the walls on either side, and the trees below were thick, like tangled vines. The night was dark, punctuated by a thick fog that was beginning to settle. It was eerily quiet, except for Tayla, who was being a bloody pain as she kept jumping up and walking along the top of the brick wall. 'Look at me, Daddy!'

'Tayla, get down from there!' I shouted. She did as she was told, but we'd only walk a few more metres before she was up there again. Several times she slipped and teetered on the edge, and I'd leap over and grab hold of her just before she went over the side.

'Daddy, you can let go, I promise I won't go up there again,' Tayla said sweetly and innocently as I put her down yet again. I let her go and, sure enough, she leapt straight back up again. 'You see, Daddy, it's okay,' she said.

Just as the last word left her lips, she slipped and went over the edge. I lunged toward the wall and managed to grab her hand, holding on as tightly as I could as I watched her dangling beneath me. My hands were clammy and sweaty, and I struggled to hold on. I mustered all my strength, tightened my grasp around her wrist, and gave one final heave, but it was no use.

Her wrist, and then her fingertips, slipped from mine and she fell. Everything played out in slow motion as I watched her body land in a crumpled heap on the railway tracks below. It was deathly silent as I rushed from end to end of the bridge, desperately searching for a way to get down to my little girl, but the gnarled, twisted trees barred my way. The silence was suddenly broken by a distant rumbling, and I looked up to see an oncoming freight train. Tayla was lying prostrate on the tracks as the train hurtled towards her. The train's horn blared, and now I could see the driver, his face a mask of utter horror as he tried absolutely everything he could to slow down the tons of steel under his control. Meanwhile, Tayla, despite her injuries, was struggling to rise to her feet, but just as she did…*thump*. The train struck her and continued on under the bridge. I searched frantically for any sign of my daughter, hoping against hope that she'd somehow managed to survive the impact, but once the train had passed all I could see were Tayla's legs, arms, fingers and toes strewn all over the tracks. I screamed out in anguish, at which point I woke up. I sat upright in bed, feeling desperately guilty that I'd let my precious baby die. I was sweating profusely, my heart was pounding, and tears were streaming down my cheeks like a waterfall.

Sue now woke again. 'Pete, are you sure you are okay?'

I buried my head in my hands and shook my head.

'You had that dream again, didn't you?'

I nodded.

Sue wrapped her arms around me. 'It's okay, honey,' she said as she stroked my head until I fell back into a fitful sleep.

Beep! Beep! Beep! The shrill sound of the alarm clock resonated in my ears, and it took several whacks before I finally managed to turn it off.

'Shit, I only just got back to sleep,' I muttered to myself as I wearily lifted myself out of bed, clicked into autopilot and headed for the shower. I closed my eyes as the hot water washed over me, and images of other dreams I'd been having flashed through my mind; retrieving fingers and other body parts from railway tracks, the hair and faces mangled together until it was impossible to tell them apart, legs bent in ways that I'd never thought possible.

What the hell is going on? Why am I having these dreams? I thought to myself as I ran my hands through my hair, took a deep breath and let out a loud sigh. I closed my eyes again but no matter what I did, the nightmares continued to play over and over.

The worst ones were the ones involving Tay. There was another one where she was falling into a dark hole. 'Daddy! Daddy! I don't want to die!' she'd scream as she looked up at me with outstretched arms. I'd lean down as far as I could and try and grab her, but I could never reach her, and she kept falling into the abyss.

I tried to push it all from my mind as I let the water from the shower flow over my body, soothing me. I would have stayed in there for hours if I could have, but I had to get to work, so I jumped out, dried myself off and quickly dressed in a pair of black trousers, a light-blue business shirt, a striped tie and black shoes and socks.

I headed downstairs, and was pensive as I ate my cereal. I really wasn't looking forward to the hour-and-a-half commute to work. The last thing I needed right now was to have nothing else to do but sit and think, allowing my nightmares to play over and over in my mind. I finished my breakfast, made my way back upstairs and crept towards my three daughters' bedrooms. All their doors were ajar, and I peered inside Jenna's room first. She was curled up and sleeping soundly. I moved on to Tayla's room. She was flat on her back and sprawled across the bed. Finally, I went to Ashleigh's room. She was lying on her right side, her messy black hair covering her face. *My little angels,* I thought to myself as I closed Ashleigh's door. *I don't know what I would do without them.* Seeing my daughters reminded me that all my dreams were just that; dreams.

I made my way back into our bedroom, kissed Sue on the forehead, and was soon out the door and wandering the hundred metres or so down the road to catch the 5.35 am bus to Penrith railway station.

The usual early starters were already at the bus stop, including two guys with whom I'd become particularly good mates over the past twelve months. On mornings like this it was really great to have a couple of fellows to shoot the breeze with. Despite it being early, they were always chirpy and cheerful, and we'd talk about the news, sport and whatever was happening with our respective jobs. It didn't matter what we chatted about; any topic that took my mind off things was fine by me. Time always passed quickly, and before long the bus would pull up outside the station and we'd make our way onto the platform to wait for the train to the city.

The same faces greeted me on the platform, and it felt a bit like Groundhog Day as the boys and I squeezed our way onto the train, continuing our conversations as best we could. Half an hour later, I said my goodbyes, got off at Westmead and walked the kilometre to the hospital. Talking with the boys had taken my mind off things, but now, left to my own devices again, my thoughts were consumed by images of Tayla plummeting off the railway bridge.

I reached the large sliding glass doors at the hospital's entrance and made my way past the kiosk and through the warm corridors. As I wandered past the wards, I tried to remind myself that everybody in here was suffering, and that in comparison, my life was really not that bad. I continued on downstairs, past the forensic pathology unit, which also housed the mortuary. I'd walked past it hundreds of times, but try as I might to resist, my eyes always found their way to the door, and I would think about the people inside. How had they died? Had they lived their life to the full? Were their families shattered? What had they left behind?

I continued on out the back door, across a small car park and grassed area, and then passed through the back entrance to the Westmead Coroner's Court. The court itself was a creamy brown-coloured building made from smooth bricks. There was only the one courtroom, a couple of cells for prisoners who were transported to and from the court, two offices for the sergeants who took the early morning reports of death and fires from the police, three Police Prosecutors' desks and four more desks for investigators from the Coroner's Support Unit. Then there was the main office for the court staff, as well as a meals room and toilets, and at the back of the building, was the Coroner's Chambers, currently occupied by Jan Stevenson.

The familiar faces of the two police officers, Senior Constable Roger 'Dolly' Dyer and Sergeant Kevin Scott, greeted me as I walked through the door. Roger was in his fifties, with light-brown hair, rugged features and a raspy voice. He was an institution in the court, and absolutely everybody knew him. He was one of those guys who did his job to the best of his ability, and promotion was something that had never really interested him. Scotty was the ultimate professional, one of those guys who commanded everyone's respect. Everything had to be done by the book, but despite his fickle ways, he was still a real man's man. He had a gruff exterior, and when he was on form, he'd scare the crap out of the coppers who came to the court. What I liked about him most was that he never took any shit. More experienced coppers would come in and try to circumvent the rules, but not only would he staunchly stick to his guns, he'd start putting the wind up them too!

'G'day, Dolly, Scotty,' I called out.

'G'day, Pete,' they replied in unison. They'd barely said their hellos when the phones started to ring. This wasn't at all unusual for this time of the morning, because if a death occurred during the day, there was always someone on hand to deal with the paperwork, but first thing in the morning, all the deaths that had occurred overnight would create a backlog. The night shift was coming to an end, and the officers reporting the deaths would all ring in at once, understandably reluctant to do any overtime.

I made my way to my office, and as I went, I could hear Dolly giving his usual advice to the police. 'What was the time of death? When did you arrive on the scene? Have you done all the paperwork? Has the P79A (reporting a death to the Coroner) been done? Has a doctor signed off on the life extinct certificate? Has the doctor determined a definitive cause of death and have the relatives been informed?'

The casual, matter-of-fact way Dolly spoke would probably have shocked most people, but I had heard the spiel so many times I had become numb to it, so I paid no attention as I made my way to my workstation, which was a pretty simple affair; a desk, a filing cabinet, an In tray, an Out tray and an overhead locker. I sat down and switched on my computer, and while I waited for it to warm up,

I looked with dread at the pile of briefs requiring my review on behalf of the Coroner, those compiled by officers who had investigated a suspicious death or fire. Suspicious deaths were the ones where a doctor was unable to determine the exact cause of death, and therefore was unable to provide a death certificate. The Coroner would then assess the matter and make a determination as to whether the death actually *was* suspicious and required further investigation. If not, the file was closed. If so, the investigating police would be instructed to gather more information from the scene, and from any witnesses.

The Coroner's main role, however, was to determine the identity of the deceased. First, the body needed to be identified, either by the family, through dental records or by means of any identifying marks such as tattoos or jewellery, which was particularly useful when a body was unrecognisable, and then the Coroner needed to determine the date and place of death, the manner of death and the circumstances surrounding it.

In the case of a fire, for example, the Coroner had to make a determination as to the nature and cause of the fire, as well as the exact date on which it occurred. Ultimately, if there was evidence to identify a known person as being responsible for the death or the fire, the Coroner would make her findings and refer the matter to the Director of Public Prosecutions (DPP) to make a further decision on whether to have the person charged and put before the court. For example, in the case of a hanging, it might seem clear-cut to begin with, but it wasn't always that straightforward. There might have been a suicide note, but that still wasn't enough. It might have been a case of homicide made to look like suicide, in which case the Coroner could order a thorough police investigation to see what the Forensic Pathologist's post-mortem revealed. Of course, the police investigators could also make their own decision to charge someone if they believed there was sufficient evidence.

My job as the Police Prosecutor (formally known as the Sergeant Assisting the Coroner when in court) was to assess the briefs for the Coroner, and once I'd read all the material, I could make a number of determinations.

1. *Make a recommendation to the Coroner as to whether there should be an Inquest (in the case of a death) or an Inquiry (in the case of a fire). This occurred when there was a known suspect, but insufficient evidence to lay charges. Then we might need to take it to a court hearing to bring out further evidence that might get to the truth of the matter.*

2. *Make a recommendation that there were no suspicious circumstances and the matter could be dispensed with by the Coroner with sufficient evidence to make the necessary determinations.*

3. *Find that there were further enquiries to be made, and direct the police to make those enquiries and re-submit the brief.*

4. *Make a determination that there was sufficient evidence to charge a known person with an indictable offence.*

In all cases except those where further enquiries were needed, the file then went to the Coroner so that she could make her own assessment and give a final decision as to how the matter should proceed.

Looking at the pile of briefs, I realised I wasn't ready to tackle them, so I grabbed my coffee mug and headed off to get my morning caffeine fix. Outside, the sun was rising and the first rays were beginning to filter through the meals room. Like most government offices, they didn't splurge on expensive coffee. I wasn't a big fan of *International Roast*, but it would have to do. Cuppa in hand, I made my way back to my office, took a sip and grabbed the first brief from the pile. When I opened it, my initial thought was, *Oh fuck! I think I'm going to have to give this one to someone else!*

The brief was a four-year-old girl who had drowned in a pool accident. *Shit*, I thought to myself, *this is not something I would ever want to have to review, let alone first thing in the morning!* Thoughts of my daughters ran through my mind. What if that had been one of my girls I was staring at? I couldn't fathom it. I didn't want to. I couldn't imagine how I'd even begin to cope.

During my time in the cops and in the Coroner's Court, one thing always hit home harder than anything else; when a child died before their parents. This had been exacerbated by everything that had happened during the Keir investigation. Throughout all the ups and downs, I had always tried to place myself in Christine's shoes, tried to imagine how she would be feeling about losing her daughter. However, perhaps quite selfishly, I'd often pushed it to the back of my mind, pretty much because I just didn't want to think about it. I'd reverted back to the defence mechanisms I'd used when I'd first started as a cop, before I was married or had my girls, and that was to not think too much about living or dying, just to do my job to the best of my ability. It was no use. Things were different now, and what had once worked no longer did.

I thought about several close calls throughout my career. One time, my partner Ted and I were working night shift. We'd been trying to serve some subpoenas on several witnesses in the Windsor area without success. Every time we went to the premises, there was no-one home. We were nearing the end of a night shift when Ted suggested it might be a good idea to serve the subpoenas early in the morning, before the witnesses headed off to work.

The next morning, we were driving down one of the main streets in Windsor on our way to test Ted's theory. I was in the passenger seat, staring out the window at nothing in particular when we passed a car dealership and something caught my eye. 'Ted, quick, pull over! There's a bloke with a metal bar in his hand hiding behind one of the cars in that car yard!'

'What? What's going on, Pete?'

'Just pull over, quick!' Ted pulled up just beyond the car yard, whereupon I jumped out of the car and immediately gave chase on foot, the bloke having seen me and started running. *Fucking hell,* I thought to myself, *I don't need this shit at this time of the morning.*

The bloke weaved his way in and out of the streets, heading into the residential areas. I kept after him, leaping over fences and running through people's yards and driveways, and I was gradually closing on him as he took more and more looks behind him. He leapt over a Colorbond fence and I followed, but unbeknown to me, there was a barbecue on the other side, and I landed right on top of it. Normally, this wouldn't have been too much of a drama, but the owners hadn't cleaned the hotplate in some time, and as soon as my feet touched it I slipped, fell and almost broke my neck.

The bloke disappeared from view for a bit, but I soon caught sight of him again. I jumped a couple more fences, gaining on the bloke with every step. I almost had him as he ran down the side of someone's house, and after following him into the front yard, I finally tackled him just as he reached the nature strip.

Meanwhile, Ted had been doing his best to follow us in the car, and he pulled into the street just as I wrestled the guy to the ground. Ted jumped out of the car and ran over to help me. The bloke stopped struggling, and we lifted him up and bundled him towards the car. 'What are you doing!' he cried. 'I haven't done anything wrong!'

'Mate, if you haven't done anything wrong, then why are you running from the police?' I said as I put him in the back and slid in beside him.

'I just got scared is all. I've had blokes chase me before.'

Ted started the car and headed off towards Windsor police station. The bloke seemed pretty relaxed at first, but after a few minutes he decided to bung it on. I reached for my cuffs, but I'd only managed to get them on one of his wrists when he unlocked the door with his free hand. Ted, aware of the commotion going on in the back, had slowed the car down, and suddenly the bloke opened the door and dived out, taking me with him. We both rolled a few feet along the road, and with arms and legs going everywhere, the free ring of the handcuffs smashed me above my left eye. It cut me up pretty good, but I didn't even notice, being more focused on restraining the bloke properly.

I did my best to secure the guy from behind, and had the arm with the cuff up behind his back while I tried to reach around and grab his other arm. Ted came up in front of the guy, put him in a headlock and yelled at him to stop struggling. Suddenly, I heard Ted yell, 'He's going for my gun. Shit, he's got it!' The guy had been able to reach up with his free hand and rip Ted's gun from his shoulder holster. I grabbed his arm just as he pulled it out from under Ted's jacket, and held onto it for dear life. I could just feel the butt of the gun as we forced him to his knees. Ted reached down, and I could feel him twisting the guy's hand back until the gun was pointing back at him. 'Mate, you pull that trigger and you're the one that's gonna get shot!' Ted screamed.

What the… I thought to myself. *If the gun goes off, the bullet will go through this guy and then through me.* To my relief, the guy let go of the gun and it fell to the ground. Ted quickly picked it up and we hauled the guy to his feet, secured him and took him to Windsor police station. At the time, it had never really sunk in that I might have died.

My mind returned to the brief I had in front of me, and I began to think about other briefs I'd looked at. I'd investigated every horrendous act that you could possibly imagine, assaults, rapes, robberies, murders, and no matter how hard I tried not to, there were times when I envisaged these things happening to my girls. Most of the time, I tried to push it to the back of my mind. I knew that if I thought about it too much, it would eventually destroy me, and there were many times when I thought to myself, *Gees, I wish I'd never investigated these matters. Perhaps I'd be better off being ignorant about it all.*

I wanted to do something else, anything, to be somewhere else. I wanted nothing more than to put this brief on someone else's desk and forget I'd ever seen it. I put it to one side and closed my eyes, only to open them after a few seconds and pick it up again. I nodded resolutely. I had to get through this one. If this had been my daughter, I would want some answers, and this family needed theirs, which began with me making my determinations. I checked the time of death, the date, the officers who had attended, who they had spoken to and when the ambos had arrived. I checked the P79A to see if a formal identification had been made, as well as the witnesses' versions of events. I also checked to see if counsellors had been contacted, and I examined the photographs of the pool gate.

Lost in my thoughts, I hadn't noticed the Senior Prosecutor, Dave Parcell, walk into the office. I looked up to see his short, wavy, mousy brown hair atop his solid six-foot frame. Dave and I had known each other for many years, as he had been the Prosecutor at Blacktown when I'd first got into the job, and I'd convinced him to come over to the Coroner's Unit at Westmead. 'Hey, Pete, how's it going?' he said casually as he put his bag down next to his desk.

'Um, yeah, mate. I'm just bloody great,' I said.

'You right, Pete?' he asked with heartfelt concern, sensing the shakiness in my voice.

'No, mate, not really. My first brief this morning was the drowning of a four-year-old girl. Don't suppose you want to do it? I'll swap you for whatever you've got.'

'I'd love to help you out, mate, but I think I'll pass. I hate those ones just as much as you,' Dave replied, plainly relieved that I'd gotten the brief and not him.

'Great help you are!' I said as I opened the file again and began reviewing the statements, trying to come to some understanding of how such a sweet, innocent little girl had come to such a tragic and untimely end. I read through the pathologist's post-mortem report, the scientific determinations and the detectives' statements, searching for anything that might suggest this was a case of foul play.

It took me almost an hour. I'd start reading, and then it would all become too much, and so I'd get up from my desk and pace up and down the office trying to convince myself to get back to it and get it finished. I'd sit down, read some more, and then repeat the whole process all over again. It was probably one of the hardest things I'd ever had to do.

No, the family need answers, I thought to myself, *I've got to keep going*.

Eventually, I came across a yellow envelope. I knew what was inside. I knew I had to examine its contents, but my hands felt like they had lead weights attached to them as I lifted the flap. I reached inside and retrieved half a dozen photographs taken by the scientific officers.

I might as well have been flicking through one of my own family albums, albeit a tremendously sad one. There was the little girl with long dark hair, lying on a hospital bed with tubes protruding from her mouth and nose. Her pale arms were hanging limply by her side, and she looked just like a porcelain doll. It was plain that the ambos and doctors had tried everything they possibly could to resuscitate her, and I wondered how they were coping with their grief. I knew they must have seen a lot in their jobs, just as I had as a policeman, but anything to do with children was always unbearable.

Due to the terrible nature of what I was viewing, I'd glanced at the picture, but hadn't really looked at it closely, so I forced myself to cast my eyes over it again, searching for any signs that this might have been a murder and not an accident. The first thing I looked at was the girl's face, and a shockwave of emotion immediately pulsated through me. I was transfixed, unable to move, unable to think. I closed my eyes and hoped that somehow, when I opened them again, what I was seeing had changed. It hadn't. I felt sick to the stomach. My mouth went bone dry as I felt the bile rising in my throat. *Fuck me dead! This girl's a dead-ringer for Tayla!*

Every tingling nerve in my body tried to convince me that I was indeed looking at my own little girl, despite the fact that I knew Tayla was safe and sound at home. Tay was a couple of years older than this poor girl, but the resemblance was uncanny, and I had to put the photo down. I just couldn't look anymore. Tears welled up in my eyes and started to trickle down my cheeks. It took every ounce of strength I had to keep it together as I pictured her parents, distraught in their grief and sorrow, and wondered how on earth they were going to cope with the loss of their beautiful daughter. Several times, I willed myself to take another look, to finish the job I knew I *had* to do, but it was no use. I couldn't take it anymore.

I grabbed my mug and headed back to the meals room, where I made myself another coffee and then walked out the back door and sat down beneath the umbrella that shaded the wooden picnic table. I stared blankly at the adjacent brick wall, my emotions alternating between horrified and petrified; horrified because of what I had just seen, and petrified by the thought that, but for the grace of God, that *could* have been my daughter.

Unbeknown to me, Lesley Newling, one of the court staff, had come out for a cigarette and had started talking to me but, completely consumed by my thoughts, I hadn't heard her.

'Pete, are you okay?' she asked as she sat down opposite me.

It took a few moments for me to register her presence, but when I did, I simply looked up at her and said, 'No, not really.'

'Why, what's up?'

'I was just reading a brief about a pool drowning, and the dead girl looks exactly like Tayla. It completely freaked me out.'

'Oh my God!' Lesley said. 'Just have your coffee and stay out here for a bit. Why don't you get Dave or Martene to do the brief?'

'Nah, I'm alright. I've read it now, and I feel like I have to finish it. I just can't believe how much she looks like Tayla.'

'Do you mind if I take a look?' she asked.

'Sure, the photos are sitting on my desk.'

Lesley walked inside and returned shortly after. 'Oh, Peter!' she said sympathetically. 'She does look like her. I can see why it freaked you out.'

'Do you know what?' I said.

'What?'

'Sometimes you have to wonder what we're doing in this job. Some days are great, like when we get through all the briefs or when we have barbies with everyone, but then you get days like this when *bam*, something comes out of left field and completely knocks you on your arse. I think I'm starting to understand how a cop or ambo must feel when they go to a car accident and find it's either a family member or someone they know. I wonder how you deal with something like that?'

'I don't know, love. I guess we have no choice but to get on with life as best we can,' Lesley smiled.

'Yeah, I guess you're right,' I said as I reluctantly hauled myself up and made my way back inside. I lingered beside my desk and looked around my office, directing my gaze anywhere but the one place I knew I had to. The photos were where I'd left them, but all I could do was take a few fleeting glimpses before I had to put them back in the envelope.

I started typing up my recommendations for the Coroner: that this was a tragic accident. All things considered, it was one of the simplest briefs I'd ever had to do, but it took me until well after lunch to type it up, and by the time I'd finished, I couldn't handle any more; I was just too messed up. I completed the paperwork and put it in the Coroner's tray. Just then, the phone rang. 'Westmead Coroner's Court, Peter Seymour speaking,' I said.

'Mr Seymour, how the devil are you, sir?'

Much to my surprise, it was Mick Lyons. Just like it had been in the old days, he seemed to have a knack of calling me right when I needed it most. 'G'day, Mick, how's things?'

'Everything's wonderful in beautiful downtown St Marys,' he replied. 'How are things with you at the Coroner's Court?'

'Mostly good, but today's been a bit of a shocker.'

'Well, if that's the case, I think it's about time you came back to the detectives and did some real work for a change!' Mick said light-heartedly.

'Why? Are you offering me a job?'

'As a matter of fact mate, I am. There's a position available if you want it. As you know, I got moved over here in charge of the detectives' office, and a spot's just come up. It's only a very junior office, and we could sure do with some experience out here.'

It's funny how things come along in your life exactly when they're supposed to. I'd been working at the Coroner's Court for six years and as a Police Prosecutor for eight, and whilst I hadn't really been considering a return to the Ds, given the morning's events, I started to wonder whether the time was right to make a change. I'd spent almost a decade prosecuting matters in court, visiting death scenes and reading about pretty much every possible way a person could be killed. I'd investigated a pilot being chopped up by two plane propellers at an aerodrome. I'd investigated an industrial accident when a worker had been mashed up when he got his hand caught in a grinder. Suicides, hangings, shootings, car accidents, pool drownings, people falling off cliffs, electrocutions: I'd seen them all. Perhaps it was all catching up with me. Perhaps the time had come for a change of scene. 'You know what, Mick, I *am* interested! Let me chat to Susie about it and I'll call you tomorrow if that's okay.'

'No worries, mate. How are Sue and the girls, by the way?'

'They're all going well. How's your tribe?'

'Yeah, they're good,' he replied. 'Listen, I'd better go, things to do, people to see. As soon as the position came up, I thought of you. It'd be great to work together again, so definitely give it some thought.'

'Will do, mate. I'll call you tomorrow.' I put the phone down and contemplated Mick's offer. I reminded myself that there were several reasons why I'd got myself out of the Ds, mostly for the sake of my family, and I needed to have a good hard think about whether I really wanted to go back. I'd opted out of the promotion race when I'd moved to the Prosecutors, so if I was to return to the Ds, at least there would be a chance for advancement. The girls were older now, and it wasn't so imperative that I spend more time at home. Ashleigh was nearly twelve, Jenna was nearly nine and Tayla was going to be seven in a month.

I contemplated Mick's offer on and off, but spent most of the rest of the day in a bit of a daze. No matter how hard I tried, I couldn't shake the images of the dead girl from my mind. No matter what I did, the picture kept finding its way back in, and the girl's face always became Tayla's. I had to finish my day's work, but I was desperate to get home and cuddle my little girl. When I finally knocked off, I hurried back through the hospital and rushed to the railway station. It was peak hour and the train was packed, so I stood there crammed in like a sardine as I examined people's faces and wondered which ones had kids of their own. I wondered how they would cope if it was their baby girl in the picture. I prayed none of them would ever have to suffer that torment. Faces disappeared, new ones arrived, and still the same thoughts continued to play over and over in my mind.

The train eventually pulled into Penrith, and I hopped on the bus. As it wound its way through the suburban streets, I stared out the window and reminded myself just how lucky I was to be blessed with three beautiful kids. I closed my eyes, and fought the urge to fall asleep. My head would drop and I would snap my eyes open, only to drift off again, the pictures of the little girl fixed in my thoughts.

When the bus stopped in my street, I leapt down from the step and quickly covered the hundred metres or so to my front door. I dashed inside, and was immediately greeted with a simultaneous cry of 'Daddy!' from all three girls. *Life doesn't get much better than this*, I thought to myself. While I love all my daughters equally, it was Tayla who I held onto the tightest that afternoon.

We went into the dining room and sat down to dinner. I revelled in the joy that my family gave me, but at the same time, I felt guilty. I couldn't shake the thought that somewhere else in Sydney, a family was sitting down to dinner one family member short, eating their meal in silence and thinking about the daughter they'd lost, thinking about all the memories they'd had and all the things they'd never get to see or experience. I looked at my three girls as I ate, and thought deeply about the offer Mick had made.

I was torn. I did like my job, and it meant I got to spend a lot more time with my girls, but at the same time, I wasn't sure I could deal with the stress anymore. I looked at Sue, and wondered what her opinion would be. I was a little concerned about bringing it up, but we always shared everything, and any decision I was going to make would affect the whole family, so it wasn't just my call; it was theirs too. *No*, I thought, *after what I've seen this morning I can't work at the Coroner's Court anymore.* 'Sue,' I eventually said.

'Yes, Pete?'

'I had a call from Mick Lyons today.'

'Oh, yes, how is he?'

'Yeah, yeah, he's all good.'

'What was he ringing about?'

'Well, actually, he offered me a job back in the Ds.'

'Wow, really? It sounds like you're thinking about it.'

'Yeah, I had a bit of a rough day today.'

'Pete, I don't think one rough day is enough to make you change jobs.'

'It's not just today, I think today just tipped the scales.'

'What do you want to do?'

'I don't know. I love the Monday to Friday, nine to five, but I'm not going to get promoted where I am, and I do think I need a change now that the girls are older. At least I'll get every second weekend off.'

'If that's what you want to do, then do it,' Susie said supportively. 'As you said, the girls are older now, so you need to do what's best for you. Besides, if it means more money, then I'm all for that!'

Sue always has a way of lightening things up and drawing me out of my darkest places. 'Yeah,' I laughed. 'I'll give Mick a call in the morning and have another chat to him about it.' It was great to have my wife's full support, regardless of whatever decision I made. She hated me doing shift work, ever since an incident when she had been stalked by a bush-rock delivery guy, and for her to put that aside and back me up meant a lot.

When I went to bed that night I found it hard to sleep, as the possibilities kept running through my mind; was I better off staying at the Prosecutors, or was it time to go back to the Ds? One minute I'd decide to go one way, only to completely change my mind a minute later and be convinced that I was going the other. With my mind reeling, I eventually drifted off, but I hardly slept a wink, as I had the same nightmares about Tayla yet again.

Chapter 2:
Careful What You Wish For

The alarm buzzed just before 5 am. I was quickly up, dressed and out the door and on my way to work, still trying to decide what I wanted to do. Where *did* I want my career to go?

When I got to work, I sat down at my desk and stared at the phone. Overnight, in between my nightmares, I'd pretty much decided what I wanted to do, but there were still some lingering doubts. I grabbed a cup of coffee and decided that this was it; the time had come. I picked up the phone and rang St Marys police station.

'Hello,' Mick said.

'G'day, Mick, it's Pete Seymour.'

'Officer Seymour! How's things, mate? Did you have a think about my offer?'

'Yes, mate. Listen, I had a chat to Susie last night and I might just take you up on it. Are they actually advertising the position, or can I just put in for a lateral transfer?'

'Leave it with me,' Mick replied. 'I'll speak to Glash about it. I reckon if you can get approval from your end, he'll jump at the chance of getting you here.'

Detective Inspector John Glasheen, or 'Glash', was Mick's boss, and once he'd approved the move, all the paperwork had been done and the transfer papers submitted, I was on my way back to St Marys to begin work as a detective senior constable, although it wasn't until the middle of June 2000 that the transfer became official.

I arrived early on my first morning back in the Ds and spent a few moments standing out the front of the station looking up and down the Great Western Highway, watching the peak-hour traffic starting to build. I headed inside and made my way upstairs, and discovered that there were two offices. One was to the left, away from the highway, and led through to the back offices. The other was to the right and led to the front offices, where the windows looked out over the highway below. There were four large wooden desks in each office, while the front office had a smaller fifth desk, which was where Mick sat.

It was strange to be back. I was awash with mixed emotions. I couldn't shake a feeling of *déjà vu*, and part of me felt like the last eight years had never happened, or that I'd somehow stepped back in time. However, despite my reservations, I was actually excited. I was coming into a very young office, and I was looking forward to passing on my experience, not only to the other detectives, but also to the uniformed guys, from both my previous work in the Ds and in the Prosecutors.

Oddly enough, the thing that scared me the most was the new computer system I'd have to be working on, because I was an absolute technophobe. I knew, and still know, nothing about technology, and I had no doubts that I was going to stuff something up somewhere along the line. I walked over to Mick's desk. He looked up and shot me a welcoming smile as he rose from his seat and shook my hand warmly. 'Good to have you back with us, mate,' he said as he gave me a hefty slap on the back.

'Yeah, hopefully it won't take long for me to get up to speed,' I replied as I sat down opposite him.

'Well, then,' Mick laughed, 'we'll just have to start you off with a couple of easy briefs just in case you've forgotten how to do it.'

'I'm happy with that,' I replied. 'Actually, you know what I really need?'

'What's that?' said Mick.

'I reckon I need a good murder case to get me back into the swing of things.'

'Careful what you wish for, mate, careful what you wish for,' Mick replied.

St Marys police station was small, yet busy, while St Marys itself was much like any other western Sydney suburb. It was very working class, and the people who lived there were your genuine, down-to-earth, do-anything-for-anyone types. The crime rates were pretty high, although it was mostly petty stuff, but we did have more than our fair share of serious investigations. Had St Marys not been so busy, I doubt I would have returned to the Ds. It was one of my strongest beliefs; you learned more and gained more experience at a hectic station. Yes, I was an experienced detective, but I also knew I still had a lot to learn, and working with others, be they higher or lower ranked than I was, would help make me a better copper.

The detectives' office was, as I had expected, a mix of uniformed officers who were up doing training duties and plain-clothes junior officers, along with a couple of detectives with a few years' experience. I spent the first few weeks back in the job liaising with the uniformed police and giving advice from a Prosecutor's perspective, which turned out to be a great help for them when it came to any Coronial matters they happened to be involved in.

I was given a new lease on life. I felt refreshed, more alive, although the flip side was that I was going to be spending more and more time away from home. However, the biggest change I noticed was the detectives' roster. Instead of working night shifts, two detectives were always rostered 'on call', and were required to respond to any serious matters that may occur during the night, which suited me to a tee.

I hated working night shift, and much preferred to be on call for a week, even if it meant that I couldn't enjoy a beer or two in case I got called in.

It was early in the morning on Saturday 15 July 2000 when the phone rang. Comfortable in my decision to move back to the Ds, I was enjoying the deepest sleep I'd had in a long time, and was startled by the call, because I wasn't rostered on. I rolled over and looked at the alarm clock: 2.30 am. I knew it must be work, but I wondered why they wanted me. Maybe they'd got the roster mixed up, and were calling me by mistake. 'Hello,' I said wearily as I picked up the phone.

'Hello, Detective Seymour, I'm sorry to call you in the middle of the night, especially seeing as you're not on call, but a male body has been found lying on the corner of Mamre Road and Edgar Street, St Marys. Inspector Weiss is at the scene, and he asked that you be called in.'

'Yeah, okay, no worries. I'll jump in the shower and get dressed. I'll be on my way shortly.'

'I didn't think you were on call this week,' Susie mumbled as she stirred.

'I'm not,' I replied as I dragged myself out of bed, 'but Frank Weiss wants me there, so I have to go. I'll give you a call later when I know what's going on. Go back to sleep, darling.'

I quickly jumped in the shower, got dressed, and was soon on my way towards St Marys. After a fifteen-minute drive, I parked on Mamre Road, about fifty metres away from the crime scene and only a few hundred metres down the road from the station itself. There were four or five police cars parked along the main road, their blue and red lights flashing brightly against the backdrop of the night sky. There were roughly half a dozen officers, including Inspector Frank Weiss, standing on the outside of the blue and white crime scene tape. Frank was a solidly built bloke who was very knowledgeable and articulate, and was studying for his Master's degree at the same time as being a top-notch officer. He was an old-school copper, in the mould of people like my old boss, Detective Sergeant Mick O'Connell, and was one of the St Marys Duty Officers. I had known Frank since 1988, when I'd worked for him for a year at the On The Job Training Unit where we were required to do research and create various resources such as a quick reference drug identification booklet that would help beat officers to do their job more efficiently. I walked over to where Frank was standing on the footpath.

'Good morning, a bit fresh isn't it?' he said as he looked up, steam streaming from his mouth as he rubbed his hands together.

'My oath it is! What have we got, Frank? What's so important that you felt the need to get me up out of my nice, cosy, warm bed in the middle of the night?'

'We have a deceased male lying over there on the grass adjacent to the footpath near the corner. It looks like he's suffered some head injuries, and there's a bit of blood coming from his right ear.'

'Has the crime scene been properly secured?' I asked.

'Sure has,' Frank replied. 'I got the tape put up straight away and nobody has gone inside it. Fieldy and Floody were the first ones here, and I'm happy that they've done everything properly.'

I took a quick look around and saw that they'd actually taped off the whole street.

'Hey, Frank,' I said, 'can I just remind you one more time that I am, in fact, not on call?'

'Yeah, I know, Pete,' he smirked, 'but it didn't matter who was on call, I was calling you in. We're going to need some experience on this one. I also called Scientific; they shouldn't be too far away.'

Whilst Frank was talking, we made our way over to Senior Constable Paul Field and Constable Mary-Jane Flood, who were both standing outside the tape to ensure nobody entered the crime scene and contaminated it. 'G'day, guys,' I said.

'Hi, Pete,' they replied.

'You guys the first on the scene?'

'Yeah,' Floody said. 'There was no one around when we got here, and we haven't disturbed the body too much,' she continued. 'We just checked for vital signs, but he was already dead.'

'Do we have any witnesses?' I asked.

'No, not at this stage,' Floody replied.

Frank and I moved over to the body, and I took a quick look around to see exactly where it lay in relation to the surrounding streets. It was on the grass on the northern side of Edgar Street, about ten metres from the adjacent to the footpath on the corner of Mamre Road, one of the main thoroughfares in St Marys. I bent down beside the body and looked it up and down, searching for anything out of the ordinary that might give me a clue as to how the man had died. The body was fully clothed, dressed in a blue jacket, a navy-blue top and a pair of grey jeans. I took a close look at his face, and my first instinct was that he was in his late forties, but he looked like he could have been older. He had bruising and swelling around his left eye, as if he'd been punched, as well as redness and swelling to his right ear, including the trickles of blood to which Frank had referred. I looked down at his feet, and noticed that he had grey socks on, but only one brown shoe. The other shoe was lying a few feet away. As I shifted my gaze back up towards his waist, I noticed that the pockets of his jeans were turned out.

Someone's gone through his pockets before the body was found; either that or he's been approached by someone and he's turned his own pockets out to show them he had nothing in them, I thought. I stood up, took another look around, and then peered back down at the lifeless body.

I could never quite reconcile the senselessness of murder. I'd visited several murder scenes before, and I'd had to deal with many unsolved murders in the briefs I'd done while working for the Coroner's Court, and I just couldn't understand how someone could be so callous as to take someone else's life. I immediately thought of the man's family. I'd seen what it had done to the Strachan family during the Keir investigation, and this was going to affect this victim's family for the rest of their lives in ways they couldn't even begin to imagine. Right at this moment, they would most likely be lying in bed asleep, with no idea that uniformed police would soon be knocking on their door and delivering the most horrible of news.

'Frank, we'll have to notify Homicide and organise a canvass of the area,' I said as I turned back to him. 'Who else did you call out?'

'McQueen was on call, so he's on his way.'

'Okay, no worries. I'll just go to the office and get my gear and make a few phone calls. I'll be back shortly. Can you arrange for a log to be started of who has been at the scene? Perhaps Floody can do that, as she was one of the first ones here.'

'Already taken care of, mate,' Frank said.

'Excellent.' I hurried back to my car and drove the short distance to the station. I rushed over to my desk to grab my gun, handcuffs and notebook, and was just on my way back out the door when Detective Matt McQueen walked into the office. Matt was a well-groomed bloke in his early twenties. He was tall, about the same height as me, with short brown hair and an athletic build.

'Hi, Pete,' he said. 'I didn't know you were on call with me tonight.'

'I wasn't, mate,' I replied, 'but Frank wanted me called in, so here I am. You nearly right to go?'

'Yeah, just give us a minute,' Matt said.

'I'll ring the Duty Operations Inspector in Sydney to notify Homicide and the Pathologist. Can you contact Glash and Mick Lyons and let them know what's going on? We're definitely going to need to call more staff in.'

'Yeah, I'll ring them now,' Matt replied.

I rang the Duty Operations Inspector in Sydney and requested the attendance of the Homicide Squad, as well as the Forensic Pathologist. By this time, McQueen had gathered up his gear, and we made our way out to my car and drove back to the scene.

'G'day, Pete, Floody has handed over the log to Senior Constable Charlton, who has just arrived. He can continue with it while everyone else canvasses the neighbourhood,' Frank said as we approached him.

'Thanks, Frank. I've contacted the DOI and Homicide, as well as the Forensic Pathologist. In addition to canvassing the streets, I'd also like someone to go to all the service stations, clubs, pubs and any place nearby that is open that might have CCTV footage, just in case we can get descriptions of anyone who may be involved, including our victim. We've also let Glash and Mick Lyons know. Mick will be able to call in a few more people from our office, so they'll be able to help with the canvass when they get here.'

I was running through everything else I needed to do as I chatted to the uniformed police about the area we needed to canvass, mostly along Mamre Road and the nearby intersecting streets, when Senior Constable Russell Frazer from Scientific arrived.

'G'day, Russell,' I said as he joined us.

'Hey, Pete, what have you got?'

'A deceased male on the nature strip on Edgar Road there. It appears that he's been bashed, and I reckon he's probably been robbed too.'

We ducked under the blue and white crime scene tape and walked over to the body.

'I think we might call out the Video Unit,' Russell said as he looked the body up and down. He then examined the surrounding streetlights.

'Pete, whilst those streetlights are pretty good, they won't be enough. It might be a good idea to have the Rescue Squad attend with some extra lighting.'

I took a look at the streetlights. Even though they weren't sufficient for the Video Unit, they were, as Russell had said, reasonably bright and on both sides of the street. I hoped that, if there were any witnesses to the attack, they had gotten a good view, even though it was the middle of the night.

'I'll organise the Rescue Squad,' McQueen offered as he moved away and phoned the Video Unit and Rescue Squad on his mobile. Russell and I started conducting a more detailed examination of the scene. I noticed some TAB tickets at the base of a nearby mesh fence surrounding the adjacent primary school, but there wasn't really much else to shed any light on what had happened. Straightaway, I knew this was going to be a difficult one to crack; quite obviously, the less evidence in a case, the harder they are to solve. Russell walked back to his car and soon returned with his camera and started photographing the scene.

I checked my watch; it was just after 4.30 am. When I looked up, I saw the familiar face of the Forensic Pathologist, Dr Dianne Little, as she walked towards me. 'Ah, Detective Seymour, fancy seeing you out here!' she said with a smile.

'Now see, Dr Little, you thought you'd got rid of me when I left the Coroner's Court, didn't you?'

'Well, it's good to see you again, although it is a very cold morning, and I would rather still be in bed asleep.'

'Wouldn't we all,' I replied. 'Anyway, I'll take you over to the body. We have a deceased male on the grass on the nature strip over here, and it looks like he may have been assaulted and robbed. He has some marks to his head, and there is some blood coming from his right ear.'

Russell continued photographing the body while Dr Little made her preliminary assessment. I took a closer look, and noticed some things I hadn't seen earlier. Scratch marks were visible on the right side of his neck, as though whoever had assaulted him had laid the boot in, and there was some bruising to his cheeks and cuts to his right hand, seemingly confirming my theory that he'd been bashed and robbed and that he had, in vain, tried to put up a fight.

The sun was still a few hours from rising, so when the Rescue Squad truck arrived, Frank began directing them as to where we needed the lighting to be set up. Not long after, the Video Unit arrived, and I also noticed the familiar faces of Detectives Paul Jacob and Gary Jubelin from the Homicide Squad arriving, along with two other Homicide detectives.

'G'day, Paul, Gary,' I said as they approached. I briefed them on what we had, or more to the point, the distinct lack of information. While the Homicide boys had a look at the body, the Rescue Squad officers and the Video Unit officer came up and asked me if there was any way the traffic could be diverted around the area so they could set up their gear and film the scene.

'Hey, Frank, can you organise all that for us?' I said. 'We'll need to block Mamre Road at the next intersections north and south of Edgar Street.'

'No worries, mate, I'll get onto it right now,' Frank said as he immediately began organising for the diversions to be put in place, his job made that much harder by the fact that the early morning traffic was now steadily increasing.

The Rescue Squad boys set up a series of spotlights and the Video Unit officer began recording the scene, taking shots from every possible angle. Meanwhile, Russell and Dr Little were busy examining the body. When they rolled the body onto its side, they found a black wallet in the back pocket of the jeans. A check of the wallet revealed that the deceased's name was Nick Hanes, and that he lived about two hundred and fifty metres down the road in Edgar Street.

Poor bugger, he was almost home! I thought as I watched Dr Little measure the air temperature and then use a rectal thermometer to check the temperature of the body. She then placed plastic bags over the deceased's hands to preserve any evidence. When she was done, she stood up, turned to me and said, 'You'll need to get permission from the Coroner for me to carry out the post-mortem today.'

'No problem, Dr Little,' I said. 'I'll organise that and get the body brought down to the morgue as soon as possible.'

'Good,' she smiled. 'No doubt I'll see you later this morning.'

'Yes, hopefully not too late.'

Dr Little then packed all her gear into her bag, walked back to her car and left the scene. As I watched her drive off, I pressed the speed dial on my mobile to ring Jan Stevenson, the Deputy State Coroner at Westmead. The phone rang several times before she eventually answered.

'Hello.'

'Good morning, ma'am. It's Peter Seymour here. Sorry to ring you so early in the morning, but I'm at a possible murder scene and need to get approval for the Forensic Pathologist to carry out a post-mortem on a suspected murder victim, and I need it done this morning. Dr Little's just left the scene. By the way, how are things?'

'Things are very good, Seymour. And normally, as you know, I would be happy to give you permission for that to be done, but right at this moment I'm enjoying a croissant and cuppa over in France!'

'What? You're joking. You're on holidays?' My mind started working overtime as I tried to figure out how the hell I was going to get permission for the post-mortem when the Coroner was on the other side of the world!

Fortunately, Jan quickly allayed my fears. 'Yes, Seymour, I *am* on holidays, and I *am* having a lovely time, but it's good to know you're on the job. What have you got?'

'We've got an older male lying on the nature strip who looks like he may have been bashed and robbed. We've got the scene secured and Homicide is in attendance.'

'No worries, then. Looks like you have things under control. You have my permission for it to be done, but you will need to advise the relieving Coroner as well,' she said.

'Thanks, ma'am. Enjoy your breakfast then while I'm freezing my butt off out here.'

'Oh, Seymour, you love it!' she joked. 'Good luck with it.'

'Thank you, ma'am.'

I hung up, but as soon as I had, I thought, *Shit! I didn't ask her who the relieving Coroner was! Doesn't matter, Dr Little will know, and in any event, at least Jan just gave me permission to get it done.*

A short time later, the government contractors attended the scene and the body was placed into a large black body bag and then into a waiting van to be transported to the Westmead Hospital Mortuary. The Rescue Squad packed up their lighting equipment and soon Mamre Road was reopened to traffic, a steady stream of cars and trucks slowing to have a gander as they drove past the crime scene.

With the body removed, I went over to the Homicide Squad detectives who were standing nearby and discussed things with them. I was pleased to have a couple of detectives of the calibre of Paul and Gary there, and they advised me that, due to the lack of information, the investigation would be left at a local level, but they said they were happy to stay around for the day to help get everything up and running and to provide any initial assistance I might need.

'Frank,' I said as I went and stood beside him and looked down Edgar Street, 'do you reckon you could organise for someone to go to the deceased's address down the road and break the news to his family? We'll need one of them to attend Westmead Morgue this morning and formally identify the body, and we'll also have to get a statement from them in due course.'

'Yeah, I'll take care of all that. I'll give them your name and the phone number for the detectives' office too. You concentrate on what you have to do, and I'll get the information you need from the family.'

'Thanks, Frank. Once you've contacted them, I'll try to get them down to the morgue as soon as possible. If they want, I can organise for a couple of our people to meet them down there, or drive them if necessary.'

I watched as Frank made his way towards his car. I didn't envy him with regard to what he was about to do. No police officer ever wants to go to a victim's house and tell their family that one of their beloved family members won't ever be coming home again, particularly when the victim's death has been violent, but that was part of the job, and someone had to do it.

Chapter 3:
An Old Dinosaur

Dawn was breaking as Matt and I made our way back to the station. I went over all the things I would have to say in the briefing that I was about to hold in the detectives' office once everyone had returned. Firstly, I had to make sure that I notified absolutely everyone who needed to be notified: the regional commander, the police Media Unit and my commander.

We set up a room specifically for the purpose of running the investigation. As St Marys was only a small station, we had no option but to use one of the interview rooms. The first thing we needed to do was get everything that we knew so far into a logical order and to enter it on the COPS computer system.

I desperately needed a cup of coffee, but for some reason I picked up my mug, stared blankly at it, and remained seated at my desk. Suddenly, I remembered that the St Marys Band Club stayed open late on Friday nights. Considering that there had been some TAB tickets near the deceased's body, it was possible he'd been at the club. 'Matt,' I said as I jumped to my feet, 'I'm just going to duck down the road to the Band Club to see if there's anyone around. They may also have CCTV available, and I want to make sure I get to them before they get rid of it.'

'It's probably too early, mate. I doubt there'd be anyone there at the moment,' Matt replied.

'Yeah, true, but the cleaners could be there. Sure as shit they won't pick up the phones, but it might be worth going down there and seeing if I can catch one of them. Either way, it's worth a shot. I'll only be twenty minutes or so. If anyone turns up here, get them to make themself a coffee.'

'No worries,' he replied.

The club was only a few minutes' walk from the station, and as I approached the entrance I noticed a woman dressed in dark clothing who had just crossed the road and was making her way towards the front door.

'Excuse me,' I said politely. She turned around with a rather apprehensive look on her face, which was entirely understandable given that a strange man was calling out to her at 5.30 am.

'Yes,' she said cautiously as she quickly looked past me to see if there was anyone else around. I immediately reached into my pocket and retrieved my ID.

'Ma'am, my name is Detective Seymour from St Marys detectives.' Upon sighting my badge, her demeanour changed completely. 'I wonder if it would be possible to ask you a few questions?'

'Sure. What do you want to know?'

'Do you work here at the Band Club?'

'Yes,' she replied, plainly a little confused as to why I was asking, 'I'm one of the managers here.'

'Fantastic! I wonder if you could help me. I'm investigating an incident that occurred last night just up the road, and I was wondering if I could get access to your CCTV footage? If I give you my contact details, can you obtain the tapes from last night until this morning and make them available for me?'

'Sure,' she replied, 'that shouldn't be a problem.'

I gave her my contact details and watched as she entered the club and disappeared into the foyer area. I then started to walk back towards the station, whereupon weariness began to kick in, the cold, crisp winter air the only thing keeping me alert. However, as soon as I was back inside the station, I sprang back to life. The detectives' office was abuzz. The Homicide Squad detectives and various other staff from St Marys were busy making phone calls, collecting all the canvass forms and putting them into folders and completing the crime scene logs as they waited for the briefing to begin.

Mick walked in just as I did. 'Officer Seymour,' he said with a wry smile. 'You said you wanted a murder to get yourself back into the swing of things.'

'G'day, Mick. Yeah, I really wish I hadn't said anything now.'

'I told you to be careful what you wish for. Never mind, you're just the right bloke for the investigation. Seriously though,' he continued, 'have you got much to go on at this stage?'

'Stuff all! Homicide said they're happy to leave it with us, but they're sticking around for the day to help us get up and running. Actually, I might need a hand with this new computer system that we've been given since I've been away. I bloody well hate computers.'

'What, the experienced Detective Seymour can't even work a simple computer?' Mick teased. 'No problem, we'll just get the young fellas to show you how it's done; they all think you're an old dinosaur anyway!'

'Gee, thanks for that, Mick,' I said as I made my way to the interview room to get the briefing underway. As I collected everything together, I sensed there was a sombre mood permeating the office. It was as though everyone shared my feelings of the wastefulness of it all, but I also sensed that there was a shared spirit of determination to start the investigation and find the killer. We wanted to get to the heart of things as quickly as possible, not least of all for the family's sake.

Shortly after, Glash arrived and entered the interview room. He made a point of politely greeting everyone before he started, because he was one of those guys who always wanted to make sure everyone, regardless of rank, felt like they were an important part of the team.

When he was finished, he looked across at me and said, 'Right, Peter, let's get this briefing underway. What can you tell us so far?'

With every pair of eyes now firmly fixed on me, I scanned the collection of expectant faces, sat down on the corner of the desk and began. 'Well, we were called shortly after 1.30 am, and found a body lying on the nature strip on the northern side of Edgar Street adjacent to the footpath near the corner of Mamre Road. The deceased had injuries to his head and hands, but his wallet was still in his pants and his front pockets were turned out. Going by the identification in the wallet, it appears the deceased's name was Nick Hanes, and he lived just down the road from where he died. Frank Weiss is looking after things as far as breaking the news to the family. My first impression is that he was assaulted, and possibly robbed, but that is yet to be determined. Enquiries are being made with all local businesses that may have CCTV footage, and any tapes we obtain will be entered into the exhibit book pending viewing. At this stage, we have no witnesses to the incident, so we don't know who or how many people may be involved. Similarly, we don't know the deceased's movements leading up to his death, and that will be one of the first things we need to determine. The body has been taken to Westmead Mortuary, and I have obtained permission from the Coroner to have an urgent post-mortem examination carried out this morning. Dr Little attended the scene, along with Scientific, Rescue and the Video Unit, and I have no concerns about the preservation of the crime scene, which was secure upon my arrival this morning. That's about all I can tell you at this stage.'

I'd barely finished when the phone rang. Mick picked up the receiver, and after a few seconds said, 'Okay, I'll let him know.' He hung up and looked at me. 'That was Steve at the switchboard downstairs. Message from Frank Weiss is that the deceased was separated from his wife and was living with a mate at that address in

Edgar Street. Frank has the address of the wife at St Clair, and is on his way there now.'

We knew from experience that the first forty-eight hours were the most critical in any investigation. Leads would start to go cold, or disappear, and witnesses would start to forget things, or their memories would become clouded. Almost five hours had passed since I'd attended the murder scene, so we needed to get cracking. The Homicide detectives provided invaluable assistance in organising the computer systems and everything else, including an operational name, *Operation Shimane*. For the life of me I didn't know how they came up with these names, but that's what we were given, so that's what we ran with.

After the briefing, I started delegating tasks to all the young officers, and found it pleasing that they were all so keen. St Marys was, as I said, a fairly busy station, but none of them had ever worked on anything this big before.

I gave Matt McQueen and Lisa Everitt the job of attending the mortuary so that they could be there with the family while they made the formal identification. Once they'd done that, the post-mortem could be performed. We also had to come up with a list of places that may have recorded CCTV footage, so I put a couple of young officers to work compiling that list: the Mobil Quix service station, the St Marys RSL Club, any other service stations within a one-kilometre radius, fast-food outlets such as McDonalds, and the Blue Cattle Dog and Parkview pubs.

I needed to ring the Media Unit and update them, a task made all the more urgent by the fact that a freelance television reporter must have been listening to the police radio that morning, and had already visited the scene. The story was a certainty to be on the evening news, which put the pressure on a bit, but that was the beauty of having a Media Unit; it was their job to deal with it, which meant one less worry for me. I spoke to a lady by the name of Sonya Sandham, and a media appeal was organised for release later that day.

The next thing I needed to do was enter everything I had done into the computer system: details of the deceased, the scene, the exact location, which police had attended the scene, and some brief statements on absolutely everything I had so far. I hated having to do it. I wanted to be out on the street, talking to people, getting down and dirty, because this was the best way to get leads. I wanted to concentrate on the old-school ways of policing, of working through the investigation and solving the crime. All the computer stuff was a damn distraction.

I turned the machine on and stared at the blue and white screen, trying to figure things out, but I had absolutely no idea what was going on. I knotted my hands together, wrapped them around the back of my head and breathed out heavily.

'Need some help?' I heard a female voice ask from behind me.

I turned around to see the blonde hair, fair skin and slightly freckled face of Plain-clothes Constable Karen Richards. 'Am I bloody glad to see you!' I said.

'Having a bit of trouble?' she smiled.

'I have got no idea what I am doing here. Don't suppose you could give us a hand, could you?'

'Sure thing, Pete,' she said as she leant over me and started tapping away. She made it look oh-so-easy, and it hit home just how out of date I really was: perhaps I really was an old dinosaur! Karen was an absolute whiz on the computer system, which confirmed my opinion that she was a very, very promising young police officer, and it occurred to me that we made a great team; she the new-style copper and me the old.

Karen patiently tried to walk me through everything, but I was extremely confused and completely lost. 'Yeah, can you repeat that bit?' I asked.

'Which bit?'

'Um, all of it.'

'You're hopeless, Pete!' Karen laughed as she started all over again. However, just as she did, Detective Evers from the Homicide Squad came up to us.

'Hey, Pete,' he said. 'The uniform guys just gave me this video tape. It's from the Mobil Quix service station up on Mamre Road, near the RSL Club.'

'Thanks, mate,' I replied as I took the tape.

'When the Exhibit Sergeant comes in we'll have to put this tape in the exhibit book,' I said to Karen as I locked the tape in my drawer and continued on with my computer lesson. I made mistake after mistake, and each time Karen would have to start all over again. To her credit, she took it all in her stride and kept trying to teach me, exhibiting the patience of a saint.

'This is shit,' I muttered under my breath as I realised there were more and more fields I had to fill in.

Karen, sensing my frustration, finally said, 'How about I just do it all for you? You just tell me what you want me to put in.'

I gave her a Cheshire-cat smile. 'About time you bloody offered! If you left me to do this, we'd be here all day! I'll deal with learning how to work this stupid thing on a quiet day.'

Glash, who had been briefing the St Marys commanders, walked back into the office.

'Everything under control, Peter?' he asked.

'Yeah, boss. We have an operation name, the Media Unit has been briefed and we'll probably organise a media appeal for later this afternoon, depending on how things turn out this morning. Matt and Lisa have already left to go to Westmead to do the formal identification and attend the post-mortem. I've done the P79A and given them the other paperwork they need to fill out and give to Scotty and Dolly at the Coroner's Court.'

I looked up at Glash, and it suddenly dawned on me that he was in uniform. I'd worked with him for a few months, and it had never really occurred to me that back when he was a plain-clothes operator or in civilian life, Glash was a very dapper dresser. Uniformed or not, he always had crisply polished shoes, and his trousers, shirt and tie were always immaculate. Like me, he was an old-school detective who didn't like mucking around, and like me, he just wanted to get in and do the job. He was always keen to offer advice, but didn't interfere and try to run someone else's investigation, and just like my old boss Mick O'Connell, he always backed his troops no matter what.

'Tell you what, Pete, it's lucky we've got you here to organise all this material, especially with your court experience,' Glash said.

'I may be an old dinosaur, but at least I come in handy for something!'

'Keep me updated on how things are going. Mick can look after the office, but you'll have to make sure you brief him on the jobs you had going, so he can make sure someone else looks after them while you work on this. Hopefully, we'll get some information; surely someone must have heard or seen something. Anyway, good luck with it all.'

'Cheers, boss,' I said as Glash turned and left the office, leaving Karen and I to finish what we needed to do on the computer. We were just about done when the phone rang. 'St Marys detectives, Peter Seymour speaking.'

'Hello, Detective Seymour. My name's Barbara Reid from St Marys Band Club. I spoke to you earlier this morning. We've got the security tape from yesterday and overnight available for you whenever you want to pick it up.'

'Thanks, Ms Reid, that's very helpful. I'll come down shortly.'

'Just ask for me at the reception desk and I'll bring it down to you.'

'Fantastic, I'll see you soon.'

I turned back to Karen and saw Mick standing beside her. 'The Band Club have got their security tape for me. I'm gonna head down there now and pick it up while I've got the chance. I'll fill you in on the jobs I've got going when I get back.'

'No dramas,' Mick said.

I hurried out of the station and back down the street to the Band Club, where I was greeted by a young receptionist. 'Hello, can I help you?' she said.

'Yes, my name is Detective Seymour,' I said as I showed her my badge. 'I'm here to see Barbara Reid.'

'Certainly, Detective. I'll just call her office.'

Shortly after, Barbara appeared and handed me a video tape. 'Hope this helps you find whatever it is you're looking for,' she said with a smile.

'Me too,' I replied as Barbara picked up a nearby notepad and scribbled something on it.

'This is my direct number,' she said as she handed me a piece of paper. 'If there is anything else I can help you with, just give me a call.'

'Great, thanks for that,' I said, and turned and headed towards the exit. Just as I reached the door, I turned back. 'Do you know what, there is one more thing you can do for me. Can I get access to your sign-in register from last night? I want to see if a particular person was at the club.'

'Sure, do you need it right now?'

'No,' I replied. 'If you can call me when you're ready, I'll send someone down to go through it.'

'Great,' she said.

With that, I left the club and made my way back to the detectives' office. I sat down and had just started writing a check list of all the things I had to do when the phone rang. 'Hello,' I said.

'Hi, Pete,' Matt said. 'I'm still down at the mortuary. The family have just formally identified Nick Hanes's body. He was separated from his wife, but they kept in touch. They're pretty distraught, as you can imagine, but they're happy to come down to the station to speak to you about what happened.'

'Good job, Matt. Can you organise all that for me?'

'Yeah, mate, can do,' Matt said, and then hung up.

I was rather pleased that the family had agreed to come in because, quite understandably, this was the most distressing of times for a family, and they were often in too much shock to be able to discuss things. Even so, it was going to be difficult for them, especially at such a horrific time, but I needed them to tell me everything they knew, because they were my main hope for information. It was going to be hard enough to get them to talk about their deceased family member, but to make matters worse, I was going to ask them if they were prepared to front the media to make a plea for witnesses to come forward. It was one of the most unpleasant things I'd experienced in my career, having to meet a family for the first time in circumstances such as this. All I could do was offer them whatever comfort I could, but I desperately needed them to do the media appeal, because it would generate public attention. People would start talking, which usually meant that witnesses' memories were jogged, and more of them would start coming forward. The other value of a media appeal was that it could sometimes make an offender, or offenders, a bit nervous, and sometimes an offender couldn't resist bragging about what they'd done, especially if it was all over the news.

Like Glash had said, someone must have seen something. There was no way a man could be bashed on a footpath of a main street without someone knowing what had happened, even if it was in the middle of the night. If he'd been drinking at the club, he must have been with mates who could fill us in on his last movements, but as it stood, we had no witnesses yet, and so a media report was the best way to get the information flowing.

I sat down at my desk, leant back in my chair and stared at the ceiling. Suddenly, I remembered that I still had to fill Mick in on the jobs I'd been working on that needed covering. He was sitting at his desk, a yellow envelope to one side, collating all the statements and information we already had. 'Hey, Mick, you got a sec?' I said.

'Yeah, Pete, what's up?'

'I've got a few free minutes, so I thought I'd fill you in on all the jobs I'm working on.'

'Shoot,' Mick said as he put his work to one side.

I gave him the details of a couple of burglaries and fraud investigations. 'There are a couple of pretty urgent briefs,' I said. 'You'll have to reallocate them to someone else, but there's a few others that aren't as important, so you can probably just leave them, and I'll get back to them when this is all over.'

'Yeah, sweet.'

'Hey, Mick, how about I make you a coffee?' I said. 'I'd like to have a quiet word with you before the family gets here.'

'Sure mate, I reckon I could go a coffee.'

We headed downstairs to the meals room, made a cuppa and headed out to the back veranda. Despite the crispness of the morning, the sun had come out, and it was quite pleasant outside. The sun's warmth soothed my soul, and I started to feel a little better about what I had to do.

'What's on your mind, mate?' Mick asked.

'You know how you were joking about me being an old dinosaur?'

'Yeah, sorry about that, mate,' he smiled.

'Nah, it's all good, you weren't far off the mark.'

'What do you mean?'

'I'm completely hopeless with the new computer system and the running sheets and all that stuff. I'm not going to have the time to get my head around it all. If it's okay with you, I'd like Karen to be my partner on this one. It'd be a great experience for her. She's a smart young operator, plus she's great on the computer. I know Matt was called out with me, so he'll want to stay on this job, but I'm happy to leave it up to you as to who else we can spare from the office to work on this.'

'Yep, Kaz is a good 'un. I'm more than happy for you and her to run the investigation, and I'll just make other people available as you need them. Everyone will be available for the first few days to get everything done, and then they can all drop back to their own work after that.'

'Sounds good,' I replied. 'To be honest, if we don't get witnesses coming forward, this one's going to be real hard to solve. If we get a media briefing done today, tonight and tomorrow will hopefully be a busy time. We'll need everyone available at least until then.'

'Yeah, that's no worries,' Mick said. He knew I was going to be pushing shit uphill, but he couldn't help throwing in one of his trademark jibes. 'You reckon you might just have the offender in the dock by spring?'

'A month and half, that's plenty of time!' I shot back. 'After all, it only took us ten years to get Keir to trial, and we're still going through the courts, so I don't see why I can't get a result in this one by September. No dramas at all! You know how I said I needed a good murder to get me back into the swing of things? I *was* only joking, you know.'

'I know, mate, I know,' Mick replied.

'Well, let's hope we get the right result. I'd better get back to it and get myself sorted before the family arrives.' As I made my way back upstairs, my mind turned to home. The girls would have woken up by now, and would be wondering where I was. *I'd better let Susie know what's going on, and that I'll probably be home late tonight,* I thought to myself, *and who knows how many nights after that.*

Chapter 4:
History Repeats

While we were preparing everything, down at the mortuary, Dr Little was conducting the post-mortem. Russell Frazer was also present, and he took possession of items of clothing, fingernail clippings and other specimens for DNA testing.

When Dr Little had finished, she passed on her preliminary findings to Matt, who in turn called me. 'Pete, it's Matt again,' he said when I picked up the phone.

'Hey, mate, has Dr Little finished the post-mortem?'

'Yeah, that's why I'm calling. It looks like the deceased had a really bad heart, and Dr Little said that a heart attack was the most likely cause of death.'

'Do you think the heart attack was brought on by an assault, or are the injuries to his head consistent with a fall?' The reason I had to ask this was because we had to prove that the assault was in fact the cause of death. If his dodgy heart had caused his death, and the assault really wasn't a contributing factor, then the charge would be downgraded to one of assault. If the offender had just given him a shove and simply walked off, and he had subsequently died of a heart attack, then there was insufficient evidence to charge anyone with anything.

'Mate,' Matt said apologetically, 'I'm not the expert. It's probably best you talk to Dr Little about that. I'll put her on.'

A moment later, Dr Little said, 'Hello there, Detective Seymour.'

'Hi, Dr Little. Can I ask you if the injuries to his head and hands are consistent with an assault?'

'In my opinion, I would say yes, he has been assaulted, but his heart was also very bad, and it is my belief that his death was as a result of a heart attack.'

'But if he suffered a heart attack as a result of being assaulted, can I assume that the stress of an assault would be enough to bring on that heart attack, especially if he had a bad heart?'

'Well,' Dr Little continued, 'I would have to say that a serious assault, as this seems to have been, would be enough to bring on a heart attack.'

'Therefore, if the deceased had not been assaulted, in all likelihood he would still be alive today, albeit with a bad heart.'

'Yes, that is about the measure of it.'

My pulse quickened. It wasn't that I was excited that we now had an offender to prosecute, it was more that I didn't want to see anyone walk free after having committed what I knew was a serious crime. I'd seen it too many times before.

From what Dr Little had said, it seemed like we were dealing with a case of manslaughter. Nevertheless, we were going to push for a murder charge because, in Australian law, there is the ability for a jury or a court to find an offender not guilty of murder but guilty of manslaughter. The onus is always on the prosecution to prove that there was an intention to take someone's life, and that it was not merely the result of an unfortunate accident or circumstance. Consequently, we always charged the offender with the higher offence of murder. It's a tricky one really. For a charge of manslaughter, you don't have to prove an intention to kill, only that an act occurred with a recklessness or disregard for the welfare of the victim that caused the death. Even an 'omission' of an act could result in a difference between a charge of murder or manslaughter.

'Thank you, Dr Little, you've been very helpful,' I said.

'My pleasure, Detective Seymour. I shall speak to you soon.'

'Pete,' Matt said as he took the phone back, 'I'm on my way back to the office now.'

'Righto, mate, see you shortly.'

I sat at my desk and thought about everything I'd just been told. In my mind, I was satisfied that Nick Hanes wouldn't be dead now if he hadn't been assaulted. The first thing I needed to do, which was absolutely critical, was to establish his last movements before he died. Most important was to find out whether he'd been complaining about chest pains or not feeling well in the weeks leading up to his death. It was a fine line. If he had been suffering ill health, then it was going to be nigh on impossible to charge someone with his murder. However, if there was no evidence of him being really sick, then the fact he had a dodgy ticker was taken more and more out of play, and there would be nothing to stop me from charging someone, but before I did any of that, I needed to discuss what Dr Little had just told me with Mick.

I got up, walked over to Mick's desk and relayed, almost word for word, what I'd been told, then added, 'We'll have to wait until all the toxicology results come back in, but assuming there's nothing untoward in that and the final determination is heart attack as a direct result of sustaining injuries in an assault, we're right to go. We can start hunting for the suspect, or suspects, with a view to charging him, or them, with murder.'

'Sounds like you've got it pretty sorted,' Mick replied.

'I hope so, mate, for the family's sake,' I said as I headed back to my desk and phoned the Media Unit, who told me they'd organised the media briefing for later that morning, just before lunch.

Whilst it was a necessity, I was dreading the media conference. I knew the family, and the media, would have thousands of questions for me, but at this stage I didn't have any answers. How do you tell a family that you're following up lines of enquiry without being able to give them anything else to hold on to? All I could do was keep myself as upbeat as possible and give them every assurance that I, along with the entire team at St Marys, would not rest until we found out what had happened to Nick Hanes, but even that felt a bit shallow. It absolutely tore me up that I didn't have anything more to give them. The next couple of hours flew by, and at around 10.30 am I was trawling through the canvass sheets when the uniformed staff at the front counter rang to let me know that the family had arrived.

I took a deep breath and psyched myself up as best I could. I was pretty apprehensive as I walked downstairs and made my way to the front foyer. The Hanes family were standing huddled together in a circle, and they immediately looked up at me as I approached them. I saw the despair etched on their faces, and it occurred to me that I was about to become a big part of their lives for all the wrong reasons. The hardest part was walking up to Nick Hanes's wife, who was at the centre of their circle, and introducing myself.

'Hello, Mrs Hanes,' I said as I extended my hand. 'I am Detective Seymour.'

'Hello, Detective. I'm Bel. This is my son, Paul, and his wife, Sharon. This is Nick's younger brother, David, and this is his wife, Kym,' she said as she pointed to the various members of her family.

I was a little taken aback when I realised there were a score or more of people there who, I would later find out, were extended family members and family friends who had all turned up to offer support. 'First of all, let me say that we're terribly sorry for your loss,' I said quietly to Mrs Hanes. I meant every word wholeheartedly, but it still seemed like a hollow statement.

'Thank you, Detective,' she replied.

I then addressed all of them. 'As we suspect this to be a murder investigation, it had to be referred to the Coroner. I will be in charge of investigating the circumstances surrounding Nick's death. Our investigations are well underway. We're making numerous enquiries, and we've taken possession of some CCTV tapes that should help us shed some light on what happened.'

'Do you have any idea who did this?' Mrs Hanes asked.

'Mrs Hanes, I'm very sorry, but it's too early at this stage for me to answer that question.'

'Do you have any idea how long it will take to catch Nick's killer?' she pushed.

'Like I said, it's still too early, but I assure you we're doing all we can.' With that, my heart shattered. How do you stand there in front of a grieving family, a family who had gone to bed last night with no idea they would be waking up to the nightmare that was now unfolding, and merely tell them that we're doing all we can?

As I watched her trying to hold back her tears, I felt the same drive welling up inside me as I'd had during the Keir investigation. I would find the answers they so desperately wanted. No matter how long it took, no matter what I had to do, I would find Nick Hanes's killer.

Media crews began pulling up outside, and before they started to set up I thought I had better ask the family one more time if they really wanted to go through with this. 'Mrs Hanes, are you sure you and your family are up for being interviewed? Remember, it is entirely up to you. This is your choice.'

'Detective Seymour, can I ask you something?' Mrs Hanes said through watery eyes. 'If we do this, will it help you to catch Nick's killer?'

'To be perfectly honest, yes, it will be a huge help to us. The media are a great way to stir people's memories, and hopefully we can get a lot of information that will assist us with the investigation,' I replied.

'In that case, I'll do it,' she said as she fought back the tears. I retrieved a box of tissues from the reception desk and gave them to her.

'Thank you,' she said quietly as she dabbed at her eyes.

'Peter,' I heard Glash call from behind me.

'Yes, boss?'

'Where do want to hold the media conference?'

'I think it's best if we do it on the grass out the front of the station.'

I went outside and directed the Channel Seven and Channel Nine film crews and journalists towards the grass, where they started setting up. Media interviews can be tough at the best of times, and I did my best to calm the family down as much as possible. I took them to one side and said, 'Look, if at any time you feel like you need to stop, that's perfectly fine. The media are fairly understanding when it comes to this type of thing.' The family nodded in reply.

When the media were ready, I went outside and began. 'Good morning everyone, thank you for coming,' I said as I looked out over the dozens of microphones and cameras. 'I would like to start by saying that, at this time, we have very little information relating to Mr Hanes's death. We are making a number of enquiries, but the investigation is still in its early stages. Beyond that, I am not prepared to make any further comment. I would, however, ask that if anyone has any information, no matter how insignificant or trivial it seems, they come forward and provide us with that information.' When I had finished, I went back inside and brought the family out.

Mrs Hanes was becoming visibly upset, and she needed to take a few deep breaths to compose herself before she began. 'Um, this is a tremendously difficult time for myself and my family. Nick was such a wonderful man who cared so much about all of us, and I am really struggling to understand why anyone would do such a horrible, terrible thing to my husband. All I can say is, I urge anyone with any information to come forward and let the police know so that they can catch whoever did this.'

Mrs Hanes did really well to get as far as she did, but as I watched her, I could see she was starting to come apart at the seams, and it wasn't long before she broke down. Her family comforted her, and after she had wiped away her tears, she somehow managed to get through the rest of her statement. It gladdened me to see how supportive her family were, and to know that whilst this was a difficult time for all of them, they would be there to help each other get through it.

The media, while considerate of Mrs Hanes's feelings, had a job to do, and kept asking her question after question. It eventually came to the point where I could see they were done, so I ended the media conference and took the family back into the foyer.

'Mrs Hanes,' I said quietly, 'what you just did was very brave. We really appreciate it. I know you and your family must just want to get home, but if you don't mind, I would like to ask you a few questions myself.'

'Certainly, Detective Seymour, what would you like to know?'

I took out my notebook. 'Can you start by telling me where your husband worked?'

'He was a panel beater and spray painter for years, mostly around here.'

'Did Nick have many friends?'

'Mostly he had his drinking buddies.'

'So can you give me an idea of what he usually did on a Friday night?'

'Um, he normally went down to the club or pub to have a few beers with his mates.'

'Do you know if he had any enemies?'

'Not that I know of. Nick was a real knockabout kind of guy. As far as I know, everybody liked him.'

'Had Nick been acting strangely at all lately, or had you noticed any changes in his normal behaviour?'

'No, not at all.'

'Had he had any serious illness that you were aware of; something like a bad heart maybe?'

'Not really. He'd had a few problems with his heart, but nothing serious that I knew of.'

'Can you tell me when you last saw him?'

'Yes, I saw him last week. We used to go shopping every Saturday, even though we weren't together.'

There was so much more I wanted to ask, but I could see she'd had enough, so I decided that it was better that I didn't push things. She needed space and time to grieve with her family, and to deal with everything that had happened.

'Thank you very much, Mrs Hanes. I really appreciate you coming in and doing this,' I said as I led her to the station exit. 'I promise you we will not rest until we find out what happened to your husband.'

'Thank you, Detective Seymour,' she replied, the tears beginning to well up again.

As I watched the family walk away from the station, my stomach began to knot at the thought of what they would have to go through. I went back up to the detectives' office, firm in my resolve to solve this case.

Thinking about how families coped with hardship made me realise I had been on the go all day, and hadn't had a chance to call home. 'Hi, darl,' I said when Susie picked up. 'I'm sorry to tell you this, but it was a murder I was called out to last night, and I'm going to have to stay late tonight.'

'Can you tell me what happened?'

'Yeah, we found a bloke's body on Mamre Road. He'd had a heart attack, but he'd also been assaulted, and I'm pretty sure that was what killed him. Apart from that, we don't know much else.'

'Oh, how terrible for the family!' she said sincerely. 'Well, do what you need to do, sweetheart, but try to make it home as early as you can.'

Damn, I thought to myself after I put the phone down, *I left the detectives because I was spending too much time away from home and my family. I've barely been back a few weeks, and here I am doing it all over again!*

Everyone worked really hard all day, but it was 8 pm before Mick finally said we should call it quits for the night. Before we left, I gathered everyone in the office and made a point of thanking them for the work they had all put in. Then, I was finally on my way home to my beautiful wife and daughters.

Chapter 5:
Staying Positive

I'd been fighting my tiredness all day, and as I wound down on the drive home, I realised I was completely and utterly exhausted. Adrenaline had kept me going throughout the day, but now that it had subsided I was knackered. When I pulled up outside my house, I didn't feel like I could go straight inside. When I'd left home that morning, I'd been close to my usual self, but having seen a family in absolute grief that day, something inside me had changed. I didn't want my girls to see me in a saddened state, so I sat in the car for a few moments and did my best to compose myself.

Death is a strange thing. Sometimes, it seems to me that we only ever pause to think about what is truly important to us when a tragedy occurs. For me, I couldn't help but think about how blessed I was to have my wife and my three beautiful daughters.

I took a deep breath, slapped the steering wheel with my hands and put on my best happy face. I walked inside and into the lounge room, where Susie was waiting for me. I forced a smile, but it was no use. Susie had always been able to see straight through me, and as soon as I walked into the room, she looked me up and down, got off the lounge and came over to me and hugged me. 'I'm glad you're home,' she whispered into my ear.

'It's been a long day,' I replied.

'Do you feel like talking about it?' she asked as she pulled back slightly.

'Not much to talk about really,' I replied. 'Like I said, looks like this bloke was assaulted on his way home last night and died at the scene from a heart attack brought on by being attacked, but unfortunately we've got bugger all to go on at this stage. Hopefully we'll get a break tomorrow after the media publicity.'

'Yeah, I saw it on the news tonight. I must say, you didn't look too bad on TV!'

'Yeah, thanks, darl.'

'Have you eaten?'

'Not since lunch.'

'Well, sit down and I'll fix you some dinner.'

A cold beer and a bowl of spag bol made me feel half human again. An hour or so later, I went to check on the girls, giving each of them a kiss on the cheek before I went to bed. I thought, given the long day I'd put in, that as soon as my head hit the pillow I'd be out like a light, but no, the projector played on the ceiling as the day's events ticked over in my mind, and I couldn't get the Hanes family's faces out of my head.

Eventually, I drifted off into a fitful sleep, and dreamt of something that had happened earlier in my career when I had first become a detective. We were in the Marrickville detectives' office when we received a call from a local bank manager to tell us that there was an armed hold-up in progress at the Westpac bank down on the main street.

'What are the details?' I said.

'There's a guy standing out the front of the bank with something wrapped up in a towel.'

'Okay, we'll be down there as quick as we can,' I said, and put the receiver down.

'We'd better jump in a car, Pete,' Eric, my senior partner, said.

'Nah, it's peak hour, it'll take too long. It's not far away, it'll be quicker if we run.'

'Yeah, you're probably right,' Eric said as we rushed out the door. We bolted as fast as we could down the two blocks to the bank.

The manager was out the front waiting for us.

'So what have you got for us?' I asked as Eric and I regained our breath.

The manager pointed inside through the large windows to a middle-aged Greek man who was scribbling on a piece of paper as he stood at the counter. In front of him was a yellow and orange towel. He was wearing sunglasses, and kept taking glances around the bank. I took a quick squiz and realised there were about six people waiting in the queue.

'What do you want to do, Eric?' I asked.

'Well, we need to sort him out,' Eric replied. 'We haven't got time to wait around. We'll have to go in. What do you reckon?'

'Probably best just one of us goes in, so it doesn't spook him. Mate, I'm single, but you've got a missus and a young kid, so I'm going in.' I reached down, raised my left trouser leg and removed my gun from my left ankle holster, and then put it back in the holster and stood straight back up.

'Eric, I can't go in holding my gun. Someone will see me and scream, and then all hell will break loose. I'll just casually walk in, hope he doesn't notice me, and then jump him. If he sees me and grabs whatever is under the towel, I won't have time to get my gun out, so I'll be hitting the deck. If it gets to that, bloody well shoot him.'

'Shit! Okay then,' Eric said, bending down and fumbling with his own ankle holster as he struggled to get his gun out.

Eric's demeanour was anything but confident, which made me a bit nervous. 'Ah, Eric, mate, how did you go in your last pistol shoot?' I asked as I glared at him.

'Yeah, I did okay, I suppose.'

'Just okay?' I said as I raised my eyebrows. 'That's fuckin' great! Just get your gun out, and if you see me hit the deck, shoot that bastard, okay?'

Eric and the bank manager exchanged decidedly concerned looks as I walked into the bank, trying my best to appear as casual as possible, even though I was absolutely shitting myself. As soon as I stepped inside the bank, the whole world seemed to slow down. As I inched my way forward, I seemed to be taking an eternity to reach the guy. *Just let me get a bit closer and don't look up at me, you bastard*, I thought to myself.

I closed in, waiting for him to turn around at any moment. I crept closer and closer, until eventually I was no more than a few feet away. At that point, I lunged forward, and just as I did he reached for the towel and unwrapped it, revealing a double-barrelled sawn-off shotgun.

Bang!

I woke with a start, breathing heavily as I wiped the sweat from my forehead.

'Pete!' Sue cried. 'Are you okay?'

'Yeah, just had another bad dream is all.'

'It's okay,' Sue said as she took me in her arms.

I looked over at the clock; 5 am, time to get up. I hauled myself out of bed and into the shower. As I stood there letting the water cascade over me, I closed my eyes and reminded myself that my dream was only that. In reality, when I'd lunged at the prospective bank robber, I'd actually managed to knock him into the wall. As soon as he'd seen this, Eric had rushed inside and held the bloke down while I handcuffed him. When we had him squared away, we checked the towel. Inside, we found a double-barrelled sawn-off shotgun with both barrels loaded, and upon frisking him, we found four more cartridges in his pocket.

I opened my eyes and prayed to myself that today would be the day when we got some good news in the Hanes investigation. I had some breakfast and was on my way back upstairs to get the last of my gear when I saw Jenna standing at the top of the stairs in her dressing gown, wiping the sleep out of her eyes. 'Daddy!' she yelled when she saw me.

I bounded up the remaining stairs and she leapt into my arms. I hugged her tightly and then put her down again. 'I'm sorry, princess, but I have to go to work again today.'

'That's not fair!' she said with a scowl on her cute little face as she stamped her right foot.

'I know, princess, I'm sorry,' I apologised as I knelt down in front of her.

'You didn't come home last night before I went to bed,' she said as her scowl became a stern pout and she crossed her arms.

'I know, I'm sorry, sweetheart, but I've got a really important job to do at the moment. A poor man died, and we have to try to find out who did it. If something happened to Mummy or your sisters, you'd want Daddy to find out who did it, wouldn't you?'

'Yes,' she said. 'But you must promise to hurry up so you can come home early.'

'I'll do my best, sweetheart, but I can't promise anything,' I said as I stood up. Talk about putting the pressure on!

On my way to work, I couldn't help but think that Sunday was supposed to be a day of rest, a day to spend time with your family and, for religious people, to go to church. Unfortunately for the Haneses, they would forever be one family member short now, and if they were churchgoers, they'd be praying for the soul of their loved one who had been taken from them too early. All I could do was hope that the media publicity would bring some witnesses forward, and that I would get the break I was desperately hoping for.

There must have been a scuffle. There must have been some yelling and shouting. The murder occurred on a public street. Surely somebody must have heard or seen something. I just had to keep telling myself that a slow, patient, painstaking attitude would yield rewards. I would spend today going through the hours of video footage, because maybe, just maybe, it would reveal the identity of the perpetrator.

When I got to work, I made my way up to the detectives' office and organised the interview room facing out onto the highway as our Command Centre. We set the room up so that everything we could possibly need was within arm's reach. It had a computer system, which I was going to leave to someone else if possible, to record any important information and running sheets. In the centre was a desk with neatly placed folders to store all the information. To the left there was a whiteboard on the wall where I wrote the daily tasks needing completion and reminders of details of any potential suspects. Once I was satisfied that everything was in order, I made my way to the meals room, grabbed a cuppa and went out to the front office. 'Hey, fellas,' I said to the uniformed staff manning the desk, 'has any information come in overnight for me?'

'No, Pete, sorry, mate,' one officer replied.

Bugger, I thought. I'd hoped that there would be some good news to greet me first thing. I was hugely disappointed, and started to wonder if we were ever going to get a break. I went back upstairs, where I ran into Karen.

'Hi, Pete, how are you this morning!' she said with her typical youthful enthusiasm.

'G'day, Kaz. I'm okay. How are you?'

'I'm excellent!' she smiled. 'Did you get a good night's sleep?'

'No, not really,' I replied. 'I had a thousand things running through my mind last night.'

'I'm not surprised,' Karen laughed. 'I'll get the computer up and running!' It was as though we shared a bit of an unspoken bond, and she knew that was the best thing she could say to me, especially given my complete lack of computer literacy.

'Thanks for that,' I said, relieved that I had one less thing to worry about.

One by one, the young crew of detectives began arriving. I was particularly relieved to see Mick Lyons, and then Glash turn up, because I knew their experience and knowledge would prove invaluable as the investigation unfolded.

'There's nothing like a murder to blow the overtime budget,' Mick said as he settled himself down at his desk. For once, he wasn't joking. Each command had a budget they were supposed to stick to, but with a murder investigation going on, everyone had to work extended hours, and the overtime bill was going to skyrocket.

'You're not worried about overtime are you Mick?' I smiled across at him.

'Nah, nobody will argue with us all being called in for a murder, especially Glash. We'll need as many people as we can get in the early stages. Did any information come in overnight?'

'No,' I replied. 'I checked the message book and spoke to the boys downstairs, but unfortunately we've got nothing more than we had yesterday.'

I'd tried all the things I could think of, but nothing had come through. The investigation seemed to be stalling. I could sense the negative feelings rising inside me, but I knew I had to keep them to myself. I had to remain as positive as I possibly could, because I was painfully aware that if I lost my enthusiasm, it would have a flow-on effect on everybody else, and the whole operation would lose direction. Past experience had taught me that positive energy often brought results at precisely the times when I least expected them, but with my nightmares intensifying and the lack of sleep starting to get to me, it was becoming harder and harder to stay upbeat.

More and more people began arriving, and some of the negativity began to subside as I sensed a determined excitement beginning to build among the crew. They were resolute that we were going to find Nick Hanes's killer, and I had to say, I found their attitude pleasantly refreshing.

The first thing I did was to get someone down to take a statement from Nick Hanes's housemate. When I read it, I discovered that Nick had gone to the Parkview Hotel for a few drinks after work on that fateful Friday, which made sense, because the hotel was just fifty metres west of the St Marys Band Club. I read on. Nick had arrived home from the hotel at dinnertime, had something to eat, and then decided to go to the Band Club.

'Hey, Mick,' I called across the room, 'I reckon we need to get a couple of people down to the Parkview to start making enquiries about Hanes's exact movements on Friday night. Apparently he went home, had some dinner, and then went back out to the Band Club, which probably explains the TAB tickets.'

'We can send Lisa and Matt down to the pub, and they can check out the Band Club while they're down there,' Mick replied. 'Have you got all the CCTV footage you needed?'

'Yeah, we've got all the surrounding service stations, pubs, clubs and restaurants,' I replied. That's when it hit me. Perhaps our perpetrator wasn't a local. Maybe he'd come in from somewhere else, and had then departed via the railway station. 'Shit, Mick, I forgot about the railway station. I'll have to get someone down there to check with them.'

'Don't stress, mate, I'll organise that one for you,' Mick replied. 'You just look after what you need to get done today.'

'Cheers, mate, that'll be a big help.'

Around mid-morning, Mick had two officers make their way down to the St Marys railway station and organised for their surveillance footage to be copied by their security section. At the same time, Matt and Lisa headed over to the Parkview Hotel. I asked them to put together a specific brief of Nick Hanes's exact movements from the moment he left the hotel to go home for dinner, and then out again to the Band Club, right up until the time of his death. I particularly wanted to know what condition he'd been in when he left the hotel and the Band Club, and I was also very keen to know if he'd been involved in any scuffles at either venue that might have carried over outside. I also needed Lisa and Matt to try to find out if Hanes had any marks on his face or body prior to him leaving the Band Club. If not, it was safe to assume the injuries we'd seen on his body had been inflicted at the crime scene.

When I read through Lisa and Matt's interviews with the staff and patrons at the hotel I felt much more optimistic, because from them, we had gained a very clear picture of the man that was Nick Hanes. He'd been extremely well liked by all who knew him, someone who would do absolutely anything for a mate.

I was sifting through all the information the guys had collected when I heard Mick's phone ring. He answered, and then listened for a few moments. 'Hey, Pete, have you got a tick?' he said. 'The uniformed boys have got a woman on the phone who said her son was with one of his mates on Friday night. Looks like they saw two blokes assaulting Hanes in almost exactly the same spot where we found his body. The media conference was a bloody top idea, mate. Apparently they saw the interview on the news and they want to speak to you.'

My mind started racing. We finally had a breakthrough! I couldn't believe our luck. Not only did we have one witness, we had two! 'Tell them to put her through to my desk, Mick.' When it rang, I picked up the receiver. 'Good morning, this is Detective Seymour, can I help you?' I said as calmly as I could.

'Hello, Detective Seymour. My name is Mrs Dupont. We were watching the news last night and we saw the story about the murder on Mamre Road. My son thinks he may have witnessed it.'

'Can I ask how old your son is, Mrs Dupont?'

'Of course. He's eighteen.'

'Could I please get his name?'

'His name is Jack.'

'Is he there at the moment? Would it be possible to speak to him?'

'Certainly, Detective. I'll just put him on.'

I could feel my heart starting to pound. This young fellow could be the key to helping me nail Nick Hanes's killer or killers.

'Hello,' said Jack Dupont. He was obviously a little nervous.

'G'day, Jack. My name is Detective Seymour. How are you today?' I said, trying to make him feel as comfortable as possible.

'I'm okay, thank you,' he replied, his voice tinged with uncertainty.

'Your mum mentioned that you may have witnessed the incident on Mamre Road on Friday night. Do you think it would be possible to tell me what you saw?'

'Well,' he started cautiously, 'me and my mate Ben were on our way home. We missed the bus, so we decided to walk from the railway station. We saw an older man walking the same way as us, but on the other side of Mamre Road. We were walking quicker than him, and just as we got in front of him, we heard some voices. There were two young guys walking towards the older guy, and they stopped him at the corner of Edgar Street. We heard them talking, and I heard one of the two younger blokes say he wanted his wallet. Ben and I turned around and I saw one of the younger blokes punch the older guy in the face and he fell to the ground. The other guy turned around and looked at us, and we thought they might come after us as well, so we took off up Mamre Road as fast as we could.'

I sensed that Jack was becoming more comfortable, so I tried to keep him talking. 'Okay, Jack, you've done a really brave and important thing by coming forward. I'm really proud of you, mate, and I'm sure Nick's family will be too,' I said. 'Do you reckon you might be able to give me a description of the two young blokes you saw?'

'Yeah, the guy I saw hitting the older man was pretty tall, and he had blond hair and he was a bit skinny. He was wearing light-coloured clothes. The other guy was shorter, and he had dark skin and dark hair and was wearing dark clothes. He wasn't as skinny as the taller guy.'

'That's brilliant, mate!' I said enthusiastically. 'Listen, I need you to come down to the police station so I can get a statement from you. Do you think you could do that this afternoon?'

'Yeah, Detective, I reckon I can do that,' Jack replied.

'Now there's just one more thing I need you to do for me. I need to speak to your friend Ben. Do you think I could have his number?'

'Yep, no prob,' he said, and gave me the number. I quickly took it down and repeated it back to him to make sure I'd gotten it right.

'By the way, what's Ben's last name?' I said.

'It's Schmidt.'

'Righto, Jack,' I said. 'Thanks for all this. Like I said, mate, you've done a really brave thing. I'll be in touch.'

No sooner had I hung up from Jack than I was ringing his mate Ben. 'Hello, is that Ben Schmidt?'

'Yes,' came the reply.

'Hi, Ben. My name is Detective Seymour from St Marys detectives. I've just been speaking to your friend Jack, and he gave me your number. He told me that he was walking home with you late last Friday night. Is that right?'

'Yes,' he replied.

'Mate, do you think you could tell me what you saw?'

'Yes, sir. We were walking along Mamre Road and these two guys demanded a wallet off another bloke on the other side of the road to us. They punched into him and knocked him to the ground, and we took off because we thought they might try to do the same thing to us.'

'Did you get a good look at these two guys?'

'Yeah, one was a white bloke, and he was tall with real blond hair and he was skinny. The other bloke looked like he was an Islander. He was shorter, and had dark hair. He had dark clothes, and the taller guy was wearing light-coloured clothes.'

'Listen mate, I really appreciate you helping us out. Do you reckon you might be able to come into the station this arvo, because I need to get a statement about what you just told me. Your mate Jack is coming in too. Would that be suitable for you?'

'Yeah, I can come in with him and we can do it together.'

'That's great mate, but there's something really important I need you to do for me. It's absolutely vital that you and Jack don't talk about what happened, because I need to get statements off both of you, but what you tell me must be your own recollection of what you saw and heard. Okay?'

'Sure, no problem,' he replied.

'I can't stress how important this is, Ben. We can't have you guys confusing each other's stories by talking about it. You need to be able to tell me what you saw and heard, and not rely on what Jack may have seen or heard.'

'No worries,' he said.

'Okay mate, I'll see you this afternoon.'

'Okay.'

I put the phone down and shook my head. I couldn't believe that, in the space of a few minutes, I'd gone from having pretty much bugger all to having two eye witnesses.

'Well, don't keep me in suspense,' Mick said, throwing his hands in the air. 'What did they have to say?'

'Mate, we've caught a bloody big break! These two boys were walking home on the other side of Mamre Road and saw two other young blokes walk up to the victim and demand his wallet. I can only assume that Hanes refused, so they started laying into him and knocked him to the ground. The two boys reckon they got a pretty good look at them, but they took off when one of the assailants turned around and saw them because they feared they might cop it as well.'

Mick, always level-headed, raised a pertinent point. 'Mate, you gotta wonder how good a look they could have gotten when they were on the other side of the road. It must have been pretty dark at that time of night.'

'Yeah, true. I did wonder about that the other night when I arrived at the crime scene, but I also noticed that there are street lights on both sides of the road. It's fairly well lit, so I can only assume they got a good look. Plus, they were pretty detailed with their descriptions,' I said as I got up from my desk and went to tell Karen the good news.

'Hey, Karen!' I said as I walked in. 'Guess what?'

'What?'

'Looks like we just got the break we were hoping for! We've got two teenage boys coming in this afternoon to give us statements. They saw two young blokes approach Hanes, demand his wallet and then punch him to the ground.'

'Unreal!' she replied excitedly.

I went back out to Mick and said, 'I'd better go over and let Glash know. Reckon it must be about coffee time then.'

'Sure is!' Mick replied jovially.

I quickly headed over to Glash's office and briefed him on the information that had just come to light. 'That's great news!' he replied. 'Once you've got their statements, can you come and show me? Excellent job, Pete. You just might get a good result in this one far more quickly than we first thought,' he said with a broad smile. That was the thing about Glash. He was a genuine bloke who, like me, was always determined to get the job done, and he took great pride when one of his boys was able to solve a crime.

'Coffee time?' Mick said as I came out of Glash's office.

'Definitely!' I replied, whereupon we made our way downstairs to the meals room.

'Regarding your previous point, mate,' I said as I stirred some sugar into my coffee, 'hopefully these two guys got a good look at the suspects, but even if they did, we're still gonna have a hard time identifying them.'

'Nah, don't worry, mate. I was just pointing something out,' Mick said supportively. 'You said you'd have them in the dock by spring, and now that you have this break, I reckon you just might do it.' I looked up to see Mick's characteristic cheesy grin spread across his face, and couldn't help but laugh as we went out the back to enjoy a well-earned cuppa.

The next few hours ticked slowly by as I anticipated the boys' arrival. They turned up with their parents at 2 pm. I took Jack into one room, and then Ben into another. Mick and I then proceeded to take Jack's statement first, and then we took a statement from Ben. Both of them were adamant that they'd heard one of the assailants say, 'Give me your wallet,' and both boys said that upon hearing this they had turned to see two males standing in front of the older man. They both saw the tall, blond male punch the older man about three times, forcing him backwards, and it was at this stage that the smaller, dark male took a step towards the older man, who said something in reply, but they couldn't make out what it was. It was then that the smaller, dark male had turned and looked at the boys.

To their credit, the two boys were absolutely fantastic. Mick's and my concerns proved to be totally unfounded, as both boys were extremely strong in their convictions about what they'd seen and heard. Their stories were very similar, but not so similar as to make you think they had got together and worked out what to say. Two absolutely identical stories always came across as a bit suspect, and it was important that there be some differences, because it would play better in court when the time came.

There were a couple of things I couldn't reconcile, though. Firstly, the offenders had demanded Hanes's wallet, but they hadn't taken it. Secondly, Hanes still had twenty-five dollars in his wallet when we'd found him. The offenders hadn't even taken the money. Nick Hanes appeared to have been killed just for the sake of it! The senselessness of it made me sick to the stomach. I just couldn't wrap my head around the fact that this poor bloke had died just because a couple of idiots had made the snap decision to bash a bloke, seemingly without any provocation.

As the boys relayed their version of events, I thought about things that were missing, or things that would need clarification. The boys' statements seemed fairly clear-cut, but the one issue I did have was that they had only seen the blond man actually strike the victim. While the second assailant had been present, and could be considered an accessory to the fact, they hadn't seen him actively participate in the assault, so it was going to be hard to pin any more serious charges on him. When the boys had finished giving their statements, we took them back downstairs, and I made a point of saying, 'I know it was tough for you guys to come in and give us a statement, but you have done a good thing here.'

'Yeah,' Jack replied, 'we know we've done the right thing, no matter what happens, but we feel a bit guilty that we didn't step in and help the bloke.'

'Don't beat yourselves up about it,' I said. 'You probably wouldn't have been able to do anything to prevent what happened, and who knows, had you stepped in, you may have been badly hurt, or worse, yourselves. If you'd stepped in, we might be investigating two more murders, and we wouldn't have any witnesses.'

Both of them nodded their heads, and I was happy I had placated them, but now came the hard part. 'Boys, I have to remind you, now that you have given statements, the day is eventually going to come when we catch these guys, and then you will be required to give evidence in court.'

'Detective, we really want to do this,' Ben said. 'You can count on us to give evidence.'

I got the impression that giving their statements had given them the feeling that they were doing the right thing, and now they wanted to see it through to the end. Perhaps they were even excited about now being the star witnesses in a murder investigation. While the boys seemed to take everything in their stride, I can't say their parents shared their enthusiasm. They looked decidedly anxious about what their sons were now involved in.

'Boys,' I continued, 'I can tell you from experience that it's really tough having to stand up in a courtroom and give evidence. The Defence lawyers will give you an absolute grilling, and will try to pick holes in everything you say. I just want to make sure you know exactly what it is you're getting yourself involved in.'

'It's okay, Detective Seymour. We really want to do this,' they both said enthusiastically. 'What happened wasn't right. That poor man's family needs justice.'

I thanked them for what they had done, and accompanied them to the station exit. As I headed back upstairs, I was quite chuffed. I did have my doubts about how two boys who were barely adults would respond to having to be Crown witnesses, but they seemed quite mature about everything, something which would be a great bonus when the time came.

I went to see Karen, and after she'd entered everything into the system, I grabbed the statements and read over them again. Before long, Mick was standing beside me.

'So what have you got?' he asked.

'Mate,' I said, tapping the statements on my desk, 'these are bloody terrific! Given that they were on the other side of the road and about ten metres further along, and the road is only four lanes wide, I'd put them at roughly twenty to thirty metres away. Aside from them standing right beside the crime scene, you can't get much more eyewitness than that!' I said excitedly.

I had to temper my excitement though. Yes, we had our first big break, but this was only the first step of what I knew would be many more. Part of me prayed that the two young blokes who'd assaulted Nick Hanes had seen the media conference, and their guilty consciences were getting the better of them and they would simply come forward and hand themselves in, but experience told me that this was highly unlikely.

'How good are their descriptions?' Mick asked.

'Surprisingly good. Neither of them could say that they'd seen these guys before, but at least we know the types of people we're looking for. One is tall and thin with very blond hair and wearing light-coloured clothing, while the other one is shorter and of Islander appearance, with short dark hair and wearing dark clothing. They should stand out like dog's balls if we can get them on the CCTV footage.'

As I spoke, I started to think about the direction from which the assailants had come. I created a mental picture of Mamre Road, and as I traced along the street in my mind, it hit me; perhaps they had come from the nearby Quix service station, or the RSL Club. 'Shit, Mick, maybe they came from the Quix servo. I wonder if they're on the CCTV footage. Nah, we couldn't be that fortunate, could we?'

'Well, you never know your luck in a big city, Pete. I wouldn't be surprised if you find what you're looking for. Might be a few hours of watching tapes though. You probably want to have a look at the RSL tapes as well.'

'Done and done,' I said as I leapt up and all but sprinted down to the exhibit room to retrieve the servo tape. 'Hey, mate, how's it going?' I said to the exhibit officer. 'I was wondering if I could have a look at the CCTV footage from the Quix servo please?'

The exhibit officer turned around and reached for his exhibit book, checked the numbers, and then rose from his seat and made his way to a large set of shelves behind him and retrieved the tape. 'I just need you to sign the exhibit book,' he said as he handed it to me. I wrote down what I was taking and my purpose for taking it, and then signed my name.

'Thanks, mate,' I said as I grabbed the tape and headed back upstairs, where I went into one of the interview rooms and locked the door behind me, because I wanted absolutely no distractions. I didn't even take a coffee in with me, because if I looked down at my cup for a couple of seconds, that might be all it would take for me to miss some vital clue.

I switched on the television and put the tape in the video player. I figured Hanes must have been assaulted near enough to 1 am, otherwise someone would have called it in earlier, so if the offenders had been in the servo, I figured it could have been up to an hour before they'd confronted Hanes. It occurred to me that they might also have gone to the servo after the assault, but I took a chance that the offenders probably wouldn't have stayed in the area after what had happened. I fast-forwarded the tape to midnight, and then settled back in my chair to watch, hoping to get a glimpse of the men I was searching for. However, my excitement was short-lived. No sooner had I started the tape on than I realised the footage was grainy, and generally of piss-poor quality. To make matters worse, the screen was split into four quarters, each showing a different camera angle, which made it extremely difficult to concentrate on all of them.

What's the point of having this 'quality' surveillance installed? I thought to myself. *You can't see shit as far as identifying faces on this tape! How the bloody hell am I going to get any decent evidence out of this crap!* I reconciled myself to the fact that the best I could hope for was to see two people who resembled the men I was looking for, but I wasn't holding my breath that I'd actually get any decent face shots.

My initial enthusiasm drained away, and watching the tape now became a slow and agonising process. Nevertheless, I leant forward, straining my eyes as I scanned the footage whilst keeping a close watch on the time counter in the top right-hand corner of the screen.

Between 12.00 and 12.05 am, there were several people that came and went but nothing matching what we were looking for.

From 12.05 to 12.10 am, there were another half a dozen people, but again, no matches.

There was nothing between 12.10 and 12.15 am. I contemplated taking a quick break, and was just about to turn the tape off when *bam*, there they were! I leant forward, completely mesmerised, and I think my heart actually skipped a few beats. They were just as the two witnesses had described them; one a tall, thin man with almost bleached blond hair wearing very light-coloured pants and a light jacket that seemed to have a thick dark stripe on the shoulder. His mate was right beside him, with dark skin, short dark hair and dark clothes. *Unmistakable*, I thought to myself. *I've got you, you bastards*.

As I watched them pay for their items, turn from the counter and head towards the exit, I didn't need to guess what their next move was. Considering they obviously had money, because they were purchasing things, I again wondered what had compelled them to confront Nick Hanes. It obviously wasn't for the cash. The only thing I could think of was that they'd done it just for the 'thrill' of it. As I watched them leave the store, I promised myself, *I will find out who you are! I will bring justice for the Hanes family. You are going down; it's just a matter of time*.

I rewound the tape and moved through it frame by frame in slow motion so that I could take note of the time when they first came into view; 12.16 am. It was then that I noticed something I hadn't seen the first time through; the blond guy was talking on his mobile phone! I continued to watch the tape until the time they left the service station, which was at 12.20 am. The whole thing was surreal. In the space of a day, I'd gone from having nothing to having witness statements and the two suspects right there on the screen in front of me. 'Hey, Mick,' I called out as I went back out into the office.

'Yeah, what have you got?' he said.

'I've just struck the jackpot, mate! The CCTV shows them in the servo between 12.16 am and 12.20 am. You can see them heading out onto Mamre Road, presumably towards where we found Nick Hanes. The other bit of luck is that one of them is using a mobile phone in the servo. The problem is that the footage doesn't show their faces clearly. The video quality is pretty shit. What bothers me is that the witnesses said they saw them assaulting Hanes at about 1.00 am, so what did they do for forty or so minutes? From the servo to Edgar Street is only a five-minute walk, max.'

'Mate, most security tapes are shit. Makes you wonder why they even bother. Who knows what they did for forty-odd minutes. Maybe they just lingered out the front before they decided to walk back into the main part of St Marys, but at least you know where they were before they assaulted him. We'll have to see about getting some enquiries done in relation to the mobile phone calls made around that area at the time.'

'True. Then all I have to do is put names to these two bastards,' I said.

'Easier said than done,' Mick replied. 'You'd better let Glash know what you've got. To be honest, I reckon you might have a bit of a hard time trying to prove that the two blokes on the tape are the same two blokes your witnesses saw. I know they match the descriptions, but you still have to prove it.'

'Yeah, I know, but I'm not really sure how I'm going to do it. I don't reckon I can just plonk the witnesses down in the front of the telly and see if they can point them out. The only way around it is if I sit them down and play the tape from a fair bit before these two come into view and see if they recognise them. Not sure how that sits from an evidentiary point of view with identification though. I'll have to have a think about it,' I said as Mick and I made our way over to

Glash's office and I filled him in on what we'd discovered from the video footage.

'Looks like things are coming along nicely,' Glash said confidently. 'Now all you have to do is find these two mongrels and lock them up.'

'Yeah, that's what we both said. I'll keep you posted on how things are going, boss,' I said as I got up and went back to my desk, where I found Karen waiting for me.

'So, where are we at, Pete?' she said.

'I reckon I've got a good handle on the two main suspects, but what I really need to do is nail down Nick Hanes's movements and how he came to end up in Edgar Street.'

Bizarrely, just as I said this, Matt and Lisa came bounding up the stairs. 'Hey, Pete!' Matt said excitedly.

'Hey, Matt, what have you got for me?'

'We've confirmed that Mr Hanes had a few to drink at the Parkview and then headed up to the Band Club later in the night. Only problem is that we don't know exactly what time he left the club.'

'Hmmm,' I said as I pondered the geographic layout of St Marys. 'What's between the club and Mamre Road that would be open late on a Friday night?'

'There's a pizza place that's just up from the club,' Matt replied.

'Yeah, the midnight pizza shop,' Lisa added.

'It looks like things are starting to *hot* up,' I said, turning to wink at Karen.

'Oh, Pete!' she said as she rolled her eyes. 'That is such a dad joke!'

'Well, I am a dad! Seriously though, do you want to stay back a bit tonight and we'll chase up the midnight pizza place?'

'Sure do,' she responded. 'But where does that put us as far as the murder goes?'

'We have to show Mr Hanes's movements right up to the point where he was assaulted,' I said as I started running things over in my mind. 'It's important that we can demonstrate that he was just trying to make his way home when these guys jumped him. It would be handy to know what sort of mood Mr Hanes was in, and also how intoxicated he was. If he was paralytic, that makes him an easy target to roll. The background statements about him will also be very important, because they'll give us a clear picture as to whether he was the sort of person to start a fight or become antagonistic, especially if he had been drinking.'

'Okay,' Karen said as she picked up on my train of thought. 'So, we're looking at whether Mr Hanes may have said something first to these guys, or whether he was just in the wrong place at the wrong time.'

'Exactly! You'll make a good detective yet!' I grinned.

'Hey!' Karen exclaimed as she slapped me on the arm.

I went back into the interview room and watched the CCTV footage again, just in case there was anything I'd missed. After finding nothing more of interest, I headed to the exhibit room to enter the tape back in for safekeeping. As I emerged, I ran into Mick. 'Have you put names to any faces yet?' he mocked.

'Not yet, but I will, never you mind,' I said confidently. 'It's all begins tonight when Karen and I go to the pizza shop.'

'Ah, riding the overtime gravy train again!' Mick laughed.

'Whatever it takes, mate. Whatever it takes.'

Later that evening, Karen and I made our way down to the pizza shop. It was located on the Great Western Highway, and as I stood outside the entrance, I realised that it was less than one hundred metres or so from the intersection with Mamre Road. I inhaled deeply, and the smell of fresh pizzas being cooked made me feel hungry as we walked inside. The man behind the counter was in his late twenties, with a thin to medium build. His head was shaven and he was wearing a chef's apron. 'Can I help you?' he said as we approached the counter.

'G'day mate, we're from St Marys Detectives. I'm Detective Seymour and this is Detective Richards. We're making enquiries in relation to the death of a man at the corner of Mamre Road and Edgar Street late on Friday night.'

Before I could say anything further he said, 'Yeah, I saw it on the news. I knew him. Nick used to come in and get a pizza off me all the time, especially if he'd been down the pub and was on his way home.'

'Can I start by getting your name?' I asked.

'Yeah, it's Barry Mason.'

'And what is your role here, Barry?'

'Um, I'm the owner.'

'Excellent, do you remember if Mr Hanes came into your shop last Friday night?'

'Yeah, he came in pretty late, and it was obvious he'd had a fair bit to drink. He ordered a pizza, but then fell asleep at the table over there before he'd finished it. I had to wake him up and get him to go home.'

'Do you recall what time this was?' I continued.

'Yeah, it would have been just after midnight, maybe ten past twelve.'

'Barry, here's my card with my details on it. I'll need to get a statement from you about Mr Hanes being in here that night. When can you come in to the station?'

'I can come in tomorrow if you want, say about eleven,' he replied.

'That would be great. See you then. Just ask for me and I'll come down and get you. It won't take long.'

'Have you got any idea what happened to Nick, or any ideas about who did it?' Barry said.

'We're still making our preliminary investigations and getting all the facts together, but don't worry, mate. We'll nail whoever did this.'

'Nick was a nice bloke, never caused any problems. In fact, he wouldn't hurt a fly. I hope you find out what happened,' Barry said.

'Like I said, mate, we'll get 'em,' I said as Karen and I turned and walked out of the shop and back up to the station.

Karen and I had only gone a few feet when I stopped and stroked my chin as I stared up and down the adjacent streets. Karen, noticing my pensiveness, said, 'What's on your mind, Pete?'

'Kaz, something not's sitting right. the timeframes don't fit. How long do you reckon it would take to walk from the pizza shop to the corner of Edgar Street?' I said as I pointed down Mamre Road.

Karen took a look down Mamre Road, back to where we were standing, and then back down Mamre Road again. 'Oh, I'd say about five minutes or so, depending on whether you got caught at the lights waiting to cross, although you wouldn't think that at that time of night you'd bother to wait at the lights if there was no traffic around.'

'Okay, so the times don't fit, which leaves us with a gap of about forty-five minutes or so. Surely it wouldn't take him that long to walk to Edgar Street, even if he was drunk to the eyeballs.'

'So what do you think he was doing? Maybe he fell asleep along the way and got woken up. After all, Barry Mason just said he'd fallen asleep in the shop.'

'Yeah, maybe, but I'm not happy about it. Anyway, we'll get his statement tomorrow and see where we go from there. Don't know about you, but after smelling those pizzas I'm starving. I reckon it's time to go home. Do your overtime form and just leave it on my desk and I'll fix it up tomorrow. But before we go, I need you to do up a quick running sheet about our conversation tonight with Barry.'

'Cool bananas!' Karen replied as we started to walk back towards the station. I stopped and shot her an odd look, which she reciprocated. 'What?' she said quizzically.

'Cool bananas? Can't say I've ever heard that one! What the hell does that mean?'

'It means "cool bananas". What do you mean you've never heard that one? I say it all the time. Get up to date with the modern language, you old thing!' she laughed.

We got back to the station, squared off the paperwork and headed off to our cars. It had been a long and exhausting day, but one that had been very rewarding as far as the investigation was concerned.

As I drove home, I tried to switch off, but everything kept playing over in my mind. I tried to push it all to the back of my mind, because I was stuffed and I needed to give my mind some rest. I'd only been away from home for a few hours, but it felt like it had been days since I'd seen my family. I thought back to earlier that morning, and the promise I'd made to Jenna, and hated the fact that I'd had to break it. *I guess I'm not going to be popular with Jenna tonight.*

It was about 8 pm when I pulled up in the driveway. I'd barely lifted the garage roller door when the internal door leading into the house flew open. There, in her dressing gown and with her flowing blonde hair, was Jenna. 'You're late, Daddy!' she scolded, putting on her best cranky face as she crossed her arms and pouted.

I did my best not to laugh. 'I'm sorry, princess, but I was really busy today, although we got a lot of work done, so that's good isn't it?'

'No, it's not! You're late, and you said you would be home early today!'

'Tell you what, to make it up to you I'll come up and read you a story when you go to bed. How does that sound?'

'Okay,' she said as her cranky face gradually turned to a smile and she uncrossed her arms. 'But you'd better promise.'

'I promise, darling.'

'Good,' she said and turned around to skip inside, but found her path blocked by Ashleigh and Tayla, neither of them giving me nearly as much of a hard time as Jenna had.

'Hey, Dad,' Ash said.

'Daddy!' Tayla yelled out.

'Hey, girls,' I called back as I jumped back into my car and carefully drove it into the garage, mindful of not running over my daughters. I parked the car, jumped out, and as I reached the doorway leading into the house, the girls wrapped their arms around my legs. Slowly dragging one leg after the other, I headed into the kitchen.

'Okay, girls, leave your dad in peace,' said Sue.

'Yes, Mum,' the girls all said as they released their bear-like grips and skipped off upstairs.

I moved over to Sue, who was standing next to the stove, wrapped my arms around her waist and kissed her on the cheek. 'What's cooking, good-looking?' I asked as I peered over her shoulder to see a casserole simmering on the stove.

'I thought this would be nice to have. Wasn't sure how hungry you'd be,' she said as she stirred the pot.

'As it happens, I'm starving,' I replied.

'Good, well I'll just dish some of this up onto a plate and you can dive in. The girls and I have already eaten, so this is all yours if you want it.'

'Sounds great,' I replied.

'How was your day?' she said as I sat down at the dining room table and she put my dinner down in front of me.

'Actually, really good,' I replied wearily. 'We were very lucky. We had a couple of young boys come forward and make statements today. They were walking home from the station and saw two blokes assault Nick Hanes after they demanded his wallet.'

I'd always thought that living with a copper for so many years had led Susie to become a bit of an amateur detective herself, and sure enough, she immediately asked the same question Mick had. 'Did they get a good look at them?'

'Yeah, they gave me a good description, and as luck would have it, it looks like I've got these two guys on some CCTV footage from the servo just up the road. You know the one near the RSL Club on Mamre Road?'

'Yeah. So have you got any idea who these two are?'

'No, not at the moment,' I said through a mouthful of casserole. 'Having the descriptions and knowing where they came from is a start, but there's still a long way to go.'

Famished after a long day, I all but inhaled my dinner and then hurried upstairs to fulfil my promise to Jenna. I read her a story until she fell asleep, and then crept out of her room as quietly as I could.

'Daddy, can you read me a bedtime story too? ' Tayla called as I tiptoed past her room. *I should have known I wouldn't get away with reading just one story!* I read to Tayla, and as I did, I got the feeling that the girls weren't really interested in the stories themselves; it was more of a comfort thing. Having me reading to them was confirmation that I was home.

Ashleigh, being the oldest, gave me a reprieve, and let me off with a simple hug and a kiss before rolling over under the blankets to go to sleep. I stared at her while she drifted off, and couldn't shake the feeling that Nick Hanes would never be able to share such tender moments with his kids again. Death in that way seemed so pointless and cruel, especially when it happened so unexpectedly.

I went to my bedroom and made a silent promise; to constantly remind myself of just how lucky I really was. Despite being absolutely exhausted, I still had trouble getting to sleep as I tried to solve the riddle of the missing forty-five minutes.

Chapter 6:
The Missing Minutes

The following day, I focussed my enquiries on Nick Hanes's friends and associates. I was particularly interested in giving the descriptions of the suspects to the people Hanes knew best, to see if any of them knew the two assailants, which would hopefully lead us to finding a motive, but unfortunately we came up empty-handed. My enthusiasm that I would have this one done and dusted started to wane as I suddenly realised that I was faced with a major dilemma. My only witnesses could describe the attackers in general, but they hadn't gotten a really good look at their faces. I knew in my mind that the two males on the CCTV footage were the ones I was after, but I still had the problem of knowing that for sure from an evidentiary point of view. My best bet was to get the mobile phone searches underway and see what came from them. 'Matt,' I said as I approached his desk, 'can you do me a favour, mate?'

'Sure, Pete, what is it?'

'Can you get onto the telco companies and get the mobile phone call lists for the area around the servo?'

'No worries, Pete, I'll get onto it straightaway.'

As I pictured the area around the servo, a thought suddenly came to me; maybe the two guys had caught a cab that night. 'Matt, there's something else I need you to do for me.'

'What's that?'

'Get the descriptions of the two suspects to the local taxi companies. Get them to ask their drivers if they remember any passengers fitting those descriptions.'

'Yep, I'll get straight onto that too.'

'Thanks, mate, you're a legend,' I said as I returned to my desk, sat down, and ran through everything in my mind again to make sure I hadn't missed anything. The main concern I had was how I handled the witnesses, because if I got it wrong it could ruin everything. I contemplated bringing them in and showing them the video tape in the hope that they would confirm that the two males in the footage were the same ones they had seen, but the problem was that there was the possibility, when the time came in court, that the identification could be challenged because I had directed them to the footage. This was all I had to go on, but if I did it, I risked completely compromising the case. I thought about it more and more. *No, I can't make this decision on my own*, I thought. *I'd better get the opinions of those I trust the most.* 'Mick, you got a sec?' I said.

'Yeah, mate, what's up?'

'Let's grab a couple of cuppas and then have a chat with Glash. There's something I want to go over with you and him.' We grabbed our cups, made our coffees and then headed to Glash's office. 'Got a sec, boss?' I asked as Mick and I stood at his doorway.

'Yeah boys, take a seat.' We sat down, and I told them about my concerns.

'Mate, that's a big risk, that much is true,' Mick said thoughtfully. 'What do you think, Glash?'

'Yeah,' Glash said as he considered things. 'The question is whether you burn the witnesses by showing them the tape. If so, the obvious answer is to just pick one to show it to and hope the one you pick distinctly recognises these two blokes. If he doesn't, it will be a big setback. Maybe you should ring Homicide and get their opinion.'

'Good idea, boss.'

'What does your gut instinct tell you, Pete?'

'As it stands, boss, it's telling me I don't have a choice. I have to know for sure that the two blokes on the tape are the ones who assaulted Hanes. If that means I have to burn one of the witnesses, then so be it. The problem with that, though, is that I will only have one of them available to give evidence when this thing ends up in court. If I do go that way, I have to have a long, hard think about which one I burn and which one I keep for court.'

'Pete, I agree with Glash. Give Homicide a call and see what they suggest,' Mick said.

I left Glash's office and called Homicide, and before long, was having the same discussion with them. The Homicide boys agreed I had a pretty big quandary on my hands, and I had to wait for some time while they discussed things among themselves. When they eventually got back to me, they said that in their opinion, I shouldn't show the tape to either witness, as I would lose whichever one I showed the tape to, and two witnesses were much stronger than one.

I hung up the phone, sat back in my chair and pondered the advice I'd just been given. It still didn't sit right. Surely if I didn't make it obvious to a witness what I was showing him, and didn't lead or direct him in any way, I should still be able to use him in court. The one thing I knew for certain was that I'd have to play enough of the tape before the two suspects came into view so as to negate the possibility of any accusations of adverse inference.

No matter how many times I ran it over in my mind, I couldn't find a solution to my dilemma, so I went and found Mick and discussed what the Homicide boys had said with him. 'What are you gonna do?' Mick asked.

'I reckon I could make another phone call, this time to the DPP at Penrith, and see if one of the Crown Prosecutors is happy to advise me.'

'I'm not sure they'll do that,' Mick replied, 'but it's worth a shot. You know what, I don't think it matters what anyone says. Ultimately, it's your call, and I reckon I know what that's gonna be,' Mick said as he winked at me.

He watched on with interest as I rang the Crown Prosecutors at the Penrith DPP and explained my quandary. Their response was firm but polite. Whilst they agreed it was a puzzling problem, they also made it very clear that they should not be giving out this sort of advice over the phone, but if they had to comment, the advice was to err on the side of caution and not potentially burn a witness. I put the phone down and looked at Mick. 'What did they say?' he asked eagerly.

'They told me in no uncertain terms that they shouldn't be discussing such things over the phone.'

'Bummer.'

'But wait, there's more,' I said. 'Despite that, they gave me the same advice as the Homicide boys. "Err on the side of caution, and don't show the tape to either of them."'

'Shit, mate, what are you gonna do?' Mick said as he shook his head.

Just at that moment, Glash happened to emerge from his office. 'How'd you go, Pete?' he asked as he came and stood beside my desk.

I looked at him ruefully. 'Boss, Homicide and the Crown Prosecutors at Penrith both say I should err on the side of caution and not show either of the boys the tape.'

Glash sat down opposite me and rubbed his face with his hands before he looked back at me. 'Pete, it's your decision. You've been around long enough to know what you're doing. Mate, throughout the Keir investigation and others like it, you trusted your gut instinct and it worked for you, so I don't see any reason why you should start changing things around. It's your investigation. I will support you with whatever decision you make. You've been a police prosecutor, so you have just as much idea as anyone else about something like this.'

Should I hold off and see if any fresh information comes to hand? No, I don't want this investigation to start going stale. Decision made. I looked back at Glash. 'I guess I'd better start working out which one I want to keep for court and which one I get to view the tape and risk burning.'

Glash sat back in his chair with a smile on his face. 'I thought you'd say that! You do what you have to do.' With that, he got up to head back to his office, but before he went, he turned to me and said, 'Let me know which one you choose.'

'Will do, boss, will do.'

'I don't know why you bothered asking us at all!' Mick laughed. 'I knew all along that you'd do your own thing. Now that you've made up your mind, I think I should tell you that personally, I don't think it can hurt to do it anyway.'

'Appreciate that, Mick. I just didn't want to go it alone, mate. You know better than anyone that it's good to toss things around and get opinions from people, but I know I don't have a choice; I've got nothing else to go on at the moment. I just have to be careful how I go about this. That's not my only problem, though. I still need to tie down that missing forty-five minutes.'

'Yeah, that's a bit strange, that one,' Mick said. 'Well, which one are you gonna choose?'

'Gees, Mick, give a fella a chance! Nah, to be honest, I don't really know at the moment. I'll have to have a good, hard think about which one I reckon will be the better one in court and which one will handle cross-examination the best.'

'Alright, mate,' Mick said as he stood up to go. 'I'll leave you with it. Let me know how you go.'

'Will do, mate, will do,' I said as I leant back in my chair and wondered which of these two unfortunate fellows I was going to make my star witness.

Chapter 7:
A Crucial Decision

Decisions come and go in any criminal investigation, but some are more crucial than others. You wrestle with the thought that you could be making a big mistake that could cost you dearly. Glash's words resonated in my mind: 'It's your investigation. I will support you with whatever decision you make.' It was something I thanked my lucky stars for. Throughout my career, I had been truly blessed to have tremendously supportive bosses who backed me no matter what. Which witness was I going to choose? Who was the most nervous? Who was the most convincing and confident?

I had to remind myself that the tapes were of particularly shit quality, and there was a distinct possibility that whichever one I chose to view the tape might not be able to make out anything at all, or not with any certainty anyway, the result being that I would burn a witness without gaining a result.

I drove home that night tossing things around in my mind, but when I walked through the door I pushed it all from my mind, kissed my girls and sat down to dinner.

'How was your day?' Susie asked.

'Tough,' I said as I sat down at the table across from her.

'Why is that, honey?'

'I have a difficult decision to make.'

'Really? About what?'

'I have to pick one witness from the investigation to view the surveillance footage and one to put on the stand.'

'And that's a problem because why?'

'Because I could end up burning one of them.'

'What does your instinct tell you?'

'I thought I had it sorted, but I'm not so sure now.'

'Never mind, sweetie, I have faith in you, and I know that whatever decision you make will be the right one. You've always done what you thought was right. You've always backed yourself, and it has always worked out for you.'

I looked at Susie, at her lovely brunette hair and delicate features, and realised how much she really completed me. It was uncanny how she was always telling me exactly what I needed to hear precisely when I needed to hear it. She had a knack for breaking things down to their simplest form, and made me realise that I didn't have to complicate things.

I stared at her beautiful face and wondered what I would have done without her. I thought back to all the near misses, the times when I may not have come home, and then it hit me. I shouldn't be thinking about what I would do without her, but more about what she would do without me. I had responsibilities. I had a wife and kids. They relied on me, they needed me, and I started to have more and more doubts as to whether I should be doing this job anymore. While I continued to gaze upon Susie's gorgeous face, I thought back to one of my near misses, when I almost hadn't made it home.

I'd been working at Newtown Ds when a call came through that there was a break and enter in progress. I'd jumped into a car with one of the other Ds and headed to the scene. When we got there, we went over to the uniformed guys. 'So, what have you got for us, boys?' I said.

'Hello, Detective, we received a call saying that there was a break-in in progress, and when we arrived we caught the bloke in the back of the paddy wagon there red-handed.'

'Good work, boys. I take it you've been through and checked the house?' I said matter-of-factly. The young officer's disposition immediately told me they hadn't. 'Tell me you went through the house!' I said, raising my voice.

'Actually, Detective, we interviewed the suspect and he told us he was working alone.'

I shot the young copper a look. 'Since when do you believe a fucking crook!' I felt bad that I was being harsh on this young fellow, but part of the reason for me doing so was because I needed to make sure he learnt how to do his job properly. It was a case of being cruel to be kind. Small oversights like this could be the difference between this bloke living and dying, the difference between him having a grieving family or not.

'Sorry, Detective,' the young officer said as he hung his head.

'It's alright, you've got an offender locked up, so it's a good job done,' I said as I nodded to my partner and headed into the house to check that it was all clear.

As I approached the house, for some reason something just didn't feel right. I scanned the house, and seeing nothing, I cautiously crept through the front door. I walked upstairs and checked there before returning downstairs. I noticed the doorway leading to the kitchen/ dining area, and as I walked towards it, the uneasy feeling came over me again in waves. I found myself reaching down and pulling my gun out of my ankle holster as I made my way through the doorway. Unbeknown to me, there was a second offender huddled in the corner to my left holding a large carving knife in front of his chest.

I had only taken a couple of steps into the room before I suddenly turned and saw him starting to rise. Fortunately, the barrel of my gun was aimed directly at his head, and he immediately stopped in his tracks. 'Put the knife down!' I said. He looked up at me as he contemplated his options. 'Put the fucking knife down now!' I yelled. Realising that he had no choice, he dropped the knife, whereupon I cuffed him and led him out to the paddy wagon, making sure I gave the young uniformed officer a stern glance when I reached him.

On those days when I'd been in danger, I would come home and Sue would ask me how my day had been. I always felt the need to answer her truthfully, but I would only ever give her a quick run-down. I never went into too much detail, because I didn't want to upset her. I'd been lucky, but there was always the possibility that I'd go to work one day for the last time. This thought had been boring into the back of my mind more and more.

When I was young and single, it had barely crossed my mind. I felt like I was bullet-proof, and nothing was ever going to go wrong. Now that I was older and had responsibilities, I was becoming painfully aware that my reactions were getting slower and slower, and I was beginning to doubt my abilities. I continued to look into Sue's eyes, and I began to picture what her life, and the kids' lives, would be like without me.

'Pete, are you okay?' Sue asked.

'Yeah, why?'

'You just seemed a bit vacant for a sec there, that's all.'

'Nah, I'm fine, just thinking.'

'So, what things do you need to consider when making your decision?' Sue continued.

'What?'

'With your two witnesses.'

'It basically comes down to who I think is the best one to handle giving evidence in court. Ben seemed to be a little more solid in his evidence, and when he spoke about what he saw, he appeared more convincing and less nervous when being questioned. Both boys saw roughly the same thing, so it isn't as if I'm going to lose crucial eyewitness material by showing the footage to one of the boys. So, I think I will go with him in court.'

'Sounds like you've thought long and hard about this. I'm sure it will work out to be the right decision.'

Just then, Tayla appeared from upstairs dressed in her PJs and slippers.

'Daddy, can you come upstairs and read me a story?'

'Not now, honey. Daddy's a bit tired.'

'Please, Daddy,' she begged.

'Not now, Tayla. Daddy's tired.'

'But Daddy, you haven't read me a story in ages.'

'But nothing, Tayla! Daddy said he's tired, now go to bed!' I yelled.

Tayla stood there stunned for a few moments, and then started bawling her eyes out. 'C'mon, darling,' Sue said softly as she moved over and picked Tayla up in her arms. 'Time for bed.'

I watched as they disappeared upstairs, and then rose from my seat, went out to the back deck, sat down by the pool and buried my head in my hands. *What was that all about? That's not like me at all.* I don't know how long I sat out there for, but when I eventually went upstairs to apologise to Tayla, she was fast asleep, so I kissed her on the forehead and made my way to bed. Sue was sitting up in bed reading, and she looked up at me when I entered the room. 'Darl, I'm sorry I snapped. I don't know what came over me,' I said as I sat down beside her.

'It's okay, Pete,' she said as she stroked my head. 'You're under a lot of pressure at the moment.'

'Yeah, maybe it wasn't a good idea to go back to the detectives,' I said.

After I'd changed for bed and brushed my teeth, I lay down and tried to go to sleep, but to no avail. I eventually drifted off, but my dreams replayed the near miss with the knife-wielding burglar over and over again. I'd wake with a start, stare up at the ceiling, then fall asleep and replay everything once more.

The next morning, as I drove to work, despite my tiredness from the restless night, I made a mental checklist of everything I needed to do that day. The first thing I had to do was to phone Jack Dupont and have him come in to the station to see if he could confirm that the men he'd seen assaulting Nick Hanes were the same men on the CCTV footage. 'Hey, Jack, it's Detective Peter Seymour here.'

'Hello, Detective, what can I do for you?'

'Jack, I have some CCTV footage that I'd like to show you if you're able to come in to the station.'

'Sure. When would you like me to come in?'

'As soon as you possibly can.'

'Um, okay, I'll be down in an hour or so.'

'That's great. See you then, Jack.'

I found it almost impossible to sit still while I waited, so I paced up and down the office and drank numerous cups of coffee to combat my weariness. The minutes slowly ticked by until Jack eventually turned up, right on time, and I took him up to the interview room and sat him down. The TV/video unit was already set up and the tape was ready to go, set to start about fifteen minutes prior to the time when the two suspects came into view.

'Jack, I cannot stress this enough,' I began, 'all I have brought you in for is to watch some video footage. You can make any comments if you wish, but you don't have to say anything.' He nodded that he understood, and then settled back into the chair and waited.

I was extremely careful to ensure that I didn't mention where the footage had been taken, lest I risk compromising the whole thing. I also made sure not to give any hints as to what he could expect to see, for the same reason, but Jack was a smart kid. He'd already put two and two together.

I hit play, and the footage began. I stood just behind Jack, watching over his right shoulder. Unbeknown to him, my face was a mixture of anticipation and intrigue as I tried to gauge his reaction. The further the tape progressed, the more he leant forward in his chair, and I sensed that he was straining to see things more clearly. He was shifting from side to side, and it was clear that he was keenly anticipating seeing something important as he gazed at the screen. Strangely, considering his apparent tenseness, after a few minutes, he leant back in his seat and began to relax. I sat down quietly beside him, notebook in hand, ready to record any comments he might make. I kept my gaze fixed firmly on Jack, but out of the corner of my eye I also watched the time clicking over. Inside, I could feel a sense of excitement, fear and anticipation. This was it; the moment of truth. I was about to find out if my gamble was going to pay off. I looked to the TV, back to Jack, and then back to the TV again.

At that point he turned his head towards me, and I had to turn mine away; I couldn't show any emotion, lest I give him a hint of what was about to happen. I tried to relax as best I could as I took another brief glance at the clock; there were only a few seconds to go before the two suspects appeared. When they walked into frame, I immediately turned my attention to Jack, who sat bolt upright before leaning forward in his chair and examining the screen more closely. 'That's them!' he said as he raised his right arm and pointed at the screen.

'Are you sure?' I asked.

'No doubt about it, that's them for sure.'

I hurriedly wrote down what he'd said in my notebook, as well as describing his action in pointing at the screen. I let the tape run for about thirty seconds after the two suspects had left the servo before I switched it off. I was surprised that Jack seemed disappointed that there wasn't more, but I was relieved that he was so adamant about what he had just seen.

Yes, it had been a gamble. Yes, there was going to be some legalistic shit that would hit the fan, but I was certain I'd done the right thing. I have never been much for the punt or putting money in the pokies, so it wasn't in my nature to take such a huge risk, but I had nothing else to go on. Sometimes the risk is worth the reward, and I desperately wanted that reward in the form of justice for the Hanes family.

I had my positive proof now. The pieces were coming together, slowly but surely. I asked Jack to describe, in his own words, what he'd seen. I typed up his statement, got him to sign it, thanked him, and told him we were finished. 'So, what happens now?' he said.

'When I find these two jokers and get them to trial, we'll have to see what the lawyers want to do. You alright with all that?'

'Like I said to you before, Detective Seymour, it's the right thing to do for the family.'

'You're a good bloke, Jack,' I said as I patted him on the back and escorted him to the station exit.

I returned to my desk and sat down. 'How did you go?' Mick called out.

'Yeah, he positively identified them. In fact, he was pretty damn sure about it.'

'You got a good result there then, mate!' Mick said.

'Actually, it probably couldn't have gone any better! You know what, I hoped I'd get the right result, but until things actually go the way you want them to, you always have that nervous feeling that something may go wrong.'

'Now all you have to do is put some names to the faces,' he said. 'And it will be spring soon!'

'Thanks for reminding me, Mick!' I replied as I started filling out my duty book for the day.

'Hey, Pete.' I didn't need to look up to know that the voice belonged to Karen. 'I've added Jack Dupont's new statement about identifying these two suspects on a running sheet in the system.'

'Thanks, Karen. If nothing else, you'll be an expert on inputting information into the system in a murder investigation,' I said.

She brushed off my taunt. 'Let's hope we find out who these two guys are and put them away for this.'

'When you're older and more experienced and leading your own investigations, always remember that everything you're doing is all about the family. It's bad enough for them that they've lost Nick, but it would be that much harder to take if the people who did it ended up getting away with it. At least if we can put them away, the family will hopefully get some satisfaction.'

No sooner had the words left my mouth than I realised their insignificance. How could a family ever gain 'satisfaction', even if we did manage to lock someone away as a result of what had happened? All we could give them was some sense of justice.

Chapter 8:
The Hand of Justice

The positive identification made, it was time to use the media again. I decided to get the CCTV footage, and consequently the two suspects, out into the public arena, and to do that I needed to get some still pictures of them. I arranged for the tape to be taken to the Video Unit, and two days later it was returned, along with the stills, which were soon on their way to the Media Unit, who liaised with all the major TV stations. That night, the pictures were shown on every channel. The hunt was well and truly on.

I just knew I was going to get some new information. I was certain that someone else would come forward, but even if nothing else happened, I wanted the two offenders to know that we knew what they looked like. I hoped that they would see themselves on the telly, that it would make them shit scared, and that they would know that the hand of justice would soon be knocking on their doors.

However, despite my renewed optimism, I needed to remain realistic. The footage was poor quality, and there was every chance that the two offenders felt confident that we had nothing much on them. Before I released the pictures, I rang Bel Hanes and told her what was happening, so that none of it would come as a surprise to her and her family. I tried to keep her positive and upbeat. I told her we were following up on all the information we had, and it was looking promising, but it was still too early to get ahead of ourselves. I made it clear that we didn't know who the suspects were, but at least we had witnesses to the assault, and we had descriptions to match the footage.

There was no immediate response to the broadcast of the pictures, and over the days that followed, one thing kept gnawing at me; the missing forty-five minutes. I just couldn't work out why it had taken Hanes so long to walk from the pizza shop to where he had met his untimely end.

One morning, I was standing out on the back veranda of the station, coffee cup in hand, when I heard a voice calling from inside. 'Hey, Pete!'

'Yeah?' I called back.

'There's a gentleman here to see you.'

I finished the remnants of my coffee, went inside, quickly washed my cup and then made my way along the corridors to the front counter. No sooner had I stepped through the doorway to the reception area than I saw the familiar face of Bill Warwick, aka 'Wazza'. Wazza was 170 cm tall and about fifty years old. He had an athletic build with short, sandy-coloured hair and rugged, pointy features. He was wearing a dark-blue King Gee shirt, blue jeans and black work boots. 'G'day, mate,' I said cheerfully as I walked across to him and shook his hand.

'How's it goin', Detective?' he replied.

'Good, mate, good. What brings you here?'

'I reckon I might 'ave a bit of info about who knocked off Nick Hanes,' he said, his face etched with an uncharacteristically stern look.

'Come through, mate, and you can fill me in on what you know,' I said, curious as to what this normally cheerful bloke might have to say. Wazza and I went back a few years. I'd first come across him during my previous stint at St Marys detectives in about 1987. Unbeknown to me at the time, he was a good mate of my older brother, who would use Wazza on jobs where trees needed to be cut down on building sites.

One day, Wazza was perched high up in a tree, lopping some branches that were overhanging the McDonald's restaurant on the Great Western Highway, which, coincidentally, was not far from the pizza shop where Nick Hanes had eaten his last meal. From high above, having cleared enough branches to give him a bird's-eye view, Wazza had spotted two well-known local druggies walk up to his truck, grab his very expensive chainsaw and take off through the car park. Quick as a flash, Wazza was down the tree, grabbed his axe from the back of his truck and set off after them. Seeing him hot on their heels, the two druggies had a decision to make; keep running and hope Wazza didn't catch them or stop and try to talk or fight their way out of it. One of them kept running, but the one with the chainsaw ran out of puff and had no choice but to turn and face Wazza. He was a large Maori fellow with tattoos covering both his arms. Given his size, he would have scared the shit out of most people, but not Wazza, who stood toe-to-toe with him.

The Maori guy held up the chainsaw. 'Put the fuckin' chainsaw down!' Wazza yelled as he raised his axe in his right hand, brandishing it at about head height, but the Maori fellow didn't comply, realising that to do so would mean he had no weapon.

'Put the fuckin' chainsaw down!' Wazza repeated, slowly and even more loudly, as he raised the axe a little higher. The Maori bloke remained frozen to the spot, and before he knew it, Wazza took a carefully aimed swing with the axe, the back of which slammed into the Maori's left knee. He immediately dropped the chainsaw and collapsed to the ground, clutching at his knee as he screamed and rolled around in agony. Wazza picked up the chainsaw and calmly made his way back to his truck, leaving the bloke writhing in pain. He locked his chainsaw and axe in the back of the truck, and then promptly climbed back up the tree to finish his work as though nothing had happened.

Half an hour or so later, Wazza noticed two uniformed officers standing at the rear of his truck and looking inside it. Before long, they called out to him. 'You up there! Come down. We need to talk to you.'

Not about to be rushed, Wazza slowly climbed down the tree. 'Yeah, officers, what's goin' on?' he said when he reached his truck.

'Can you please tell us your name?' one officer said.

'Yeah, it's Bill Warwick. Why?'

'Mr Warwick, you're under arrest.'

'You fuckin' what?' Wazza said, incensed.

'You do not have to say anything unless you wish to,' the officer continued, 'but anything you do say may be taken down as evidence and used against you in court.'

'What the fuck's goin' on? You've got the wrong bloke! Them druggie bastards stole me fuckin' chainsaw!'

'Sir, you need to come down to the station with us,' the officer said calmly.

Realising the futility of his situation, Wazza put his arms behind his back and allowed himself to be cuffed and led to the back of the waiting paddy wagon. When they got to the station, he was booked in and taken straight to an interview room.

'Mr Warwick, we are going to interview you about assaulting a male with an axe in the McDonald's car park a short time ago,' the officer began.

'What the bloody hell are you talking about?' he said. 'That prick and his druggie mate were stealing me chainsaw! It's worth a lot of money, and now you're arresting me for assaulting that big bastard? You've got to be fuckin' kiddin' me!'

'Do you have anything else to say about this matter?' the other officer asked.

'I'm not sayin' another fuckin' word!'

The uniformed officers shook their heads and left the interview room, leaving Wazza sitting there fuming. One of them came and got me, because it was a serious assault involving the use of a weapon, and they wanted my advice on how to deal with it. They filled me in on the details. The alleged victim had limped across the road to the Astley Medical Centre on the corner of the Great Western Highway and Mamre Road to get treatment for his busted knee, and it was the medical centre staff who had alerted us as to what had happened.

I listened intently to what the uniformed guys were telling me, and once they were done, I entered the interview room, and immediately had a different view on things. As a D, it never paid to see the world in black and white, but rather to always look at the bigger picture. Common sense dictated that we had a good old fair dinkum, hard-working Aussie just trying to make a living, and these scumbag druggies had tried to steal his work equipment. It didn't take much to figure out who the real victim was, and of course I was going to look after the real victim and go after the arseholes who, to my mind, were just bludgers and a blight on society.

Wazza was sitting with his hands clenched together on the table in front of him. I was struck straightaway by his rugged features, weathered skin and messy blond hair. He was, as I'd thought, your typical hard-working, hard-drinking type. 'G'day, mate, my name is Detective Seymour. Can I start by asking your name?'

'Bill Warwick!' he replied tersely.

'The uniformed cops tell me you hit a bloke across the side of his knee with the back of an axe a little while ago. Have you got anything to say about that?'

'Yeah, well, the bastard was lucky I hit him with the back end of me axe! If I'd hit him with the sharp end he wouldn't have a fuckin' leg from the knee down.'

The way he spoke was such that, even when he was angry, you couldn't help but smile. It took everything I had to stop myself from chuckling.

'Look,' he continued, 'I'm up a bloody tree tryin' to earn a fuckin' living and these two drug addicts decide they want to knock off me chainsaw. That thing's worth a lot of money to me. Then they take off and I chase after them, and the one with me chainsaw stops and confronts me, so I whacked him with me axe. So, Detective, I don't really get what it is that I've done wrong. They were knocking off *my* chainsaw!'

His face bore a look of sheer exasperation, and I started to feel sorry for him. 'Mr Warwick,' I began, 'I'm going to do what I can to help you, and get this whole mess sorted out. Can you start by describing these two blokes to me?'

'Yeah, one was a fair-skinned Aussie, a redhead with freckles and a bloody tear-drop tat down his cheek. I got close enough to see that. The other bloke was a big Islander bastard. Fair dinkum, mate, when I say big bastard, I mean *big* bastard. He was the one who had me chainsaw.'

I started making some notes. 'Okay, I'll get a quick statement from you outlining what you just said to me, which I'll need you to sign.'

'What,' he said incredulously, 'am I gonna get charged over this?'

'No, mate,' I assured him. 'You are now a victim of a theft. That's why I need to get a statement from you about what happened. I take it that you only used your axe because you thought this Islander guy was going to assault you, and you were just protecting yourself?'

When I said that, Wazza's demeanour suddenly changed and he began to relax. 'Yeah, that's exactly what happened,' he replied.

Before long, I had his statement, whereupon I quickly typed it up and then he read it and signed it. 'You know, that big bloke is still down at the medical centre getting his knee fixed up,' I said when we'd finished.

'Yeah, well, like I said, he was lucky I hit him with the back of the axe,' Wazza said with a yellow-toothed smile. 'Honestly though, I was just trying to get me chainsaw back. They were the ones doin' the wrong thing. I'll tell you somethin' though, the redhead was shitting himself when he saw me coming with the axe; made him run a lot fuckin' faster. The last I saw of him he was heading towards the car park near the Band Club, and I reckon he's probably still runnin'!'

We emerged from the interview room to find the uniformed boys sitting outside waiting. They looked up at me expectantly. 'It's all right, boys, just a misunderstanding. I'll take it from here.'

The uniformed boys just shrugged and headed off to other duties, while my young offsider and I gave Wazza a lift back to Maccas so he could continue his tree lopping. Once we'd dropped him off, my colleague and I immediately made our way to the medical centre where the Kiwi was still receiving treatment. I thought it better that we didn't make a scene in the medical centre, as there were several families in the waiting room, plus he was a man mountain, and I didn't particularly feel like having to wrestle him to the ground if he decided to bung it on. When he came out of the doctor's office, I took him to one side and quietly informed him that I was investigating the incident and required him to come back to the station with me. When we got back to the station, I took him to the downstairs interview room, as he couldn't really manage the stairs, and as soon as I had him seated, I cautioned him and told him he was under arrest for stealing the chainsaw. As it turned out, the guy never did appear in court, but was arrested on warrants a few years later, and ended up pleading guilty to the theft.

About six months later, my brother called me one day and said, 'Hey, did you interview a bloke by the name of Bill Warwick a while back?'

I immediately recognised the name, and replied, 'Yeah, why?'

'He's a good mate of mine. We were just down the pub having a beer and he was telling me this funny story about how he chased these two druggies who had stolen his chainsaw while he was up a tree and he ended up getting arrested by the cops for hitting one of them across the knee with his axe.'

My brother was cracking up laughing as he told me the story, and as I recalled the events, I couldn't help but join him.

'He didn't know you were my brother until today. I'll tell you what, that bloke is lucky he still has a leg! Knowing Wazza, I'm surprised he didn't take it off. He reckons one minute he was being locked up, and the next minute you turned up and sorted it all out and he was back at work. He reckons you're alright.'

'That's good to hear. I'm glad he likes me, because I'd hate to get on his bad side!' I laughed.

'Yeah, well, Pete, he knows a lot of people around the place. He's a bit of a rough diamond, but a bloody good bloke. I tell you something else, he's the best tree lopper around.'

'Is that how you know him?' I asked.

'Yeah, I use him all the time. He just said, "Thank God your brother turned up, those fuckin' uniformed blokes were gonna lock me up and throw away the fuckin' key!"'

Now, Wazza's and my paths were crossing again. I took him through the station and into the detectives' office. When he sat down, the first thing he said was, 'Last time I was in this place with you, I thought I was gonna get locked up!'

'Mate, you still owe me a beer for that!' I joked.

'Champion, I'll get you a beer, or seven, any time you like. You just tell me when you're free!'

'So what information do you have for me, Bill?' I asked inquisitively as I sat poised with my pen and notebook ready.

'Look, this comes from the son of a mate of mine, but I know this kid and he wouldn't bullshit, especially about somethin' like this. Apparently there's talk goin' around that some young blokes by the names of Hohopa, Walton and Black were the ones involved in Nick Hanes's death. Anyway this kid saw the news report with the pictures of the two blokes you're after, and he reckons one of them is Hohopa. This young bloke's not real keen on coming forward, so I thought I'd come in and see you about it.'

'Mate, I'll take whatever information I can get! We do know that there were two persons involved, and I was hoping that the media coverage would bring some fresh information. Hopefully this is it.'

'Like I said, this kid might be young, but I trust him.'

'When you say young, how old is he exactly?' I asked.

'He's around eighteen or so, but like I said, he knows a lot of people around here, and he's fuckin' shit scared about coming forward, if you know what I mean.'

'Look, Bill, I'll level with you, mate. We've had absolutely no one else come forward about the identity of the two suspects yet, and it's vitally important that we get a lead on who they are. Do you reckon you could have a word with this kid and convince him to come in and talk to me?'

'Yeah, I'll do me best. Nick was a mate of mine, and there are a lot of his mates out there trying to find out who did this to him. I wouldn't want to be those bastards if we catch 'em!' Wazza said with a sudden burst of anger.

'Bill, what I really need is for people to come and talk to me about any information they have, not to try to find these blokes themselves. That doesn't help me do my job, in fact it will make it a lot harder. If blokes go out and act like vigilantes, it will bugger up everything.'

'Detective Seymour, I don't need to tell you that there aren't too many cops these blokes around St Marys trust, you know. Like they're not real criminals or anything, but they don't go around talkin' to coppers, but you helped me out, so I trust you. I'll make sure anyone who has any information comes and speaks to you.'

'Thanks, mate, that's exactly what I needed to hear. It would be a great help if you could give this kid my name and number and get him to ring me so I can have a chat with him.'

'No dramas, I'll go around and see him and his old man tonight and see what I can do.' He must have sensed a little bit of uncertainty in me as we rose from our seats and I walked him out of the station, because just as we reached the exit, he turned to me and said, 'Detective Seymour, I've known Nick for a lot of years, and he was a bloody top fella, a real good bloke. Believe me, I want to do whatever it takes to catch these bastards just as much as you do.' With that, he turned and walked across the Great Western Highway to where his truck was parked. *I hope this kid comes through*, I thought to myself as I watched until he drove out of sight before walking back upstairs, *otherwise we're screwed.*

I immediately found Mick and Karen and told them what had just happened. When I was done, I said, 'Right, I'm off to get some lunch. Do you guys want anything?'

'Nah, we're good,' they both said.

'Suit yourselves.'

I headed back downstairs, out the back door, along a small laneway, out onto King Street and towards Queen Street, St Marys' main shopping thoroughfare. While I was standing at the corner of Queen Street waiting for the traffic to clear, I looked up and down the streets and started to think about the missing forty-five minutes. Where the hell *had* Hanes been?

I had all but resigned myself to the fact that those minutes may forever remain a mystery when, out of the corner of my eye, something suddenly stood out. To my left were the flashing neon lights of one of the local brothels, *The Final Touch*, which was just down from the corner of the Great Western Highway where it intersected Mamre Road to the south and Queen Street to the north. *I wonder if that's where he went?* I thought to myself. *He was separated from his wife, so maybe, just maybe.*

Completely forgetting about my lunch, I turned around and rushed back to the station.

'That was bloody quick! I know you like to stay trim, Pete, but you really must eat more,' Mick said as I ran back into the office. 'Or did you forget something?'

'Nah, mate, I was standing at the corner down on Queen Street when I had an epiphany.'

'Gees, mate, that sounds painful!'

'You know those forty-five minutes that I can't account for?' I said, ignoring his obvious attempts to bait me.

'Yeah, what about them?'

'You don't suppose Hanes went to *The Final Touch* on his way home that night?'

'Definitely a possibility, Pete,' he said as he nodded his head. 'Are you gonna take someone with you, or are you going alone?' he laughed as he gave me a sly wink. 'Are you offering to come with me, Mick?' I shot back. 'Everyone else is out.'

'Nah, mate, I'll be right,' he laughed. 'I think you can handle this particular enquiry on your own. Tell you what though, mate, I'll be keeping a close watch on how long you're gone!'

'I see! Well, at least allow for the fact that it will take me a bit of time to walk down there and back again. Anyway, you know me, Mick. I've got respect for my marriage vows!' Leaving the banter behind, I grabbed my notebook and a picture of Nick Hanes that his wife had given me and headed down to the brothel.

I'd like to be able to say that this was my first time in a brothel, but if I did, I'd be lying, in fact Mick and I had been into dozens of them. Back in the eighties, when we worked together at Penrith, we'd been assigned the task of obtaining the names of all the ladies for our Intel section, because we wanted to make sure there were no underage or illegally imported foreign girls working in the houses. Our job was made harder by the fact that the girls rarely gave us their real names, but Mick and I would always take down the rego number, make and model of the cars parked outside and run checks against the traffic records.

Even though I'd been into all those brothels, every time I went into one, it was still an odd feeling. As I walked into *The Final Touch*, I fully expected them to be a bit cagey around me, given my job and the nature of their business, and as I climbed the staircase, which was flanked on either side by hot-pink walls, I wondered what kind of reception I would get and how the hell Hanes managed to get up the stairs in the first place. I turned left at the top of the stairs and saw a middle-aged woman with long brown hair seated behind a counter. She looked up and smiled. 'Hello, sir, how can we help you today?'

I could see from the look on her face that she thought I was a prospective client, so I made a point of quickly showing her my ID. 'My name is Detective Seymour, from St Marys detectives.'

The polite smile on her face evaporated instantly, and was replaced with a look of guarded curiosity. When I reached the reception desk, I produced the photo of Nick Hanes and handed it to her. 'I'm making enquiries in relation to an incident involving this man. Can you have a look at this photo, and also show the girls? I need to know if he was here on the night of Friday 14 July. It would have been around midnight.'

She studied the photo for a minute and then said, 'Yeah, I've seen him here before. I'm here until closing time on Fridays, and I definitely remember him coming in that night. From memory, he was pretty drunk, but I think he's been in a few times before that too. Let me show the girls. I'll be back in a minute.' With that, she headed off through a doorway behind her. She returned a short time later and handed the photo back to me. 'Yeah, one of the girls was here that night, and she's confirmed that he did come in.'

'Did he actually manage to … you know?'

'No, the girl said he actually went to sleep,' she laughed. 'And we sent him on his way.'

'Look, I'll need to get a statement from you about him being here. Is it okay to do it now?'

'That's fine,' she said, so I took my pen from my shirt pocket and wrote down the details as she gave them to me. She basically told me what she'd already said; both she and the other girl were certain he'd come in on the night of Friday 14 July, and that he'd been quite intoxicated. The additional details she gave me were in keeping with what everyone else had said about Nick Hanes; he was an easygoing fellow, never angry or aggressive, even after a few beers. When she was finished, I thanked her for her assistance and made my way back downstairs. As I approached the exit, something suddenly occurred to me: *Murphy's Law says that as soon as I step out of here, I'll run into somebody I know!*

I stepped hesitantly out onto the footpath, but fortunately the street was empty. I rushed across the road and made my way back to the station. When I entered the Ds office, Mick was busy devouring a sandwich, and as soon as he saw me, he started. 'Officer *Seymour*,' he said emphasising my last name. 'How did you get on?' Before I could respond, he made a show of checking his watch. 'Wow, that *was* quick!' he said.

I wasn't about to be outdone, so I fired straight back. 'Pretty sure that's what your wife says to you all the time, isn't it, mate? Nah, they confirmed that Hanes was there, which explains the missing forty-five minutes.'

'One problem solved,' Mick said in a more serious tone. 'Now, if you're lucky enough to get more witnesses coming forward, you should be right to go.'

'One can only hope,' I said as I sat down at my desk and looked over everything again. As I did, it suddenly occurred to me that everything was now pretty much out of my control, so I spent the rest of the day ensuring that I had any loose ends squared away. It was frustrating the hell out of me that I couldn't do more, but on the plus side, a quiet day meant I could get home on time for a change. It really burned me that I still hadn't discovered the identity of the suspects. Yes, I had several promising leads, but I'd been in that situation before and it had all come to nought.

As I drove home, I countered my frustrations by reminding myself why I had gotten into the cops in the first place. I had always loved watching shows like *Homicide* when I was growing up, and then one day when I was out shopping with my mum in Parramatta, a couple of cops had pulled up alongside us at the lights. I'd looked at them in awe, and thought to myself, *Wow, cops are cool. They're the real good guys, and that's what I want to be – one of the good guys.* So, in 1980, I'd joined the cops as a fresh-faced eighteen-year-old.

The longer I spent in the force, from Blacktown to Penrith to St Marys to Newtown to Marrickville, the more I revelled in the respect that came with the uniform, and every time I put it on it felt like I was making a difference. To be honest though, in those early days I was bloody green, and ignorant regarding a lot of things. The world of crime and crooks that I'd been thrust into was not a world I was at all used to. My family, my parents and my two brothers, had all been close while I was growing up, and as the middle one of three boys, I had been shielded from most of the 'real' world problems. All my grandparents were amazing, and all my aunties, uncles and cousins got along really well and caught up with each other regularly, so it was a dramatic change of scenery for me to be going to domestics and dealing with drug addicts and people from a totally different background.

As time went on and I saw more and more, I was able to deal with things because I kept reminding myself that I'd joined the cops because there were a lot of bad people out there who needed to be dealt with, while at the same time there were a lot of good people who relied on the cops for help. It made it easier for me to deal with crooks, because I knew I was on the right side, and the decent people of the world needed protecting.

I had only been in the job for a few months when I started to see the other side of life, and that was when I really began to develop a dislike for the criminal element. My sense of being a cop and my reasons for being one began to change, from simply wanting to help people and be a symbol of doing the right thing to wanting to lock up crooks who made life miserable for others. Not being able to lock someone up always made me feel like I'd somehow failed the people I'd sworn to protect.

I remembered back to 1987, when I'd investigated the rape of four women around the Penrith area. The arsehole of a bloke would break into his chosen victim's car, then lock the doors again and hide in the back seat while he waited for them. As soon as they jumped in, he'd leap up, hold a knife to their throats and make them drive to some isolated location, where he'd rape them. The last one was a nineteen-year-old girl who'd been out with friends at the Colyton Hotel. She had barely driven out of the premises when he held a knife to her throat, ordered her to drive to some nearby soccer fields and then raped her on the bonnet of her car.

A few weeks later, in a strange twist of fate, the bastard happened to be in the Salvation Army store at Minchinbury at the same time as the young girl. She heard him speak, and immediately recognised his voice. She hid behind a rack of dresses and waited until he left before taking down his rego number, and then came into the station to tell me what had happened. I checked the vehicle details and found the owner, a local bikie who lived on a rural property out near Cranebrook and was known to police, as he had a criminal record for drug and assault-related matters. I took the girl's statement and phoned the other girls to see if they were happy to come in while we put the bloke in a line-up, that is, if he agreed to do one. Apart from the young girl, however, only one other lady had gotten a decent enough look at his face to be able to confidently identify him.

I organised for the two girls to come into the station on the same day we executed a search warrant on the property where the offender lived. Another detective, two junior officers and I carried out the search and found an unlicensed shotgun. We were looking for items of clothing that the girls had told us about, but unfortunately we didn't find anything matching their descriptions.

There was, however, one key piece of evidence. The victims had told us that the offender was not circumcised, so while the others were searching the house, I remained in the lounge room with the suspect and told him to drop his pants. 'What, are you a poof or something?' he said as he shot me a strange look.

'Keep your mouth shut, mate.'

'I'm not dropping my pants.'

'Just fucking do it, mate!' The suspect complied just as the other detective walked back in, and we both immediately noticed that his old fella had the extra coat on. 'Bingo,' I said as I looked at the other detective and smiled.

You would think that a man saying 'bingo' as soon as another man dropped his strides might draw some strange comments, but the suspect didn't say anything. He knew exactly why I'd done it. We took him back to the station and interviewed him, but he vehemently denied everything. I asked him to go in a line-up, not for a minute expecting him to comply, but to my surprise he agreed to it, so then we had to quickly send some of our guys out to find a random group of males from off the street or in nearby shops to take part in the line-up. The suspect was Caucasian with a reasonably big build, so we had to find guys that looked similar to him. If we couldn't find any, we couldn't do the line-up.

Fortunately, we found enough suitable guys, and were able to put the bloke in the line-up. The older of the two victims came into the room and only walked up and down the line-up once before she stopped directly in front of the suspect. She eyeballed him for what seemed like an eternity, and I could see that she recognised him, but there was one slight problem. Since his last attack, he'd been involved in a serious motor cycle accident, and his injuries had left him with a number of facial scars that had dramatically altered his appearance. Eventually, she stepped back and walked out of the room. I followed her outside, and before I could say anything, she broke down. 'It's okay,' I said as I tried to comfort her. 'You just did a really brave thing.'

'I think it's number four,' she said through her tears, 'but I can't be one hundred per cent sure. The scars on his face make him look really different.'

I wasn't going to subject her to any more suffering, so I brought the younger girl in, confident that she'd quickly identify him, as she'd seen him at the Salvos just a few days earlier. She walked into the room, took a brief look at the line-up of men, panicked, and rushed back outside again. 'It's okay,' I said as comfortingly as I could. 'Take your time. You can have another try in a minute.'

'I can't! I don't know! I can't identify him. Can I please just go?'

I was in shock. I knew he was the one, but my identification was shot to pieces, and I had to console myself with the fact that at least I had him on the firearm offence. I was shocked, angry and frustrated. This animal, this pig, was going to get away with raping *four* women, and I was *so* close to nailing him.

The younger girl's mother rang me later that day to tell me that her daughter had recognised the man in the line-up, but she'd been too frightened by the sight of him and had decided she couldn't go through with it. I felt sorry for her, but I couldn't help but think about the next possible victim, who we could have saved by putting this guy away for a long time. When shit like that happened, I'd start to question why I was doing this job, and whether I was really making a difference.

I pulled into my driveway, and could hear shouting coming from inside my house. 'What the bloody hell's going on?' I said as I walked inside.

'She stole my doll!' Jenna cried. 'She's always going into my room and taking my stuff!'

'I am not!' Ashleigh retorted. 'If I do go into her room, it's only to get back stuff that she's stolen from me. That's my doll, anyway!'

'Okay, girls, let's sort this out calmly.' No joy. Now Tayla joined in, a three-way tug of war over possession of the doll began, and the screaming match intensified. 'Girls, now give Daddy the doll, and we'll talk about this,' I tried to say.

'It's mine!'

'No, it's mine! Give it!'

I could feel the frustration and anger building up inside me. I tried to suppress my feelings, to calm down, but I'd reached the point of no return. 'Quiet, all of you!' I snarled as I walked over and snatched the doll from them. 'I swear if I have to put up with any more of this kind of thing, there's gonna be hell to pay!' The rage in my voice shocked the girls, who all stood in stunned silence with frightened looks on their faces.

'Girls, time to go to bed now,' Sue said gently as she took the doll from me and ushered all three girls towards the stairs.

'But, Mum!' they all argued.

'Go to bed,' Sue repeated as I retrieved a beer from the fridge and headed out the back to sit by the pool. I stared into the blue water as I sipped on my beer, and then bowed my head and closed my eyes. *What the hell is happening to me*, I thought to myself. *I've never snapped at my kids like that before. I don't like this bloke that I've become. I need to get the real Pete back.* I'd always been there for my girls, always promised to protect and nurture them, and here I was hurting them.

'Are you alright, Pete?' I heard Sue say as she came to the back door.

'I don't know what's wrong with me,' I said as I buried my head in my hands. 'I'm sorry, Susie. I really am. I'm just under a lot of pressure at work.'

'I know, honey,' she said as she sat down next to me and wrapped her arms around me. 'But you'll find whoever killed that poor man, and it will all be over soon.'

'Yeah, I guess, you're right.'

Sue's attempts to console me helped, but I couldn't stop feeling horrible about myself. I had a couple more beers before I eventually went inside and upstairs to bed. Susie was already asleep when I slid into bed beside her. I lay back and tried to go to sleep, but it was no use.

Chapter 9:
A Stronger Man

The next morning, I headed in to work knowing that I needed to bring this investigation to a head one way or another, not only for the Hanes family but also for myself, so that I could get back to being the man I knew I was. I hoped and prayed that Wazza's mate's son was going to do the right thing and contact me. However, witnesses can be a tricky proposition, and whether they are prepared to come forward with information often depends on what's going on in their world, who they know and what they think they have to gain or lose.

It was around mid-morning when the guys at the front desk told me there was someone there to see me. I walked out to the reception area and saw a young lad standing there who I could only assume was Wazza's son's mate. 'Hi, mate, I'm Detective Seymour,' I said as I extended my hand.

'Hello, Detective, my name is Byron Smith.'

'Wazza told me you might have some information for me.'

'Yes, sir, I think I do.'

'Righto, mate, come on through then.' I escorted him into one of the interview rooms and sat him down, then sat down opposite him. 'What have you got for me, mate?'

'Well,' he began nervously, 'we've all seen the footage and stuff on the telly, and one of me mates told me that he knows some of the blokes involved.'

'Do you have some names?'

'Yeah, John Walton, Charlie Hohopa and Dale Black.'

'And how did your mates come to know this?' I asked.

'I dunno, the blokes must have said something to them,' he said.

It didn't surprise me. I'd come across many a crook whose undoing was the fact that they couldn't keep their secret to themselves and just had to brag about it, in fact it was something I was relying on. 'Can you describe Mr Walton for me?'

'Yeah, he's a tall, blond-haired guy.'

'And what about the other two?'

'Hohopa is a Maori, or some type of Islander anyway, and Black looks pretty similar to Walton.'

'Do you know where I might be able to find them?'

'Yeah, Hohopa lives in the next street over from where the guy was killed. Walton lives in St Clair, and Black lives in a street further up the highway.'

'Can you give me the names of your mates who told you this?'

'If it's all the same, Detective, I'd rather not.'

I wasn't going to push the point. I knew it had taken a lot for this young fellow to come forward in the first place, so I wasn't about to scare him off now. 'Okay mate, just give me a tick,' I said. I finished writing the last of my notes, and then headed outside to have a chat with Mick.

'Is that the young bloke Wazza mentioned?' he asked.

'Sure is. Looks like our killers have opened their traps.'

'Do you have names?'

'Yeah, he gave me three. Reckon I'll have to show him the CCTV footage for confirmation, but even if he does positively identify the suspects, I'm not sure I can do much with it at the moment. It's not enough for me to bring these guys in; it's all just hearsay.'

'Hmmm, well in that case, I guess it can't hurt to show him the tape,' Mick mused as he carefully considered what I was telling him.

'Right,' I said, and then turned and headed back into the interview room.

'Byron, I'd like to show you some CCTV footage, if you don't mind.'

'No, not at all.'

I disappeared down to the exhibit room, signed for and retrieved the tape, and headed back upstairs to the interview room. I put the tape in the video and pressed play. I forwarded the tape the correct time and let him watch. He leaned forward in his chair, watching the screen intently. The two suspects eventually came into view, and I watched his reactions with interest. As he strained his eyes, my hopes began to fade, his body language suggesting that he didn't recognise anyone, but just as the suspects were exiting the servo, their faces could be seen more clearly, and he suddenly pointed at the television and said, 'That one there, that looks like John Walton.'

'Which one?' I asked.

'The tall blond guy wearing the light-coloured clothes.'

'What about the dark guy? Does he look familiar?'

'Well, it could be Hohopa, but I can't be sure.'

I took a formal statement and thanked the kid for coming in and giving me the information. I then escorted him from the station and went back to my desk. Leaning back in my chair with my hands clenched behind my head, I called across the office to Mick. 'He wasn't prepared to tell me the names of his mates who reckon Walton, Hohopa and Black were the guys involved.'

'But he did say that the tall blond guy in the tape looked like him, didn't he,' said Mick.

'Yeah, but he couldn't be sure about the other fella.'

'Where are you going to go from here, then?'

'I don't know, mate. I reckon I'll have to do some surveillance on them, and see what information I can find. I'll get Karen to run some checks and see what comes up.'

Karen was kept pretty busy for the rest of the day, and although nothing much came up in terms of criminal offences, she was able to find addresses for the three suspects.

'Hey, Pete!' she called across the room. 'The description of the Walton guy is very similar to the tall, blond-haired dude we're looking for. Hohopa, is an Islander which fits the description of the second offender, although he seems to be a bit taller than our offender seems to be. Not sure about the third guy, Black.'

I got up, jogged over to the computer, peered over Karen's shoulder and scanned the screen. *This may be just what we're looking for*, I thought to myself.

'What do you reckon?' Karen said.

I checked my watch. It was 4.10 pm. 'I reckon we go and pay Walton a visit and see what he has to say about his movements on the night of 14 July. Grab a set of car keys; we may be working some overtime tonight.'

'Do you think he may be the one?' Karen asked excitedly.

'Well, we'll soon find out, won't we,' I replied as Karen retrieved a set of keys. We headed down to the car park, and made our way to an address in St Clair.

It was around 4.30 pm when we pulled up outside a small brown-brick home with two steps leading up to the front veranda. The front yard was plain, with only a lawn, and no real garden to speak of. I knocked on the screen door, and a young male with short blond hair answered.

'Yeah?' he said as he peered through the screen door, first at me, then at Karen.

'Good afternoon,' I replied. 'Are you John Walton?'

'Yeah, who are you?' he said.

'My name is Detective Seymour, and this is Detective Richards. We're from St Marys police station. I'd like to have a chat with you about a matter we're investigating. Can we come in?'

'Yeah, sure,' he said, and opened the screen door. We walked inside, and into the lounge room. A quick scan around the room revealed a tidy house, with small ornaments and various photos scattered around the place. Karen and I sat on a two-seater lounge, while Walton sat opposite us in a single lounge chair. As we sat down, I heard a door close toward the rear of the house, and a few moments later an older man walked into the lounge room. I stood up, introduced myself and told him I was there to ask John some questions.

'Well, I'm his father, and I want to know what this is all about,' Mr Walton said firmly.

'Mr Walton, we're investigating the death of a man on Mamre Road, St Marys, in the early hours of the morning of 15 July. We have descriptions of two young males who may be able to assist us with our enquiries. We have information that leads us to believe that your son may be one of those persons.'

I turned to John Walton and said, 'Do you remember where you were on the night of Friday 14 July and into the early hours of 15 July?'

'Yeah, I was with my girlfriend from about 7.30 pm. We went to the St Clair shops to get a bottle of vodka and some orange juice. We caught up with some friends at St Marys and ended up at the RSL Club for a while. Then we went to the Band Club, but I couldn't get in, so I went to Penrith and had a few drinks there before getting a taxi back to the Band Club.'

'What were you wearing that night?' I asked.

'A cream jumper and blue jeans.'

'Go and get them, son,' his father said sternly. As he watched his son disappear towards his bedroom, he turned back to me and said, clearly worried, 'Are you saying my son is involved in this murder?'

'As I said Mr Walton, we're making enquiries into this matter, and we need to speak to your son about it.'

John Walton soon returned carrying a cream-coloured long-sleeve Billabong brand jumper and a pair of dark-blue denim jeans.

The jumper matches, but the bloke we're after wasn't wearing dark trousers, I thought. *Still, he does look reasonably similar to the grainy image on the screen, and there was certainly enough there to warrant him being questioned further.* I reached for my folder and pulled out the stills from the CCTV footage. 'I want you to have a look at this photo, John,' I said, and handed the photo to him. He held it in his lap and examined it carefully. 'Is that you in the photo?' I asked.

'Yeah, it looks like me, but I don't remember being in a service station that night. I was pretty pissed.'

That was enough for me. My pulse rate skyrocketed as it dawned on me that we may have just identified the first offender! I stood up and reached out for the photo, which he handed back to me. I put it back in my folder, and then turned and looked him squarely in the eye.

'John Walton, you are under arrest for murder,' I said. 'You will be taken back to Penrith police station, where I will interview you further in relation to this matter. You are not obliged to say anything unless you wish to do so, but whatever you say will be recorded and may be used in evidence. Do you understand that?'

'Yeah,' he said rather nervously.

I looked across at his father, the worry lines across his forehead now more apparent. 'I want to come as well,' he said.

I looked back at John Walton, and as I looked him up and down, I said, 'How old are you?'

'Twenty,' he replied.

'He's over eighteen, so you can't come with us, Mr Walton. It's fine if you want to come down to the station, but you'll have to make your own way there.'

'Yeah, no worries,' he said, and proceeded to follow us while we walked Walton out to the unmarked police car and put him in the back seat, along with the clothes that he'd shown us.

I sat beside him, while Karen drove. As she pulled away from the kerb, she said, 'Peter, how come we're going to Penrith?'

'While we were on our way out here, I heard the uniformed boys talking about how they were bringing someone back for a drink-driving matter, so they're using the interview room. Besides, if we decide to lay charges, we'd have to go to Penrith anyway.' St Marys was only a small station, with no charging facilities or cells, so whenever we arrested someone, we had to take them back to Penrith.

About fifteen minutes later, we pulled up in the basement car park at Penrith, led Walton to the elevator and made our way to the ground floor, where he was taken to the custody officer and booked into custody. By this time, his father had arrived and was seated in the foyer, nervously waiting for word on what was happening with his son. Before long, I was taking Walton and his father upstairs to the detectives' office where, instead of doing an electronically recorded interview, I decided to sit Walton and his father down and ask Walton some more questions.

Before I began, I examined them both carefully. There was something nagging at me. Despite my initial excitement, I wasn't convinced this guy was the one I was after. He just didn't look sufficiently like the person in the video, and now the more questions I asked, the more convinced I became that he wasn't my man. He was able to answer every question I asked him about his movements that night, and he provided several solid alibis.

Eventually, I showed him the photo again. 'Take a good hard look at the picture. You said when I interviewed you at your house that you thought it was you in that photo. Do you still think it is you?'

'No, that isn't me. I don't know why I thought it was me when I said that earlier. I guess I was panicking about you speaking to me, and I know I was really drunk that night and ended up in a fight at the Band Club when we went back there about 1 am. The other thing is, the Islander bloke in the photo actually looks a bit like a mate of mine who I was with that night.'

'What's your mate's name?' I said, knowing that I would have to speak to this person in order to rule them both out.

'Charlie Hohopa,' he replied.

'Will you excuse us for a couple of minutes?' I said to Walton and his father as I nodded to Karen to join me outside. 'He isn't the person we're after,' I said as soon as I'd shut the door behind us. 'We'll have to let him go.'

'Dammit,' Karen replied, clearly disappointed. 'I really thought we had him, especially when he said at his home that it was him in the picture.'

'Yeah, as soon as we started talking to him, things just weren't sitting right. Anyway, we'll still interview his mate Hohopa and see what he has to say, and then go from there. But for now, we have to let this guy go.'

We went back into the interview room, and I explained to Walton and his father that he was free to go, but he was not to contact Hohopa and discuss what had just happened.

'Don't worry, he won't,' his father said adamantly. 'I'm just glad this whole thing is sorted out, and I hope you get whoever did this.' I shook his hand, and then led them both downstairs and watched as they walked out through the front doors of the station. *So close and yet so far*, I thought to myself. The same old sunken feelings now returned. I'd gotten my hopes up, and now I was back to square one.

I went back upstairs to the detectives' office, where I found Karen staring out the window onto High Street. Deep inside, I was deflated, dejected, but there was no way I was going to let Karen see that. She was still young and inexperienced, and as the senior officer, I had to keep her upbeat and enthusiastic.

'I know it's disappointing when things don't go the way we want them to, but that's just the way it is. We have to put that behind us and get back into it,' I said, trying to reassure her that yet another setback wasn't the end of the world, even if I didn't really believe what I was saying.

'Yeah, I know,' she sighed, 'but I was getting so excited about this, and now we're back to not having much to go on again.'

'This is probably one of the best lessons you can learn,' I replied. 'Sometimes things just don't go the way you'd like. You're going to go through this a lot more times during your career. If you don't learn how to leave things, they'll end up eating away at you and messing with your head. Come on, let's get back to St Marys, put our overtime forms in and get home.'

As I drove home, I continued to consider all the things that were going through my mind. Throughout my career, I had simply done my job to the best of my ability, but if things hadn't gone how I wanted them to, no matter how frustrating or annoying, I'd just put it behind me and got on with it, but at some point, something deep down inside me had changed. I'd first started to notice the changes during the Keir investigation. There had been times when I felt like I was never going to solve the case, but somehow I'd still managed to keep myself upbeat and positive. However, with this investigation, I was racked by a fear of failure I'd never felt before. I didn't want to let the Hanes family down, and I felt an acute sense of personal responsibility. In the Keir investigation, I'd been part of a team, and we'd all been in it together, but with this one, the buck stopped with me. I was the commander, and I was beginning to feel isolated and lonely. If the investigation failed, I had nowhere to hide. In the Keir investigation, there had been a group of detectives, including some from Homicide, with whom I could share the load. I'd had other people to help provide answers as to why things weren't progressing as we'd hoped, or why we didn't have the evidence we needed to do anything, but this time it all fell on me.

Yeah, I had Mick and Glash there for support, but at the end of the day, they were busy with their own work, and if this one fell down, it would be my fault, and no one else's. Suddenly, I felt overwhelmed by the weight of my burden, and I wanted nothing more than to pull over and cry my eyes out.

Somehow I managed to keep it together, and eventually arrived home. I took a few moments in the car to compose myself before I walked inside, and tried to put on my best happy face, but as soon as Sue saw me, she knew something was up. She didn't say anything, she didn't have to; the look on her face gave it away. She made me a cuppa, and asked me where the investigation was up to. I explained everything, and told her of my frustrations. 'Perhaps you need a couple of days off,' she suggested.

As always, Susie was right. I'd been pushing myself hard as I tried to get a result as quickly as possible, but this latest setback had shown me just how jaded I was. The best thing I could do for everybody right now was to spend some quality time with my family, in order to unwind and rejuvenate myself. I went to bed early that night and managed to get some sleep, but woke at 3 am after having the nightmare about Tayla falling off the railway bridge again, and struggled to get back to sleep after that.

When morning came, I dragged myself out of bed and in to work, and as soon as I got there, I went straight into Glash's office. 'You got a sec, boss?' I said.

'Yeah, Pete, what's up?' Glash said, his face wearing a look of concern.

I updated him on everything, and then said, 'As you know, boss, I'm due to take two rest days after today. I'll get Karen and the others guys to do some surveillance on Dale Black while I'm off, and we'll see where that leads us. I'm really interested to see if Black has a mate who matches the description of the second offender. The problem is, my new witness didn't recognise the second offender, but that doesn't mean too much, I guess.'

'Okay, Pete. You take your days off. You've earned them, and at least there are still some lines of enquiry that the other guys can follow up on. I'm ordering you to relax over the next couple of days with your family, and come back fresh so you can get back into this investigation with a clear pair of eyes.'

'Will do, boss. Thanks.' I left Glash's office, and decided that before I went, I should give Nick Hanes's wife a call. I had been calling her every couple of days, but each time I did, my words sounded hollow. I wished I could give her the words that she wanted to hear, that we'd caught her husband's killers, but all I could do was reassure her that the investigation was progressing. Much to her credit, she always told me she understood how difficult our job must be, and that she appreciated that I was keeping her in the loop. I wish I could say that each case I'd ever worked on was unique, but there were always similarities. It was uncanny how much Bel Hanes reminded me of Christine Strachan, who had lost her daughter to a violent murder at the hands of her husband. She had that same hopeful smile, but behind the smile there was pain and suffering caused by the uncertainty.

While I was talking to Bel, Karen brought up the information she'd uncovered while doing checks on Hohopa. She called the phone number she'd located and spoke to his father, and made arrangements for him to bring his son in to the station. They arrived just after lunch, and I soon had them upstairs in the interview room. The moment I laid eyes on Hohopa, I could see that he wasn't the person in the pictures. He was too solidly built, and his face was fuller and more rounded and he had a much longer, dense helmet of tight curls surrounding his face. I only needed to ask a few questions before I was certain that he and his mate were not the two people I was after.

That afternoon, I headed home and tried to put everything out of my mind. My two days off were a godsend, exactly what I needed to recharge my batteries and get me thinking clearly again. I dropped the girls off at school and picked them up again in the afternoon, and tried to be the dad that they knew, but when everyone else was out of the house and I was left to my own devices, I had nothing else to do but sit and think.

On my first day off, I was out the back relaxing by the pool enjoying a cold beer, staring idly up at the bright blue sky and watching the fluffy white clouds skip by when suddenly I felt like I had travelled out of my body. It wasn't what I would call an out-of-body experience as such, but it was as though I was in a mental and emotional vacuum. It was like I was there, and yet I wasn't; my mind and body felt like they had completely switched off.

I actually found it therapeutic to be able to float in this emotional void, but eventually, no matter what I tried to do to prevent it, my entire career, including the bank robber and the knife-wielding burglar, began to play over and over in my mind, as though I was watching an old movie.

I didn't want to think about all that, so I busied myself with the chores that I generally never had time to do. That worked for a while, but as soon as I stopped, the horrible thoughts would return. That evening, when all the girls were back home, I sat on the couch and tried to engage with them, to be a good dad, but I wanted nothing more than to return to my emotional void.

The next day, I managed to sneak in a quick eighteen holes of golf, which had the same therapeutic effect. That was one thing I loved about golf; it didn't matter if I was playing like shit, I could still find a sense of solitude.

Despite having a lot on my mind, the couple of days off rejuvenated me, and as I drove in to work on my first day back, I resolved to find out absolutely everything I could about our next suspect, Black. I would set up surveillance on him, and depending on what I found, I would then make a call as to whether we had sufficient information to take things further and arrest him.

As soon as I walked into the office, everyone brought me up to date on what they had discovered while I was gone. Firstly, they'd learned that our main suspect worked in the building trade, and secondly, he was currently working on a building site about five minutes away at Werrington. I went straight into Glash's office. 'Hey, Pete,' he said as he lifted his head. 'How was your time off?'

'I hate to tell you, boss, but if I didn't have to come back, I wouldn't have.'

'Ain't that the truth,' Glash replied. 'So the guys have updated you on everything?'

'Yeah, they tell me that our last suspect, Black, works as a builder in Werrington.'

'Right, well, I want to set off early tomorrow morning. We'll sit outside his house and follow him to work. It's possible the second suspect might be one of his workmates, so that way we'll be able to find out who he is.'

Glash was more animated than usual, and I sensed that he wanted to be more heavily involved. Back in his younger days, Glash had always been a very good investigator, but now his job was managerial, so he no longer got to do much of the hands-on stuff. He'd told me a couple of times how much he really missed it, and the prospect of us having another suspect had obviously gotten him excited.

We set out before dawn the next day in an unmarked car. It was an eerie feeling driving through the western suburbs of Sydney as the sun came up. After weeks of leads, it felt like this was the culmination, as though the sun's rays were bringing illumination to everything we had worked so hard for. We pulled up on the opposite side of the street from the suspect's house, far enough away so that we wouldn't be noticed but close enough so that we would still have a clear view of anyone leaving the house.

Both Glash and I had steaming cups of coffee in hand, and sipped away as we tried to wake ourselves up. I looked over at him as he stared intently at the target premises. 'I really could have done without being up this early,' I joked.

All I got from Glash was '*Hmmm, hmmm,*' as he nodded his head. I was just about to say more when he suddenly said, 'There he is. Let's go.'

The target got into his car, pulled out of his driveway and drove off in the direction of the Great Western Highway. Glash started the car, pulled out from the kerb, swung round the corner and set about tailing him, but we hadn't been following him for long when he pulled in to a building site.

Glash quickly pulled over and turned off the engine, then looked across at me. 'Well, he didn't pick anyone up,' he said quietly.

'Yeah,' I said as I strained my eyes trying to get a look at the rest of the workers on the site. 'And from here, there doesn't appear to be anyone else on the site resembling the second offender. To be honest Glash, this guy's hair isn't as blond as the one in the footage, but he could have coloured his hair to try to change his appearance since the murder.'

'Anything's possible, which is precisely why we need to keep an open mind to all the possibilities in cases like this,' Glash replied.

Working on a hunch that the second offender might still turn up, we stayed in position for another half an hour before we decided we weren't going to get anywhere, and then headed back to the station. On the way, I said to Glash, 'I need to know more about this guy. I wonder if I can get a warrant to bug his home phone to see if he's talking to anyone about the murder. I'll contact headquarters and see if I have enough information based on the footage, the witness identifying the two suspects, and now the new information alleging that Black could have been involved. Given all of that, I reckon I should be a chance.'

'That's a great idea, Pete,' Glash agreed. 'Let me know how you go.'

When we arrived at the station, I quickly collected everything I needed and sent it to headquarters. I hoped like hell that firstly, it was enough for them to put to the Supreme Court Justice, and secondly, that the Justice would deem there to be sufficient evidence for us to put a trace on Black's phone.

While I was waiting for a response, I contemplated what my next move would be if they didn't grant my request. A few hours later, however, I received the go ahead, and within a couple of days the phone had been bugged and Telstra were delivering daily reports on all the calls to and from the house. The only thing I'd forgotten about was that I'd have to go through every number myself! After hours and hours of sifting through them, much to my disappointment, I didn't find anything of interest. It was time to bring Black in and interview him.

Karen and I went to Black's parents' house, and I arranged for Black to come down to the station. When I interviewed him, he vehemently denied being involved, and the alibis he gave were watertight. Another lead gone, another suspect crossed off the list.

To say I was livid, not at the bloke, but at the case itself, would have been an understatement. I'd been so sure that this was it. I had a suspect who fitted the bill, and I was eagerly anticipating making an arrest and getting the court proceedings underway, but now, yet again, I was back to square one, and it completely pissed me off. I don't know what was the hardest thing; not having any solid information about who I was chasing, or having seemingly good evidence and not being able to get to the point of identification. I felt like I was on an emotional roller coaster that was never going to stop, and as I made my way home that night, I thought that all the frustrations and aggravations bubbling away inside me were going to overflow.

When I walked in the door, Tayla and Jenna came up to me for a hug, but I walked straight past them and slumped down onto the couch. Ashleigh was lying on the lounge room floor doing her homework and, as soon as I sat down, she said, 'Dad, can you help me with my homework?'

'Not now, honey, Daddy just got home. Maybe later.'

'Pete, there's a problem with the fridge,' Sue called out from the kitchen. 'I was wondering if you could have a look at it for me.'

'For God's sake, I just got home! Can't a man have five minutes to himself!' I bellowed as I leapt off the couch and went out the back to be by myself. Jenna and Tayla followed me out, 'Daddy, are you okay?' they both said.

'Girls, let your father be,' I heard Sue say. I know I should have been a stronger man and kept work and my family life separate, but unfortunately my frustrations exploded like a volcano, and there was nothing I could do about it.

I paced around the pool, trying to figure out why I was feeling this way. I knew it was wrong to snap at my girls and my wife for absolutely no reason, but I just couldn't help it. It was like all my emotions had been sucked out of me. I was putting everything I had into the investigation, and by the time I got home, I had nothing left to give.

Eventually, I walked back inside and sat down in the lounge room. 'Girls, come here for a minute,' I called. The three girls all came into the room, and Ashleigh sat beside me while Jenna sat on one knee and Tayla on the other. 'Girls, I'm really sorry I've been yelling at you lately,' I said. 'I'm under a lot of pressure at work, but I'll try not to be so grumpy, and do more stuff with you.'

'It's okay, Daddy, we understand,' Jenna said as she kissed me on the cheek. 'We still love you.'

That broke my heart. I hated how I was feeling, and it was made all that much worse by the fact that I knew the kids had no way of knowing or understanding what was going on. It must have confused them no end to see their normally happy, loving father behaving in such an uncharacteristic way.

'Okay, girls, time for bed,' Susie said. With that, the girls happily skipped off upstairs, got into their jamas and went to bed. 'The kids really love you, you know,' Susie said as she came and sat beside me on the sofa.

'I know, I know. I really don't know what's going on, Susie. I feel like I'm coming apart at the seams.'

'My poor baby,' she said as she held me. 'Everything's going to be alright, I promise you.' She kissed me on the cheek, and then let me be. I sat on the couch and looked at all the family photos scattered around the room. It reminded me of happier times, of times when I was the man I knew I really was, and I resolved that, when this was all over, I'd find that man again.

As time went on, the days began to blur into one another. The thing that really kept my anger levels high was the fact that I had to drive past the crime scene every day on my way to and from work. Every morning when I passed by, I prayed that today would be the day that the break would come, that the evidence would appear so I could finally identify the two suspects.

I rang Bel Hanes regularly, and her words gave me hope, and the strength to continue. 'It's all right, Detective Seymour,' she said. 'I know something will come up. I know you will find Nick's killers. I have faith in you.' It worked both ways, too, and Bel often rang me for a chat when she was feeling despondent.

One night, at around 8 pm, she rang me at home in a real state. 'It's all becoming a bit too much for me, Peter,' she said as her voice began to waver. 'I'm really beginning to struggle.'

'I know the feeling, Bel,' I said. 'We're doing everything we can. Something will come up, I swear to you, and when it does, we'll get to the bottom of everything. In the meantime, I'll come over right now if you like.'

'Okay, Peter, that would be great. Thank you.'

I put the phone down. 'Sue, that was Bel Hanes. She's in a bit of a state. I need to go over there.'

'Uh-huh,' Sue said. 'Just make sure you're not home too late.'

'Okay, darl, I won't be,' I said as I grabbed my keys and was out the door. I drove to Bel's, had a cuppa and a chat, did my best to allay all her fears and eventually left her place at around 10 pm. When I got home, I went upstairs to discover that Sue was only half asleep.

'Is she okay now?' Sue said as she rolled over.

'Yeah, I think she'll be right.'

'Pete,' Sue said as she propped herself up on one elbow, 'I love you because you're the kind of man who would do anything for anyone, but there comes a point where enough is enough.'

'What do you mean?'

'Don't get me wrong, Pete, what you do and who you are is wonderful, but you need to leave work at work. Rushing over to Bel's place at 8 pm is perhaps going just a little overboard.'

'Sue, the poor woman's husband was murdered. What do you expect me to do?' I snapped.

'Pete, I know she has suffered, and is still suffering. I respect the fact that you have to be there for her and her family, but you have a family of your own, and we need you here.'

She was right, of course. 'You're right, honey. I'm sorry. I'll make sure I make time for all of you. I promise.'

I didn't sleep much that night, and spent a long time contemplating simply leaving things be. I knew I'd promised Bel Hanes that I would solve the case and give her the answers she so desperately sought, but it was starting to have a profound effect on my family, and they came first. I needed to do whatever it took to return to being the man Sue had fallen in love with and the daddy that my girls knew and loved, regardless of anything that was going on at work.

Chapter 10:
Got 'em

I was sitting at my desk one afternoon when a uniformed officer walked up to my desk and handed me a yellow envelope. 'Here, Pete, this came for you,' he said.

'Ta, mate,' I said as I took it from him. I turned it over and saw that it was from the Coroner's Court. I opened the envelope and retrieved the toxicology report from the post-mortem examination of Nick Hanes's body. Hanes was clear of drugs, apart from alcohol, but I was surprised to find that his blood alcohol reading was 0.285! *Damn, he wouldn't have been able to swat a fly with that much alcohol in his system!* I thought to myself, and then continued to read. It was Dr Little's view that the assault, combined with the deceased's enlarged heart and the alcohol reading, had all contributed to his death.

Knowing that Hanes's blood alcohol reading was so high didn't really help me. In fact, it made me feel incredibly sorry for him. All things considered, he never stood a chance. He would've had a hard enough time defending himself against two younger and fitter men if he'd been sober, let alone while he was paralytic. Still, this didn't get us any closer to discovering the identities of the two suspects.

One night, we were having dinner when Susie said, 'Pete, we've been having a few problems lately.'

'Yes, dear, I know. I'm sorry.'

'It's alright, darling. I just think it would be a good idea if we got away for a few days. What do you think?'

'Yeah, sounds good to me,' I said.

That weekend, we packed up the kids and headed up to the Central Coast to spend a couple of days with Sue's parents. Somehow, being geographically removed from the western suburbs helped me to recharge. The kids loved visiting their grandparents, and we walked on the beach and went fishing in a little runabout around Brisbane Waters. Sue's dad, Ted, loved taking the girls for walks up the mountain near his house to collect gumnuts, and took them up there that weekend. As always, the girls came back dirty, and their legs were covered in scratches, but as always, they had big smiles on their faces after their little adventure with Poppy. Susie's mum spoiled them rotten too.

A few weekends later, my parents took the girls off our hands and treated them to a day out at Featherdale Wildlife Park at Blacktown before going home to enjoy Mum's home-cooked treats and special milkshakes.

Both the girls' grandfathers were great men, and their grandmothers were, and are, great women. Sadly, both my father, John Seymour, and my father-in-law Ted Kneale are gone now, but their passing did make me realise one thing; no matter how unfair or unjustified someone's passing may be, life stills goes on.

While I was up the coast, I had a good hard think about things, and realised that I might never find Nick Hanes's killers. I had done everything I could, covered every lead, but perhaps solving this one just wasn't meant to be, and so I resigned myself to that fact.

One day, not long after, a call came in to the switchboard at St Marys police station at around 4 pm. It was an adult female, who wanted to remain anonymous, but said she had information about the two men we were after. She gave the operator two names before she hung up; Aaron Cooper and Ricky Mahia.

Karen and I were out checking up on Bel Hanes at the time, and no sooner had I walked back into the station than the uniformed boys came rushing up to me. 'Hey, Pete!' one of them said excitedly. 'Guess what?'

'What?'

'We got a call this arvo!'

'And?'

'Some lady rang in and gave us the names of the two guys she reckons killed Nick Hanes!'

'You're kidding me!' I exclaimed, amazed that just when the investigation seemed like it was going nowhere, our biggest lead might have just presented itself.

'Nah, I'm dead serious, mate. She rang at around 4 pm.'

'Did you get her details?'

'No, she didn't want to leave them.'

'Damn! Why wouldn't she leave her details?' I said out loud without thinking. Armed with this new information, Karen and I raced upstairs and started running checks on the two names. Mahia, who was twenty-two, had a conviction for drink-driving as well as another traffic offence. Cooper, who was eighteen, only had a couple of minor matters on his record. 'Doesn't really give us much to go on,' Karen said despondently as she looked up at me from the computer.

'Yeah, usually guys who assault people have a lengthy criminal history.'

'So, what's next?' she asked.

I closed my eyes and rubbed my head with my palms. 'You know what?' I said. 'The RSL has a late-night disco on Fridays. In the video footage, they seem to have come from that direction. It's possible they were at the RSL Club earlier that night.'

'Yeah, right,' Karen said as she started cottoning on to my line of thinking.

'I reckon I'll ring the club,' I said, picking up the phone.

'Hello,' the receptionist said.

'Hello, my name is Detective Seymour. I'm following up on some enquiries, and I'm wondering if I could speak to your Duty Manager?'

'Yes, certainly. One moment please.'

A short time later a female voice said, 'Hello. This is the Duty Manager.'

'Hello, my name is Detective Seymour from St Marys police. I wonder if you could check if you have your sign-in register for Friday night 14 July?'

'One sec,' she said. A few moments later, she returned. 'Yes, I've got them here. You're welcome to come down and have a look if you want.'

'Yeah, that'd be great. Thanks, I'll come straight down,' I said, and hung up. Karen and I grabbed our gear, made our way out to the car park, jumped into my car and drove the short distance down the road to the RSL.

The Duty Manager was waiting for us when we walked in. 'Hello, Detectives,' she said. 'If you'd just like to come into my office, I can show you the sign-in registers.'

We followed her to her office, and she handed us two large books. Karen took one, I took the other, and we began to flick through them. I'd only gone through the first few pages when I found what we were looking for; A. Cooper and R. Mahia. 'Got 'em!' I shouted. Karen leant over, saw the names, and then looked up at me with a huge smile on her face. 'This is all starting to come together rather nicely, Kaz,' I said as I returned her smile. 'Can I get a copy of this?' I asked the Duty Manager.

'Sure,' she said, and took the register and walked over to the photocopier. She quickly copied the page we needed, and brought it back to me. 'There you go,' she smiled.

As Karen and I drove back to the station, I said, 'We need to find out the identity of the lady who rang the station and gave us these names.'

'Well, der!' Karen taunted. 'But the question is, how are we gonna do that?'

'The only way is to get checks done on all the incoming calls around that time. Hopefully there won't be too many!'

When we got back to the station, I was straight on the phone to Telstra asking for a list of all the calls that had come into the station between 3.50 pm and 4.10 pm that afternoon.

There were nine, which was eight more than I'd been hoping for, but it could have been worse. The first one I resolved pretty quickly, which was unusual. It was a call was from Nepean Hospital. I rang the number, and found that it was the medical records section and they had rung to leave a message for one of the cops about medical records for a victim he was chasing. One by one, I started to work my way through the numbers.

It took me a couple of days to get through the rest of the numbers because they were all residential. I had to establish the address for each phone number and go out to each one to speak to the occupants of the house to establish who made the call and what it was about and to gather as much intelligence about each address and the people who lived there as I could. That took time, given the need to catch someone at home at each location. Eventually, I managed to rule out eight of the calls. The last one had to be the one I was searching for.

'Kaz, you got a tick?' I said.

'Yep.'

'Right then, we're off to Minchinbury.'

We got into a car and drove for about fifteen minutes until we reached the address. We pulled up outside a standard single-storey cream-coloured brick house with a neat and tidy garden and a carefully mowed lawn in a reasonably new area. 'I've got a funny feeling about this place, Karen,' I said as I leant over from the passenger seat and gazed at the front door.

'Why's that, Pete?'

'Dunno. I've just got a gut feeling that this is it. Anyway, it has to be, doesn't it. This is the last number we've got to check.'

We got out of the car and made our way up the path to the front door. I rang the doorbell, and could soon hear approaching footsteps. A short, middle-aged woman, possibly in her fifties, with a plump yet delicate build, appeared behind the mesh of the security door. When I got my first glimpse of her, the thing that immediately stood out was her dark-brown hair, which was tied up in a tidy bun. She struck me as the type of person who always wanted to do the right thing, something I thought I might be able to use if the time came. 'Yes,' she said, plainly unsure who we were.

'Good afternoon, ma'am. I'm Detective Seymour and this is Detective Richards from St Marys police,' I said as I showed her my badge.

Her bewildered expression changed to one of concern as it dawned on her exactly why we were there. 'I was wondering how long it would take before you came to see me,' she said.

If she knew we'd be knocking on her door sooner or later, why didn't she leave her name in the first place, I thought to myself. 'You rang us a couple of days ago and informed us about Nick Hanes's death?' I asked.

'Yes, that was me. I think you'd better come in,' she said, as she opened the security door and ushered us inside. At that point, my stomach started to turn. It doesn't matter how experienced you are as a copper, when you're on the verge of a huge breakthrough the butterflies always start to flutter. She led us through to the lounge room, and as I examined the ornaments and photos that were on display, I realised that this was a *very* neat woman. She motioned with an open palm for us to sit down, and then she sat down, keeping her head slightly bowed as she fidgeted with her hands. 'Can we start by getting your name?' I asked gently.

'Ah, yes, my name is Mary McDonald,' she said shakily.

The uncertainty in her voice convinced me that I needed to be careful with this lady, or I was going to lose her. I had to gain her confidence and trust, but deep down, I already knew I wasn't going to be able to get her to give me a statement, just some leads. I also realised that this was the time to play the 'you're doing the right thing' card.

'Mrs McDonald,' I began, 'this investigation has already been going for some time, and we need to bring it to a head for the sake of the Hanes family. I speak to Mr Hanes's wife on a regular basis, and it's been really tough on her. I'm sure she's really glad you took the time to ring the station. You gave us two names, which is a great help, but it would be fantastic if you could tell us how you came to know these names?'

She turned her head to the left and grasped the bridge of her nose between the thumb and forefinger of her right hand as she pondered what I'd said. Then she let out a sigh, and looked up at me. 'My son was at a party near Penrith the other night, and there was a girl there who he knows who is going out with a boy who knows the two guys. She told my son it was them. He asked her how come she knew, and she told him that they work with her boyfriend, and they had told him.'

What she was telling us confirmed my hunch that the two suspects worked together; it was just that we'd been chasing the wrong ones. 'Would your son be prepared to come forward and speak to me about what he knows?' I asked.

'No!' she said forcefully. 'He doesn't want to get involved. He's scared of what may happen. He doesn't know I rang you.'

'Mrs McDonald, I cannot stress how important this is,' I began, choosing my words carefully. 'We have descriptions of the two men responsible, but until now, we didn't know their names. The man who died had a wife and six children. They need us to find out who did this. We're not talking about a simple robbery, or something like that. A man has died, and we need to find the people responsible for his death. I'm sure you can appreciate that.'

She lowered her head and stared at the floor for a few moments before she looked back up at me. 'Look, all I can tell you is that the girl's name is Karina Reynolds, and she lives on a property at Cranebrook off the Northern Road. I don't know the number of the house, but it has a white timber fence around the front of the property and the house is set back from the road. It's on the right-hand side, not far from the roundabout that continues on to Windsor. She lives there with her older sister and her partner. That's all I can tell you. Please,' she pleaded, 'I need this to stay confidential.'

'Mrs McDonald, I can't thank you enough for what you have done. I promise your name won't be mentioned. If you speak to your son and he decides he wants to talk to me, this is my direct number.' I gave her my card, and Karen and I rose from our seats. Mrs McDonald accompanied us to the door and watched us walk to the car. I'd made it about half way across the yard when I paused and turned back to Mrs McDonald. 'Thank you again for this. I certainly appreciate it, and I know Mr Hanes's family will too.' She gave me an awkward smile and hurriedly closed the door.

Karen and I walked the rest of the way to the car in silence, but as soon as we were inside, she said, 'I dunno, Pete. Do you think what she told us was reliable?'

'I get the feeling that she's telling the truth. Did you see her body language? She was too nervous and too worried for it not to be good information. I don't want to get too far ahead of myself, but we may have just gotten the break we needed.'

We drove back to the detectives' office, and Karen started compiling the running sheet while I ran a check on Karina Reynolds. 'So how do we go about this, Pete?' Karen asked when she was done.

'Well, Reynolds has no record, so I'm not sure yet. Let me just have a coffee and I'll have a think about where we go from here.' It was around 6 pm, and everyone else in the detectives' office had gone home. I walked down to the meals room, made a coffee and sat down to have a think.

I had two choices. One, go and speak to this girl straightaway, or two, conduct a surveillance operation on her and the boyfriend and go from there. I sipped away at my coffee, and soon made my decision. I walked back up to the office, where Karen was sitting at her desk filling out her duty book. 'Are you happy to do a bit of overtime tonight?' I said.

'Sure,' Karen replied. 'What have you decided?'

'We're going out to the girl's house and bringing her back to the station to interview her.'

'Good, that's what I was hoping you'd say. The only thing is,' she continued, 'I'm supposed to be taking two weeks leave tomorrow to go down to the snow. What if we get enough information to make an arrest?'

'Don't get too far ahead of yourself. She may not tell us anything. Let's just see what happens tonight and take it from there.'

With that, we jumped back in the car and headed out to Cranebrook. Karen's enthusiasm reminded me that she was still learning, so I thought the twenty-minute drive would be a good opportunity to pass on some wisdom. 'Look, we may have to play this a bit cagily at first, just to suss out what these people are like. I'd like to talk to the sister or the sister's partner first and see what reaction I get, because their reactions should give us a good idea of how to proceed. As I said, we'll just have to play things by ear.'

It was getting quite dark when we arrived at Cranebrook, which made finding the house we were looking for a little difficult, but when we eventually found the distinctive white timber railing fence that Mrs McDonald had described, the property stood out like a lighthouse. We pulled into the driveway and headed towards the house, which was set about one hundred metres back from the road. As we approached the weatherboard dwelling, I noticed a woman who appeared to be in her mid to late twenties standing next to a small white car parked in front of the house.

'Okay,' I said to Karen, 'we're here to make enquiries about a matter involving a car similar to that white Toyota. Leave the talking to me.'

'Cool bananas,' Karen replied as we pulled up right behind the Toyota. The woman immediately began to walk towards us.

'Good evening,' I said as we hopped out of the car. 'We're from St Marys police. I'm Detective Seymour and this is Detective Richards. Do you own this car?'

'Yes,' she replied, her voice indicating that she was plainly unsure why we were there. 'What's wrong?'

'We're just making enquiries in relation to an incident involving a car similar to this one. Can you tell me your name?'

'Ah, yeah, it's Sarah Reynolds,' she replied.

'Can you please tell me if anyone else lives here with you?'

'Yeah, my partner, Chris Carter, and my little sister, Karina.'

Bingo, the name matches! I thought. Before I could ask my next question, another car pulled into the driveway behind us.

'That's Chris now,' Sarah said.

I walked straight over to the car as it came to a stop and Chris got out. 'G'day mate, I'm Peter Seymour from St Marys Detectives. Are you Chris Carter?'

'Yes, that's me. What's the problem? Is everything okay?' he asked, genuinely concerned.

'Yeah, mate, we're just making enquiries in relation to an incident, and I was hoping you might be able to help me with those enquiries. Can I talk to you over here for a minute?' I said as I pointed back up the driveway.

'Sure,' he replied, and followed me as I set off up the driveway.

As we walked, I considered my feelings about these people. They seemed to be decent enough, and certainly didn't strike me as at all dodgy, so I felt increasingly confident about obtaining some good information from them. I stopped and turned to Chris. 'Okay, mate. I'll level with you. We're investigating a murder, and we've been told that your partner's younger sister may have some information that may assist us.'

'Shit, ay!' he exclaimed as he ran his hands through his hair and started pacing up and down the driveway. 'She isn't a bad kid,' he said suddenly as he stopped and turned to look at me. 'She's been in a bit of trouble before, so we took her in to try to help her out. You don't reckon she was involved in a murder, do you?'

'No, not directly,' I reassured him, 'but I believe she may know who did it. It involves a couple of young blokes who assaulted a man at St Marys in July as he was walking home.'

'Oh, yeah, I remember seeing that on the news. Look, you'd better tell Sarah. She'll make sure Karina tells you what you need to know.'

'Thanks, mate,' I said as we walked back up the driveway. Before we reached the cars, I said, 'Is Karina home at the moment?'

'Yeah, she should be,' he replied.

'Sarah, I'm going to level with you,' I said when we reached the cars, where Sarah was standing somewhat uncomfortably. 'I know I said we were here investigating a matter involving a car similar to yours, but in actuality, I really need to speak to your sister. I believe she may know the identity of two men we're looking for in relation to the murder of a man at St Marys in July.'

'You're kidding!' she replied as she put her right hand to her mouth. It took her a few moments to gather herself before she asked the question I knew was coming. 'How do you know that Karina knows anything about this?'

'We received information today that Karina's boyfriend knows the two offenders. Is she home at the moment?'

'Yeah, she's inside.'

'Look, I'd rather talk to her down at the station, if that's okay with you. Would it be possible for you to bring her down now?' I wanted to speak to her at the station because it was far more intimidating and daunting. I'd found in the past that interviewing a witness at the station meant that the seriousness of the situation quickly sank in, which made it much easier to obtain the required information. People, especially younger people, tend to shit themselves and tell you everything you need to know when you take them out of their comfort zone. If nothing else, we'd be able to put the fear of God into her, something she would pass on to the offenders, via her boyfriend, and they would know that we were closing in on them.

'Yeah, that's not a problem,' Sarah said. 'If she does know something, she'll be telling you, I can assure you of that.'

'If it's all the same, I'd rather you didn't tell her anything about it at this stage. Leave it to me to speak to her when you bring her in.'

'Okay, we'll come down straightaway. When we arrive, do I just go into the station and ask for you?'

'Yes, there'll be some uniformed officers at the front desk. They'll let me know you've arrived. See you shortly. Hey, thanks for this.'

'That's okay,' Sarah replied as she turned to Chris. 'I'll take her. You stay here. It will be better if I just go with her to sort this out.'

'No worries, babe,' Chris replied. 'Just let me know if you need me.'

Karen and I watched them walk inside before we left, and then headed straight back towards the station. We'd barely made it back onto the Northern Road when Karen said, 'Do you really think she's gonna bring her straight in?'

'I think she will. Like I said, I wanted to gauge what type of people they were before I made my decision. They seemed decent enough, and the sister was genuinely worried about what was going on.'

'Well, I hope we get what we need from this girl,' Karen said with some concern. 'We've come too far not to.'

'So do I, Kaz, but you know, I really do have a good feeling about this. If she does know something, and it seems fairly certain that she does, we may get very busy in the coming days.'

'Bloody hell, Peter!' Karen said. 'Just when I'm taking two weeks off! I don't want to miss out on arresting these guys, but we've already booked and paid for the trip!'

I turned to her and smiled. 'Look, we're not there yet. We'll worry about arrests after we speak to Karina tonight.'

As soon as we got back to the station, I told the uniformed officer at the front desk that I was expecting some people shortly, and then Karen and I headed upstairs to wait. While we did so, I took the opportunity to give Susie a quick call to let her know there was a good chance I was going to be late yet again. She was disappointed, but after I explained what was happening, she changed her tone. She knew how cranky I'd become, and knew equally well that a major breakthrough would go a long way to bringing her 'normal' Pete back. I'd barely put the phone down when it rang again. 'Detective Seymour,' said the uniformed station officer.

'Yeah?'

'The people you were expecting have arrived.'

'Thanks, we'll be down in a sec.'

Karen and I walked down to the foyer and smiled at both girls, paying close attention to the younger one. She was in her late teens, with short brown hair and a slim build. Her eyes were as blue as the sky, and held an innocence that convinced me that she was, as Chris had said, really a good kid.

'This must be Karina,' I said gently. 'Hi, I'm Detective Seymour, and this is Detective Richards. Could you please come upstairs with us?'

I led them up to the detectives' office and sat them down in the interview room. I kept my gaze firmly fixed on Karina as she sat down opposite me, while her older sister sat on a chair just to the right of her. The young girl was very nervous and uncomfortable as she shifted in her seat and directed her stare anywhere but at me. 'I haven't told her anything about why she's here,' Sarah said.

'Thanks,' I replied.

'Karina,' I began, 'I don't want to keep you here for long, but I need you to answer all my questions. Just after 1 am on Saturday 15 July, two men assaulted another man as he was walking home. As a result of that assault, the man died, and I've received information today that you know the names of the two men responsible for this murder. Can you tell me anything about that?'

Karina kept her eyes firmly on the table in front of her, and remained silent.

'Karina, this is a very serious matter,' I continued. 'A man was murdered, and if you know anything about it, particularly the names of the offenders, you need to tell me.'

'I don't know anything about it,' she whispered.

'I'm sorry, what was that?'

'I don't know anything about it,' she repeated, this time in a voice only barely audible.

'Okay, can you at least tell me your boyfriend's name?'

'Yeah, Mark Formoza,' she replied shakily.

Sensing that she was not about to give up what she knew readily, I decided it was time to wind her up and get a rise out of her. I needed her information, and sensing that I had few other options, I started to push. 'Hold on a sec, you just told me that you don't know anything about this. So why did someone give me your name and tell me that you know who these two offenders are because your boyfriend knows them?'

'I don't know!' she shouted as she looked up, suddenly becoming very angry and agitated.

'How about I go a bit further and tell you that I've also been told that your boyfriend works with the offenders. What can you tell me about that?' She folded her arms, pouted and looked away to her left. Experienced as I was in dealing with pouting girls, I decided to try a different line of attack. 'Detective Richards,' I said, 'can you get me a copy of the Crimes Act please?'

'Sure,' Karen replied as she rose and left the room, returning shortly afterwards with a copy of the Crimes Act, which she handed to me. I flicked through until I reached the section that dealt with the offence *Misprision of a Felony*, and then slammed the book down on the table, causing Karina to nearly jump out of her chair.

'Did you know, Karina, that when someone knows about a felony, when a very serious offence has been committed, but refuses to notify the police about it, they can be charged with what's called *Misprision of a Felony*?' I said, my voice becoming louder and louder. 'Karina, this is no minor matter we're talking about here, we're talking about a murder! A man was killed! If you don't tell me what happened, you're looking at a maximum penalty of two years in jail! Is that what you really want?'

'No!' she snapped back.

'Well, then tell me what you know,' I said more softly now, but still firmly enough that she knew the seriousness of the situation.

'I don't know what you're talking about!' she yelled as she dropped her gaze back to the table.

I knew she was lying through her teeth, and I was becoming increasingly frustrated that she was stuffing me around. I picked up the Crimes Act, stood up and walked around the table. When I was standing next to her, I slammed it down a second time, this time with much more force. 'Read that,' I said as I pointed to the relevant section. She read silently, and when she'd finished she sat back in her chair biting her bottom lip. 'Now this offence carries a maximum penalty of two years jail,' I repeated. 'Is that what you want?'

'No,' she replied.

'Well then, tell me what you know!' I said, raising my voice again.

'I told you!' she yelled. 'I don't know anything about this!'

Inside, I respected her loyalty to her boyfriend, or any other people she knew that were involved, but I wasn't about to show her that, so I shook my head and looked at Sarah, who was obviously worried about Karina's continued denials.

It was time for the make or break, so I leant in close and whispered into Karina's ear, 'I didn't have your sister bring you here tonight just for the fun of it. I *am* going to get more information about this, and when I do, I'll have sworn statements proving that you have lied to me tonight. Rest assured, I will come and find you and arrest you! I *am* going to charge you with this offence and put you before the courts, and I guarantee you the courts won't go lightly on someone who has withheld information about a murder. Two years in jail is a *very* long time!' I then walked back around the table and stood near the door, keeping my gaze firmly fixed on Karina. 'Sarah, can I see you outside for a moment please?' I said.

'Yeah, sure,' she said and stood up.

'Stay with her, Detective Richards,' I said to Karen, who nodded as I walked past her, with Sarah right behind me. I closed the door behind us and walked to the far end of the detectives' office. 'Look, she knows who did this,' I said, 'but she's obviously too scared at the moment to say anything. Do you think you can take her home and have a talk with her and see what you can get out of her?'

'Yeah, I'll try to talk some sense into her and get her to tell you what she knows. I think she's just really scared. Can she really be charged with that offence you were talking about?'

'Yes, as a matter of fact, she can. As I said to her in there, it doesn't get any more serious than a murder. We'll go back in and I'll let her go home with you. Here's my card with my number on it if you need to ring me.' We headed back into the interview room and I sat down opposite Karina. 'Okay,' I said, 'I'm going to let you go home for the moment, but you can expect to see me again *real* soon. I will be interviewing more people about this, and it won't be long before I have all the information I need, and when I do, I'll be coming for you. Before I let you leave, I want you to remember one thing, Karina. If you don't tell me what I need to know, you're looking at two years in jail.' With that, I nodded towards the door.

'Come on, let's go,' Sarah said quietly, rising from her seat.

Karina got up and walked quickly out of the room, followed by her sister. Karen and I watched as they approached the stairs. Before they started to descend, Sarah stopped, looked at me, smiled and said, 'Thank you.' I merely nodded.

'Well, that was a bust!' Karen said, disappointed. 'She's obviously lying.'

'Somehow I have a feeling her sister is going to give her a real rev up when they leave here,' I said reassuringly. 'Don't be surprised if we get a call from her shortly.'

'What do we do if she refuses to talk to us?' Karen asked.

'We go and get her boyfriend and bring him in.'

Barely a few minutes had passed when my phone rang. 'Hello, Detective Seymour speaking.'

'Detective Seymour, this is Sarah Reynolds. I'm bringing Karina back in. We'll be there in a minute.'

'No worries.' I put the phone down and grinned at Karen. 'Gees, didn't take as long as I thought. That was Sarah; they're coming back right now.'

'Cool bananas!' Karen beamed.

A short time later, we had Sarah and Karina back in the interview room.

'Karina and I have had a talk, and she wants to tell you what she knows,' Sarah said.

'Okay, let's hear it then,' I said impatiently.

Karina took a deep breath, exhaled, and began. 'So, I was at a party with my boyfriend, and I overheard some people having a conversation about how Aaron and Ricky had bashed an older guy on Mamre Road at St Marys. I heard them talking about how Aaron had been thinking about handing himself in. One of them, I don't remember which one, gave my boyfriend the boots he was wearing that night because they had blood on them.'

'Where are those boots now?' I asked.

'Mark still has them at his house.'

'Can you describe them to me?' I said.

'Yeah, they're creamy-coloured Colorado boots,' she replied. As she outlined the rest of what she knew, she started to cry. Considering how slowly things had been moving, it felt a little strange that everything was now starting to fall into place extremely quickly, especially as Karina's descriptions matched the suspects in the CCTV footage exactly. By the time she'd finished, the tears were flowing freely down her cheeks, and she had her hands clasped tightly together. I hurriedly typed up her statement, and got her to sign it.

'Karina, you've done a very good thing here tonight,' I said, my tone now reassuring. The man who died, Mr Hanes, had a wife and six children, and I am absolutely positive his family will be very appreciative of what you have done. Before I let you go, I must stress just how important it is that you don't speak to your boyfriend, or anyone else, about what you have just told me. Do you understand that?' Karina held her hand up to her mouth and nodded. 'Are you sure you understand? If you say anything about this, it could have serious consequences for our investigation.'

'Yes, I understand.'

'Okay, thank you again, girls. You can go now.'

No sooner had they left the room than Karen said, 'Bloody hell, Pete! What happens now?'

'Based on what we now have, I reckon there's enough to get search warrants for the three addresses, Formoza's and those of the two suspects. We need to get the boots from Formoza's place and interview him before we do the other two. I want him on paper first. Either he becomes a police witness or he gets charged for knowing these guys committed a murder and not doing anything about it.'

'Is that going to happen tomorrow?' Karen asked. 'I'm thinking about cancelling my leave. I really don't want to miss out on this.'

'Kaz, that's entirely up to you. At this stage, I'm just gonna do up the search warrant applications, but there are absolutely no guarantees that the court will approve them. If we don't get approval, then the whole thing will be off for the time being. Besides, even if the warrants do get approved, we don't even know if these idiots are all going to be home when we go there, so like I said, there are no guarantees. I know what you're saying, and believe me, I want you involved in the arrest more than anything because you've been with me on this one from the start, but I don't want you to give up your two-week holiday in the snow with your friends and then not have this come together. At the end of the day, you have to do whatever you think is best.'

Karen's anguish at the difficult decision she had to make was plain to see. She was a young officer who had tremendous potential as a detective, and to be involved in a murder arrest and interview would be an opportunity not many police at her level would ever get.

'In one way, I hope you don't get the warrants tomorrow,' she said.

I did have a real soft spot for Karen, and so I tried to make her decision a little easier. 'At the end of the day, Kaz, you've been able to experience a murder investigation as a main investigator, and so you know what's involved now. Not many people of your length of service can say that, so either way, this will help your career enormously. The only regret, if this does come together while you're away, is that you don't get the opportunity to sit in on an interview with the offenders. However, there's no guarantee they'll say anything anyway, so I reckon you should go and enjoy your holiday. I'll keep in touch with you and let you know what happens.'

'Yeah, I know,' she said, 'but we've done so much work together on this, and I really wanted to be involved in the arrests and the interviews. I suppose the main thing is that we get these bastards.'

'That's a good way of looking at it. You might as well head off home. I can finish things here.' Karen nodded, collected her gear and headed home. Before I left, I checked the next day's roster to see who was on. Luckily, there were loads of people available. *That's good*, I thought, *I'm gonna need everyone if this comes off.* I looked up at the wall clock; it was 10.30 pm.

By the time I got home, all the girls were asleep. I climbed the stairs as quietly as I could, made my way into their bedrooms, kissed each of them on the forehead and then went to my bedroom. I tried to be as quiet as I could, but Susie stirred and half-opened one eye. 'How did you get on today?' she asked sleepily.

'Really, really good, sweetheart,' I replied. 'I've got names for the blokes I'm after, and tomorrow I'll be holding a briefing at work and we'll try to get search warrants so we can arrest them and lock them up.' I got undressed and climbed into bed. My head had barely hit the pillow when I sat bolt upright. 'Bloody hell! Tomorrow is 1 September!'

'Yeah, the first day of spring. That's good, I hate winter,' Susie replied in a tired voice.

'No, you don't understand,' I chuckled. 'Mick Lyons and I joked about having the offenders in the dock by the beginning of spring and it looks like that may just happen. Can you believe that?'

'That's good, honey, but I don't think it would matter to you when you got these guys, as long as you got them.'

'Yeah, you're right there,' I said as I leant over and gave her a kiss.

For the first time in a long time, I had a deep and comfortable night's sleep, no nightmares, no reliving the dark times in my career, only dreams of the good old days when I was young enough and fit enough to play for the police rugby league team. The next morning, a good breakfast and some time spent sitting down with my girls meant that I went off to work with a real spring in my step. I felt energised, full of enthusiasm and expectation as I bounced into work at around 7.30 am.

'Hey, Pete, you know what today is?' Mick said as soon as I walked into the detectives' office.

'Shit, Mick, doesn't take you long, does it?'

'No, mate, it doesn't. So, do you know what day it is?'

'Yes, Mick, it's the first day of spring!'

'And yet you haven't got them in the docks. So how close are you?'

I told him everything that had happened the previous night.

'Fuck ol' Daisy!' Mick said when I'd finished. 'Looks like you might just have them in the dock by this afternoon!'

'Piece of cake, mate. Piece of cake.' We both had a good laugh, and headed downstairs to make a cuppa.

'You gonna do a briefing with everyone this morning?' Mick asked as he stirred some sugar into his coffee. 'If so, you'd better let Glash know, because I'm pretty sure he'll want to be in on it.'

'Yeah, I'll go and see him when I finish my coffee.' We grabbed our coffees and moved out onto the veranda.

'All jokes aside,' Mick said, 'I'm really amazed at how quickly you've managed to get this one together.'

'Yeah, it was great to be able to get the junior staff involved as well,' I said.

After we'd finished our coffees, we headed back inside, whereupon I made my way to Glash's office and filled him in on everything. 'That's fantastic news, Pete!' Glash exclaimed. 'So, you'll brief everyone when they come in and then go to Penrith Court with the warrant applications?'

'Yeah, that's the plan, boss,' I replied. 'I'll go and start typing up the search warrant applications now so we can get moving on this asap.' I left Glash's office, went back to my desk and started typing out the search warrant applications. While I was madly hammering away, all the other officers began to arrive. Mick was quick to tell them all to hang around, as there was going to be a briefing about the murder investigation.

At around 9.30 am, everyone gathered in the office, eagerly anticipating what I had to say. Glash and I stood at the front of the briefing room as I filled everyone in on the events of the previous night. Everyone was given sheets with the names of the two suspects, along with their background checks and addresses. I also gave them the information pertaining to Formoza, who was my first target for the day, pending me being able to obtain approval for the warrants. I finished by telling everyone that we would be having another briefing at midday, after I'd been to the court, so that I could arrange the operational plan for the execution of the warrants.

Having come this far, I certainly didn't want any stuff-ups, so I took Mick and Glash aside and asked their opinions on how best to execute the warrants. 'I reckon we should split into teams,' Glash said. 'Yeah,' Mick agreed. 'You, me, Dukesy and Sergeant Thornton will execute the first warrant. Depending on how that one turns out, we'll see how we go with the next two.'

'Sweet,' I said, and then went back to my desk to telephone the Penrith Court office and make an appointment to meet with the Chamber Magistrate.

As I drove to Penrith, the butterflies in my stomach started fluttering madly. I was pretty sure I had enough evidence to support the applications, but I still wasn't one hundred per cent positive it was enough to convince the Chamber Magistrate. When I arrived, I entered the Court office and one of the girls at the counter called me over and ushered me in. I handed my applications to the Magistrate and gave him a brief overview of their contents. He carefully read every piece of documentation before straightening them up and tapping them on his desk. 'I'm happy with all that,' he said as he looked up at me. 'I'll sign off on these and you can be on your way.'

The butterflies went ballistic, and as I watched the Chamber Magistrate sign all the warrants, I couldn't help but think about what this would mean to the Hanes family, and the chain of events that was about to follow.

Chapter 11:
Tough Choices

I went back to St Marys and made my way upstairs to the detectives'
office. As I walked through the office, I passed dozens of expectant
faces, all waiting for some sort of reaction, or for me to say something.
I tried my best to keep a straight face, and managed to get as far as my
desk, but when I put the warrants down and turned to face everyone,
I couldn't hide my elation. 'Okay, everyone, the warrants have been
granted, so we're ready to go,' I said. 'Mick, Dukesy and I will go
with Geoff Thornton to execute the first warrant, and hopefully we'll
get Formoza to give us a statement. Sorry, I know the rest of you all
want to get stuck into this, but you'll just have to wait until we see
how we go. Once we execute the first warrant, we'll come back here
for another briefing, and hopefully we'll split up into two teams to
execute the warrants on the suspects' premises.' Mick, Mark Dukes,
Geoff Thornton and I then went into the interview room.

'Okay, the warrant authorises us to enter the premises to search for the Colorado boots because, primarily, that's what we're after.' I checked my watch: it was 1.15 pm. We went downstairs to the garage, where Mick and I jumped into an unmarked car while the other two got into a marked car.

A short time later, we arrived at the Formoza residence. It was a small brown-brick home with a tidy yard and a three-foot-high metal fence surrounding it. I approached the front door with Mick and Geoff, while Dukesy stayed standing on the cement driveway to the right side of the house. I knocked on the door, and an elderly man soon answered, the look on his face indicating the same confusion as had that of Mrs McDonald. 'Good afternoon, sir. My name is Detective Peter Seymour. Are you Mr Formoza?' I said as I held up my badge.

'Yes,' he said cautiously as he looked past me at the other officers. 'What's this all about?'

'Sir, we have a warrant here authorising us to search this house for items of clothing, in particular a pair of Colorado work boots that we believe were worn by an offender at the time of a murder that was committed on 15 July this year.'

Mr Formoza opened the door, whereupon Geoff handed him the Occupier's Notice and explained the details: the date that the warrant was issued and was to be executed, the address, my name, the station we were from and the exact items we were looking for.

While Geoff was doing this, a car pulled up in the driveway and a young man who looked to be about twenty got out and started walking towards us. 'Are you Mark Formoza?' I asked as I held up my badge.

'Yeah,' he said as his head dropped.

'I have a warrant in my possession allowing us to search these premises for some property, that being a pair of Colorado boots. The Occupier's Notice has just been given to your father outlining the nature of this warrant. Do you understand that?'

'Yeah, I understand.'

His father handed him the Occupier's Notice, and then turned and walked inside the house without saying anything further. Mark Formoza followed him inside, with the four of us right behind him. The Formozas sat down in the lounge room, while we remained standing. Geoff started by outlining his role. 'I am what is called the Independent Officer. I am not involved in the investigation. Any questions you have about what my colleagues are doing should be directed to me.'

Once the formalities had been dispensed with, I turned to the younger Formoza and said, 'We've received information that you may know something about the persons responsible for the death of a man at St Marys on the morning of 15 July 2000.'

'Yeah, my girlfriend rang me this morning and told me what happened. I've been expecting you.'

I was angry that Karina had gone against my specific instructions not to say anything to anyone, but at the same time, I wasn't at all surprised. 'Have you spoken to Aaron and Ricky about this?' I said. This concerned me more than anything else, because if he had, it would make our job of locating them that much more difficult.

'No, I haven't spoken to them,' he replied.

I felt a huge surge of relief. 'Where are the Colorado boots your mates gave to you?' I said. 'You may as well tell us. It will save us the trouble of having to go through your whole house.'

'They're in the laundry,' he said without hesitation. 'I'll show you.' We followed him to the laundry, where he retrieved the boots from a cupboard and gave them to me. Dukesy recorded everything on a video tape, as stipulated by the conditions of the search warrant, and we made our way back into the lounge room, where the two Formozas sat down again.

'Mate,' I said to Mark, 'I know that you have information about this matter. The problem you have is that you are in possession of evidence. Now, you can do one of two things. You can come to the station with me now and make a statement about what you know, or I will arrest you for either being an accessory to murder or withholding evidence in relation to the murder. Your choice, champ. You can either be a witness or a defendant.'

Formoza had his hands clasped in front of him, and was fidgeting in exactly the same manner as his girlfriend had when I'd interviewed her. 'I guess I don't have a choice, do I?' he sighed as his eyes found mine.

'Yes, you do,' I replied. 'I know you want to look out for your mates, and I can respect that, but what happens to you depends on the choice you now make. It's as simple as that.'

'Okay, I'll come with you and make a statement, but what happens then?' he asked. 'I'll explain it all to you when we get down to the station. You've made the right choice, Mark. It's far better for you to be a witness for the police than to be charged by us.'

We escorted Formoza to the unmarked car and drove back to the station, where I took him straight to the interview room while Mick entered the boots into the exhibit book.

After sitting him down, I took a seat opposite him and began. 'Right, Mark, I need to get a statement from you, a copy of which I will give you when we're done. Now what I am about to tell you is absolutely imperative. You cannot, under any circumstances, have any contact with Aaron and Ricky. If you do, you could be charged with hindering a police investigation.' I could see from his body language that he really didn't want to betray his mates, but he knew he had no choice if he wanted to keep himself out of trouble, so he nodded in reply. 'Right, Mark. Can you start by telling me where you work?'

'I work at a chicken factory.'

'And Aaron and Ricky both work there with you?'

'Yes.'

'You know them pretty well then?'

'Yeah, they're some of me best mates.'

'And can you tell me how you came to find out about the assault?'

'Well, one day Aaz came to me, not long after you showed the footage on the TV, and he says, "Mark, you know that bloke that they showed that got killed on the telly?" I said, "Yeah, I saw it." He said, "I think me and Ricky might have done it." I said, "What do you mean you 'think' you might have done it?" He said, "We were the ones who bashed him. We didn't think we'd done him in though. Mark, I need you to do me a favour." I said, "Yeah, what's that then?" He said, "I need you to take me work boots and shirt and hide 'em for me.'"

'So you obviously did this?'

'I had no choice. He's me mate.'

'Where's the shirt then?'

'I lost it.'

'Mark, you know it's a crime to lie to a police officer.'

'Yeah, I know, but I swear I lost it.'

'What about Ricky? Did he talk to you about the assault?'

'Nup.'

I knew he was just giving me the bare minimum, especially where it concerned Mahia. Nevertheless, it was enough that he'd confirmed what I needed; there had been an assault, and Cooper had admitted his involvement to Formoza. I typed up his statement, which he then signed. 'What happens next?' he asked.

'You're free to leave the station, but you must not, under any circumstances, contact either Aaron or Ricky about anything you have just told me. If this ends up in court, and I am fairly certain it will, you will be required to give evidence.'

With everything happening so quickly, I don't think he'd really considered the fact that he would have to take the witness stand and give evidence against his mates, and now that it dawned on him, he began to shake. Mick and I drove him home, and to say that he was happy to get out of the car and get back inside his house would be an understatement.

Mick and I then returned to the station and put together our second team. Detectives Dukes, Everitt, Ozen and Ralph were asked to meet over at Mt Druitt for a quick briefing in relation to executing the next search warrant at the house of our main suspect, Aaron Cooper.

In all the planning, neither Mick nor I had had time to contemplate the fact that we were returning to our old stomping ground, but as soon as we walked upstairs into the detectives' office, the flashbacks came thick and fast. I thought back to the Keir investigation, all the hours I'd spent hoping and praying for the right result, and experienced a sense of *deja vu* like I'd never had before.

We did the briefing, just like old times, and then the team headed to Aaron Cooper's house. We pulled up outside a light-coloured fibro Housing Commission cottage. Mick and I walked up to the front door, accompanied by Inspector Moore from Mt Druitt, while the other detectives waited at various points around the perimeter of the house. I checked my watch: it was 4 pm. Mick and I walked up a couple of steps onto a landing leading to the front door. I knocked, and a plump woman in her mid-forties soon answered. 'Yes?' she said, her face displaying the same perplexed look as the others.

'My name is Detective Peter Seymour,' I said, as I showed her my badge. 'Are you Mrs Cooper?'

'Yes,' she replied.

'I have a warrant here to search your house for items of clothing belonging to your son.'

'What's this all about?' she asked, worry in her voice.

'Mrs Cooper, is Aaron home at the moment?'

'Yes, he is.'

'This is the Occupier's Notice,' I said as I handed it to her. 'I suggest you read that document, as it sets out everything about the warrant.'

Mick, Inspector Moore, the other detectives and I then entered the premises, with Dukesy following close behind us filming everything we did.

Aaron Cooper, who was dressed in fawn-coloured trousers and a dark-coloured shirt, was standing in the centre of the lounge room waiting for us. I immediately recognised him as the guy in the service station footage. 'Aaron Cooper?' I said as I walked into the room and stood directly in front of him.

'Yes.'

'My name is Detective Seymour, and these other detectives are from St Marys and Mt Druitt. We are here in relation to the death of a man by the name of Nick Hanes at the corner of Mamre Road and Edgar Street in St Marys on 15 July this year. You are under arrest in relation to this matter. You are not obliged to say anything unless you wish to do so, as anything you say will be recorded and may be used in evidence. Do you understand that?'

'Yeah, I understand.'

'Can you please show me where your bedroom is?'

He didn't say anything, but simply turned and walked to the back of the house. I stood beside him at his bedroom door while the other guys carried out a search for any clothing resembling the clothes he'd worn on the night of the incident. While they searched, I studied Cooper's body language intently, and was immediately struck by the fact that he didn't appear remotely anxious or nervous. It was almost as if he'd already resigned himself to his fate. He knew his time was up, and his shoulders slouched as he watched the detectives searching his room. His mother stood nearby, silently watching on. Her face, however, bore a look of sheer disbelief, every wrinkle conveying her fear and uncertainty.

'Ma'am,' I said as I leant in close to her, 'don't worry. We're not going to pull the place apart. We're only searching for specific items; the ones mentioned in the Occupier's Notice that I just gave you. We won't be here for long. Once we find what we need, we're going to have to take your son back to Mt Druitt police station for questioning.'

'How is it that my son came to be involved in all of this?' she said.

'Ma'am, we are acting on information we have received. Witnesses have identified your son as one of two men responsible for the assault that led to the death of the man at St Marys back in July.'

She put her hand to her mouth and scrunched up her eyes, willing herself not to cry. I felt sympathy for her, and could only imagine the sheer heartache she was going through as a mother, but I had to remind myself that her son's actions were responsible for the Hanes family's suffering.

'Aaron,' I said, 'I need you to take off the trousers you're wearing and hand them to the officers doing the search.' He went into his bedroom, manoeuvred around the searching officers and retrieved a pair of track pants. I followed him to the bathroom, where he changed and then handed me the light-coloured trousers, which I then handed to Detective Everitt, who placed them in a brown paper exhibit bag, wrote on the tag and sealed it.

'Hey, Pete,' one of the detectives called as he held up a white Billabong jumper with navy stripes across the shoulders and a navy blue Nike jacket, both of which looked identical to the ones in the CCTV footage. They too were bagged and sealed.

'Aaron,' I said as the search of his room came to an end, 'as I have already stated, you are under arrest in relation to the death of Mr Hanes. You will be taken back to Mt Druitt police station, where I intend to ask you further questions about this matter. You are not obliged to say anything unless you wish to do so, but whatever you say will be recorded and may be used in evidence. Do you understand that?'

With his head lowered, and in a quiet voice, he said, 'Yeah.'

The other detectives briefly searched the backyard under the watchful supervision of Mrs Cooper, but they didn't find anything of note, and when they came back inside, I told Cooper to put his hands behind his back. He complied, and I cuffed him.

'Is that really necessary? He isn't going anywhere!' his mother protested.

'Too right he isn't going anywhere,' I replied loudly. 'He's under arrest for murder. This isn't some minor offence like stealing. He's now in my custody, and will stay handcuffed until we get him back to Mt Druitt police station.'

I felt bad that I'd raised my voice. It hadn't been my intention to upset her, but rather to get Cooper to really start shitting himself so that when I got him back to the station for the interview he would be very cooperative. We concluded the search warrant at precisely 4.24 pm, and I led Cooper outside and across the road to a waiting car. I opened the rear passenger door and assisted him inside before flicking the door lock. After he was squared away, I looked back to his mother, who had her hand to her mouth again and was sobbing. I really did feel sorry for her. She was an innocent, loving parent, and it must have been tough for her to watch her son being taken away by the police.

I shook my head. Here was another family suffering from a senseless crime, and when I joined Cooper in the rear of the car, I looked at him and wondered what the hell has been going through his head when he'd decided to do this terrible thing.

Throughout the drive back to the station, you could have heard a pin drop. It was a deliberate silence, a deathly silence, and I hoped it would have a profound effect on Cooper's emotions as he contemplated his fate.

Chapter 12:
Passing the Exam

On our arrival at the station, Cooper was booked straight into custody. While the Custody Sergeant was processing him, I said to Mick, 'Mate, Fran Ralph has been part of the team and has been sitting here at Mt Druitt waiting for us to come back, what do you reckon I use her with me on this. She would really benefit from the experience, and I know she would jump at the chance to sit in on the interview.'

'Good idea,' Mick replied.

Fran was another plain-clothes constable in the St Marys detectives, and was also a good friend of Karen's. I felt bad that Karen had missed out on such an important day, especially as she had put in so much work, and it only felt right that even though Karen was going to miss out, another junior officer should benefit.

Mick and I made our way up to the detectives' office and began to get the audio and video tapes ready for the Record of Interview. 'Fran,' I said when I saw her, 'can I have a quiet word?'

'Sure, Pete, what's up?'

I took her to one side. 'How would you like to sit in on the interview with Cooper?'

Her eyes lit up and a huge smile came over her face. 'Would I ever!' she said enthusiastically.

'Okay, he's just being processed at the moment, so it shouldn't be too long. Now when we do this, I don't want you to just sit in the room and merely listen to what's going on. I need you to make notes of anything you think needs clarification, or anything you think of during the interview. I don't profess to know everything, or to be able to think of everything I need to ask him. When I'm finished, I'll ask you if there's anything you want to ask him. That's the time for you to ask him whatever you want. You'll be just as big a part of this as me, okay?'

'Yeah, no worries Pete,' she said excitedly, 'but I feel bad that Karen's missing out. She'll be spewing!'

'Yeah, I know,' I replied, 'but there's not much we can do about that now.'

I had a quick chat with Mick and the others, and we decided that if anything of interest regarding Mahia came up, I would suspend the interview and let the others know. If and when we had everything we needed, Dukesy would lead the team in executing the search warrant at Mahia's address and effecting the arrest.

Word came through that Cooper was good to go, so Fran and I went down to the custody room and led him upstairs to the interview room. I filled out all the details on the three audio tapes and the video tape, and then placed them all in the Electronically Recorded Interview with a Suspected Person (ERISP) machine. Cooper was seated in front of the machine at one end of the table, while Fran and I sat opposite him.

'Aaron, I intend to ask you some further questions in relation to the death of Nick Hanes at St Marys on 15 July this year,' I began. 'My questions, and any answers you give to those questions, will be recorded on audio and video tape as the interview takes place. Do you understand that?'

'Yes,' he said quietly.

'You are not obliged to say anything unless you wish to do so, as anything you say will be electronically recorded and may later be used in evidence. Do you understand that?'

'Yes.'

'At the conclusion of the interview, you will be given a complete copy of the master audio tape. Do you understand that?'

'Yes.'

'At a later date, arrangements can be made for you or your legal representative to view the video tape, if required. Do you understand that?'

'Yes.'

At this point, he looked up at Fran, and then at me. His forlorn expression gave me the impression that he wanted to talk, so I began the interview. 'Aaron, I want you to start by telling me your exact movements on the night of 14 July 2000.'

'I started out drinking at home with a few of me mates, and then we decided to go to the disco at the RSL. I got into an argument with a girl, so we left.'

He seemed very willing to comply, so I decided to come straight out and ask him if Mahia was his accomplice. 'When you say "we", do you mean you were with Ricky Mahia?'

'Yes,' he said, and nodded.

'After the disco and the argument with the girl, what did you both do?'

'We walked down to the servo, then we went to visit a mate, and then we were gonna go to the Band Club.'

'And this is when you came into contact with Mr Hanes?'

'Yeah.'

Here was the part I was desperate to find the answer to: why on earth had it gotten to the point where a man had died? 'Why did you assault Mr Hanes?'

'We'd had a few to drink, and I was still pretty angry about the argument with the girl. I thought he mouthed off at me, so I hit him.'

'You thought he mouthed off? What exactly did you think he said to you?'

'I don't remember exactly.'

'Did your friend Ricky also hit Mr Hanes?'

He nodded. 'Yeah, we punched and kicked him, then left him on the ground and walked off.'

'You just walked off?'

'Yep.'

'You didn't demand Mr Hanes's wallet before you assaulted him?'

'Nope, like I said, I thought he mouthed off at me.'

'Alright, at this point, I am going to suspend the interview. It's 5.28 pm,' I said as I checked the clock on the wall and then paused the tape. 'Aaron, I am going to take you out into the detectives' office, and I am going to show you some photos, okay?'

He nodded, pushed himself up out of his chair and followed Fran and me out to the detective's office, where I sat him down at a desk and showed him the photos from the CCTV footage. 'Is that you and Ricky leaving the service station?' I asked as I pointed to the stills.

'Yeah, that's us.'

'I need you to sign the back of the photos and write the date under your signature.' He did as asked, and then I took him over to a nearby television set and played the actual CCTV footage. 'Is that you and Ricky in the footage?'

'Yeah, that's us.'

Fran and I took him back to the interview room, sat him down and restarted the tape.

'Interview recommenced at 5.35 pm,' I said. 'Aaron, do you admit that you identified yourself and Ricky Mahia in the CCTV footage and the photographs that I just showed you?'

'Yes.'

I asked him a few more questions, and then had to stop the interview to load new tapes. When I was done, Fran asked a few questions on things she wanted clarified, and when she was done I left her with Cooper while I ducked out to get Station Sergeant Roser to come to the interview room and ask the mandatory adoption questions, that is, basically to question

Cooper as to the manner of our interview and to ask him if he had any complaints about the way the interview had been conducted. Fran and I had to vacate the room while Sergeant Roser asked his questions, so while we waited, I went and spoke to Mick and Dukesy, and told them everything I'd gotten out of Cooper. 'That'll do us,' Dukesy said as he and Mick grabbed their gear and left to execute the next warrant.

Shortly after they'd departed, Sergeant Roser emerged from the interview room. 'All good, Pete,' he said. Fran and I went back into the interview room, retrieved the tapes and sealed them in front of Cooper. We gave him a copy of the two tapes, and he signed the receipt. 'Aaron Cooper,' I said as I looked him squarely in the eye, 'you will be charged with the murder, and with the assault with intent to rob, of Mr Hanes. Do you understand that?'

He looked despondently down into his lap and said, 'Yeah.'

Fran and I led him downstairs to be formally charged, and then headed back up to the detectives' office to await the outcome of the second search warrant. 'Well,' I said to Fran, 'we could be waiting for a while. Feel like a cuppa?'

'Yeah, why not.'

We headed off to the meals room, found a couple of washed cups in the cupboard and helped ourselves to a coffee. 'I'm sure they won't mind us using their facilities,' I joked. 'One of these cups in here is probably mine or Mick's anyway!'

'I'm sure they won't, Pete,' Fran laughed.

I stirred some sugar into my coffee and *bang*, everything finally hit me; the finish line was actually in sight.

'That was a great experience, Pete,' Fran said as she sipped away at her coffee. 'Thanks heaps for letting me sit in on the interview. I really learned a lot.'

'You're welcome, Fran,' I smiled. 'You did a good job in there. The questions you asked were very relevant.'

Fran I and finished our coffees and the boys still weren't back, so I thought it would be a good opportunity to give Susie a quick call and let her know what was going on. 'Hey, sweetheart, how are things at home?' I asked when she answered.

'Good,' she said guardedly. 'You're having another late one, aren't you?'

'Yes, darling, I'm afraid I am. We had a great day today, though. I've got one offender in the dock being charged, and hopefully the boys will be on their way back with the second offender soon.'

'Congratulations! That's great news!' Susie said with genuine excitement. 'Any idea when you might be home?'

'I'm not sure. Once the second bloke is in the dock, I want to contact Bel Hanes and give her the good news.'

'I'm sure she'll be grateful,' Susie said.

'Yes, I'm sure she will. Give the kids a kiss and hug for me, and I'll see you later on tonight.'

'Okay, darl, I'll see you when you get home.'

I hung up the phone and suddenly felt as though a huge weight had been lifted off my shoulders, the same feeling you got when you walked out of the room at the end of an exam, but I had to remind myself that it wasn't over yet. Even though the offenders had finally been caught, there was still a lot of work to do. About half an hour later, the phone in the detectives' office rang. 'Pete?'

'Hey, Dukesy, how'd you go?'

'Yeah, good, mate. We executed the warrant and we arrested Mahia. We're on our way back to the station now.'

A wave of relief washed over me, especially when the boys arrived a short time later with their man safely in custody. While Mahia was being processed, Mick came upstairs and filled me in on the arrest. The whole thing had gone down almost identically to the way it had at Cooper's place.

Mahia was eventually brought upstairs, and as he came down the corridor, I stood outside the interview room with my arms folded, my gaze firmly fixed on him as he was ushered inside.

The arresting officers conducted the Record of Interview while I waited outside, pacing up and down the office and hoping like hell that Mahia was doing the same as Cooper, and making a full admission of guilt, but eventually Dukesy emerged and said, 'Well, he's not saying much. I put it to him that Cooper had implicated him, but he's still denying everything.'

'That's not necessarily a bad thing,' I replied. 'If we can prove he's lying about what happened that night, that's gonna go in our favour, because we can show that he can't be believed. He can protest his innocence all he wants, but he's shooting himself in the foot, because we'll prove that he's a liar.'

'Yeah, s'pose you're right,' Dukesy said.

Sergeant Roser did the adoption questions, and with Mahia having voiced no objections, he was led downstairs to be formally taken into custody. I advised the bail officer that I strongly objected to bail being granted for both men as, in my opinion, they were both a fair chance to do a runner, and based on the seriousness of the offence, they should be remanded to appear in court the next day, where they could then make another bail application.

After the custody process was completed, Dukesy and Mick took Mahia into the charge room to formally charge him. It was around 9 pm when I headed off to make the phone call that every police officer loves to make, the one that makes all the hard work, all the sacrifices, all the time away from your family completely and utterly worth it. I picked up the phone, and a huge smile spread across my face as I dialled. It rang four or five times before Bel Hanes answered. 'Hello.'

'Hello, Bel, it's Peter Seymour here. How are things?'

'Oh, not too bad,' she replied.

'Have you had a good day today?'

'Yes, as a matter of fact, I have,' she said. 'I went out with the kids and bought myself a new car.'

'Oh, yeah, what did you buy?'

'A little Mitsubishi Colt. It's lovely,' she replied.

'Wow, sounds like you *have* had a nice day. How about I make it just that little bit better for you?' I said elatedly.

There was a long pause, and it almost seemed like I could hear her tears welling up.

'What…what are you saying?' she finally asked.

'We already have one offender in the cells charged with murdering Nick, and the second one is being charged as we speak. I'm sorry I couldn't let you know what was going on earlier, but it's been one hell of a day!'

Bel began to sob uncontrollably. It was an indescribably immense feeling of satisfaction to be able to give the family the news they had so desperately longed to hear, and I felt very honoured to have had the opportunity to experience that feeling for a second time. 'Is it too late for me to come over and have a coffee with you?' I said. 'I can fill you in on everything.'

'No…no…please come over. I'll…I'll put the kettle on. I'd love to see you,' she stammered through her tears.

'Righto, I'll see you soon.' After I'd hung up, I turned to Fran and said, 'This is what makes this job so worthwhile.'

'Not that I want anyone to die, but I hope I'm lucky enough to experience what you're feeling right now,' she said as we made our way back downstairs to see how things were going with the processing of Mahia. With everything under control there, I headed back upstairs and sat down with Dukesy to square everything away on the computer system so that police headquarters, the Media Unit and the commanders had all been notified of the arrests and charges. However, there was one thing that couldn't be handled through the computer system, and that was notifying Glash. I rang him at home. 'Hello.'

'G'day, Glash, it's Pete here.'

'Hey, Pete, what's up?'

'Sorry to call you so late, boss, but I have some news I think you might want to hear.'

'Yeah, what's that?' he said, the excitement in his voice suggesting he already suspected what I was about to tell him.

'We got 'em!'

'Great work, Peter! Bloody fantastic news!' he said. 'See, good old-fashioned police work and a good team working on the case always leads to a good result. Congratulate everyone there for me. Now take a well-earned couple of days off, and I'll see you next week.'

'I'll have to come in tomorrow, boss, as I want to make sure everything is right at the bail hearing, and I wouldn't mind spending a day in the office just so I can get everything together, but then I'll gladly take a couple of days off.'

'Alright, mate, but I know what you're like, Seymour. Once again, I'm ordering you to spend some time with your family,' he said forcefully.

'Will do, boss, will do,' I said, and then hung up.

Satisfied that everything was in order and there was nothing left for us to do at Mt Druitt, Fran and I left and drove to Bel's house. I'm sure I was speeding, because I couldn't wait to knock on the door and see the look on her face. When Bel opened the door, I could see the tears flowing down her cheeks. She stepped outside and hugged me tightly. 'Thank you so much, Peter,' she whispered in my ear.

'You're most welcome,' I replied. 'Now have you got that kettle boiled?'

'Yes, come in.'

'This is Detective Ralph,' I said, introducing Fran. Bel shook hands with Fran, and we walked inside, where we found a lady whose face I thought I recognised.

'Peter, you remember my daughter-in-law, Sharon?' said Bel. 'I had to ring her when I got off the phone from you, and she came straight over.'

'Yeah, I remember. Hi, Sharon, how are you?'

'I'm really good, thanks, especially after getting the terrific news!' she beamed.

Bel hurriedly made the cuppas, and we all sat in the lounge room while I proceeded to describe the day's events and exactly how they'd unfolded. Bel leant forward in her chair, hands wrapped tightly around her cup, hanging on my every word. I looked at her, and could see that behind her glasses, her eyes were very red. *As a policeman it simply doesn't get any better than this*, I thought to myself.

'So, what happens next?' Bel asked me when I'd finished.

I then proceeded to explain the process to her. Hopefully, the offenders would initially be refused bail, and would then appear in court in the coming days, when they could apply for bail again. I explained to her that it would be up to the court to determine whether bail was granted or whether they should remain in custody. I would then have to put a brief of evidence together with all the statements, and that would eventually be served on the defendants or their solicitors, and then they'd be asked whether they pleaded guilty or not guilty to the charges. If they pleaded guilty, they'd be remanded in custody for sentencing in the Supreme Court, but if they pleaded not guilty, then we'd have to go through the trial process.

'There's still work for us to do, and some other things we need to follow up on,' I explained. 'Just because we've charged these two guys doesn't mean we've finished. The main offender has made a full admission, and has implicated the co-offender, but the co-offender refused to admit to much at all.'

Fran and I stayed with Bel and Sharon for another hour or so before heading off back to the station so we could square things away before heading off home. It had been an exhausting yet extremely fulfilling day, but I had to temper my feelings. The job was far from done, and I needed to keep my emotions in check. There was, however, one thing still bothering me: the two witnesses hadn't actually seen Mahia assault Nick Hanes. Yes, we could place him at the scene. Yes, Cooper had told us that both he *and* Mahia had kicked and punched Nick while he was on the ground, but I strongly doubted that Mahia would admit that in court. Anyway, enough was enough for one day.

I was engulfed by a feeling of completeness as I drove home. It felt wonderful that I had got the right result for the victim and his family, as though the universe had somehow come together to right a terrible wrong. I pulled into my driveway and opened the garage roller door. The only light that was on was a small one in the garage, and after I'd turned it off, I stumbled around a bit in the darkness as I tried to creep through the house without waking anyone. I managed to get as far as my bedroom, but while I was undressing, I woke Susie. 'Congratulations, honey,' she murmured as she rolled over in bed. 'You must be very proud to have solved this murder.'

'Yeah, to be honest, there were times when I didn't think it was going to happen,' I whispered. 'Are the kids okay?'

'They're fine. Does this mean you're going to have some days off?'

'I have to go in tomorrow to finish off all the paperwork. These two will front the bail court tomorrow, but we're opposing bail, and hopefully it won't be granted, but I guarantee they'll make another application, so I need to make sure that everything goes okay, but I'll definitely be off on Sunday.'

'I suppose that's better than nothing,' she replied as I slid into bed beside her, put my arm around her and softly kissed her neck, cheeks and ears.

Chapter 13:
Just Like Old Times

The next day, thankfully, both offenders were refused bail at their hearing at Parramatta Local Court, and were remanded in custody. All that remained for me to do was to put a brief folder together with everything I'd gathered from the investigation.

One makes full admissions and the other denies the whole bloody thing, I thought to myself as I compiled the folder. *Well, there's not really much more I can do at this stage. I'll just have to let things run their course.*

I looked at the roster and marked myself off for the next two days so I could spend a full day with my family and then have a day at home by myself just chilling out. I actually arrived home early for a change, which meant that I was able to enjoy a great lamb roast dinner with Susie and the girls. While we were having dinner, the news came on TV, and there was a brief story about the arrest of Cooper and Mahia and the refusal of bail. I watched from the dining table, and when the report had finished I looked up to Susie and smiled. 'So, you've made the news again!' she said.

'Yeah, at least it's for the right reasons!'

The next day was Sunday, and we drove up to the Central Coast to spend the day with Sue's mum and dad. We took the kids for a picnic lunch and enjoyed a walk along the beach. We had a lovely dinner, and then headed off back home at about 8 pm. It made me feel like I was whole again, like the Pete I wanted to be.

On Monday morning, I drove the girls to school and then picked them up that afternoon. Sue had gone off to work, so in between, I had the house to myself. I managed to get a quick nine holes of golf in, and then spent the rest of the day relaxing beside the pool, so that I could totally immerse myself in my own world and clear my mind of anything work related. I waited for the flashbacks to come, but for a change, my mind remained totally blank. I was completely spent; my mind and I had nothing left to give. I was so tired that I think even my negative feelings felt like they needed a break. The only real job I had to do that day was to prepare dinner, and seeing as I couldn't cook to save my life, it was a barbie all the way.

When I went back to work the next morning, the first thing I did was ring the Westmead Coroner's Court to speak to my old boss, Sergeant Dave Parcell. 'Hey, Dave, how are you, mate?' I said when he answered.

'I'm good, Pete. Hey, congratulations on locking those two blokes up. I suppose you want all the Coroner's paperwork for your brief?' he said, as if reading my mind.

'Yeah, Dave, that's exactly why I'm ringing. I can come down this morning if that's okay.'

'Sure, mate. Come down and have a cuppa with us. I'm sure everyone here would love to see you. It'll be just like old times.'

'Righto, mate, I'll leave shortly.'

When I arrived at Westmead, it felt very odd to be back, and I momentarily wondered whether, considering the investigation that I was running and the toll it had taken on me, I should have left at all. As I entered the back door to the office, I could hear Dolly's familiar voice on the phone. Just as I walked past him, he put the phone down, and as soon as he looked up and saw me, he called out, 'Hey, look what the bloody cat dragged in! Can't keep away from the place, can you?'

'G'day, Dolly, did you miss me?'

'Nah, not really. Actually, it's been a lot quieter around here without you joking around.'

'C'mon, you missed me, admit it!'

'Okay, I'll admit it, Pete, I missed you! You here to see Parcell?'

'Yeah, I need to pick up the P79A, the post-mortem reports and all the other stuff for the brief folder. Is he in his office?'

'No, mate. He's not.'

'Shit,' I said despondently. 'I really need to speak to him.'

'Calm down, Pete, it's alright!' Dolly laughed. 'He's standing right behind you!'

I turned around and, sure enough, there he was. 'Hello, Pete, good to see you, mate!' he said as he shook my hand warmly. 'I'm glad you got those two bastards.'

'Yeah, mate, it was a top result. Now we've just got to get them through the courts, into a trial, and then hopefully we put them away.'

'Pete, I've got everything you need in my office,' Dave said, 'but first I reckon it's time to say g'day to everyone and have a cuppa.'

We walked into the court office and all the staff came up to say hello, which was a nice touch. It was good to know that even though I'd left, people still made the effort to come and see me, and I revelled in catching up with them all over a cuppa and a few bikkies. The Clerk of the Court, Noel Drew, came up with a coffee in his hand and said, 'I heard you rang the Coroner when she was in France on holidays.'

'Yeah, I caught her having a cuppa and croissants,' I laughed.

'Mate, I reckon you're the only person who could have done that and got away with it!'

Just as he finished speaking, the Coroner, Jan Stevenson, came into the meals room. 'I thought I heard your voice, Seymour. How are you?' she smirked.

'Really well, ma'am,' I replied. 'I was just talking to Noel about ringing you over in France. I hope I didn't ruin your breakfast that morning.'

'No, Seymour, you didn't spoil my breakfast, but I must admit that a phone call from Australia was the last thing I was expecting!' she laughed. 'I hear you arrested the two young blokes responsible for that murder. Great result.'

'Yeah, thanks for that, ma'am. I'm just picking up the formal documents I need for the brief, so I can't stay long.'

'Seymour, you seem to have a knack for solving murders, or maybe you just attract trouble. Either way, don't be a stranger.'

'I won't be, ma'am, I promise.'

'You done catching up, Pete?' Dave finally said.

'Yeah, mate.'

'Shall we go then?'

'No worries.'

I said my farewells to the staff and accompanied Dave to his office. He handed me an envelope, which I opened. I examined the contents to make sure I had everything I needed, basically all the stuff I would have expected in a brief back when I was working at the Coroner's.

I thanked Dave, said my goodbyes and made my way back to St Marys.

Over the next couple of days, there were only a few things I needed to follow up. Firstly, I needed to check with the Band Club to see if the two offenders *had* been there, and sure enough, their names appeared in the sign-in register. What really bothered me, nay pissed me off entirely, was that their names had been entered in the register *after* they'd assaulted Nick Hanes. I couldn't understand why anyone would attack someone with absolutely no provocation in the first place, but to viciously assault someone and then carry on to the Band Club for a drink as though you didn't have a care in the world was something I found altogether sickening.

With that thought at the forefront of my mind, I wanted to gain the maximum amount of watertight evidence so that there was absolutely no way they could walk. The key piece of evidence I needed was a DNA sample from the two offenders, so that we could match their DNA with what we'd collected from the crime scene. I made arrangements for the Police Medical Officer, Dr Stuart Anderson, to meet Mick Lyons and myself at the Silverwater Correctional jail where Cooper and Mahia were being held. I also contacted the jail and arranged to have their new prisoners brought to the clinic so the doctor could take mouth swabs.

On Tuesday 11 September, Mick and I arrived at the jail at 11 am and met the tall, thin, balding Dr Anderson at the reception office. The staff then escorted us to the clinic where both Cooper and Mahia, dressed in their prison greens, were seated and waiting.

'This is Detective Sergeant Lyons,' I said, pointing to Mick, 'and this is Dr Anderson. He is the Police Forensic Doctor. We intend to take either mouth swabs or a blood sample from you for the purpose of DNA testing and comparison. We have authority under the provisions of the Crimes Act to conduct the necessary medical procedure with or without your consent. Dr Anderson will explain the procedure to you individually.'

As I spoke, they both remained completely expressionless, and it was obvious they weren't enjoying prison life, which was something I was rather pleased about. I then took Cooper into a side room, where Dr Anderson explained the procedure and got Cooper to sign a consent form. Dr Anderson took three mouth swabs with cotton buds and placed them into individual containers, which were then sealed, and I took Cooper back out to the waiting area.

The same procedure was repeated with Mahia, and when he was done, they were taken from the clinic and returned to their cells. Dr Anderson gave me the containers and Mick and I left the jail and drove to Lidcombe to give them to the Forensic Analyst at the analytical laboratory.

A few days later, the results came back, and we discovered that there were no matches between the forensic examination of the swabs and the DNA that had been taken from the crime scene. Whilst this didn't damage our case in a major way, DNA matches between the accused and what we'd collected from Nick Hanes's body and the surrounding crime scene would have strengthened our case no end. There was nothing more I could do now but wait for the court dates to be set, and so I went back to my other cases.

A few days later, I was called to a death at Wallacia, near Warragamba Dam on the outskirts of Sydney. This time I was actually on call overnight, and the phone rang at about 1 am. When I arrived at the house a couple of uniformed guys met me at the front door. 'Hello, Detective Seymour,' one of them said. 'Come through and we'll show you what we've got. Scientific are on the way.'

I walked through the house and into the main bedroom to find a deceased male on the bed. There was a .22 calibre rifle lying on the bed near the deceased's hand, and there was a hole in the wall near his head. A quick look out into the hallway revealed a second hole higher up on the wall on the opposite side of the hallway, while the deceased had a trickle of blood coming from the left side of his mouth, which appeared to be where the bullet had entered. 'Pretty clear-cut case of suicide,' one of the officers said.

'Maybe,' I said as I walked around the bed and examined everything. It was clear to me that the young uniformed police officers thought that the hole in the bedroom wall and the hole in the opposite wall in the hallway were both from the fatal bullet, but there was something wrong with that scenario. 'Okay, boys,' I said, 'I don't want to come across the wrong way, but treat this as a training exercise.'

'What do you mean, boss?' they both said.

'I don't want you to touch anything, but have another look around and tell me what is wrong with this scene.'

The two uniformed boys looked at each other and then looked back at me.

'Just take a look.'

The officers examined the scene again, and as they did so, they came up with several weird and wonderful explanations.

'Boys, think more simply,' I said.

They had another look around, and then looked at me blankly.

'Boys, there's no exit wound. When someone puts a gun in their mouth and shoots themself, where should the bullet travel?'

'Out the back of their head,' one of them said.

'Exactly. In this case, there's no exit wound, nor is there any blood splattered on the wall behind the body. Therefore, the bullet that killed him hasn't exited his head. So the hole in the wall behind him and the one in the other wall out there were not from the fatal shot.'

'So what's happened?' one of them asked.

'That's what we need to find out,' I replied.

'How did those bullet holes in the two walls get there?' the other officer asked.

I leant down and looked at the gun. 'Boys, this gun looks like it's pretty old. I reckon he might have had a dummy shot to see if the gun still worked before he did the deed.'

Scientific eventually arrived, and I assisted in the examination of the body. A search of the house revealed the deceased's identity and some contact numbers for friends. It wasn't long before we were able to establish that the deceased had been suffering from depression following a recent relationship breakdown, and had spoken about 'ending it'. The subsequent post-mortem revealed that the bullet was still lodged in the deceased's head, and it was ultimately found to be a suicide. I wondered about the guy, and how suicide is such a final act that can't be reversed. Being involved in two major murder investigations had solidified the value and preciousness of life in my mind, and I wondered what this guy had found so difficult in his world that made him feel that he had no option but to end it all.

I really felt for him. I had attended numerous suicides, and I always felt bad for the person that things in their life had gotten to such a point where they felt like they had no other option.

Although I was now back on the cases I'd set aside while I focused on the murder, every couple of days I'd give Bel Hanes a call, or drop in on her whenever I could to give her detailed explanations of how the court process worked and exactly what she was going to have to endure, similar to the way I'd spoken to Christine Strachan some years earlier in the Keir case. I always thought it was quite important to talk people through the trial process, because most people have never been to court, and other than what they might have seen on TV, would have no idea what to expect. I sat down with Bel in her lounge room on several occasions and explained how the jury would be formed, and what their role entailed. I talked to her about the judge's role, and those of the Crown and Defence lawyers, as well as how witnesses were questioned and all the ways in which evidence was either allowed or denied in a courtroom. I explained that it was then up to the jury to reach a verdict.

Having to live through the news of the death of her husband and then wait for the offenders to be caught was one thing, but to then have to endure the court process was another thing entirely. Deep in the recesses of my heart, I hoped and prayed that these two clowns would do the right thing and plead guilty to spare the family the heartache of having to listen to the evidence in court and endure the wait for the jury's verdict. I'd tried to put it behind me, but I still had thoughts of Rosalina Canonizado's trial buzzing around in my head, and it certainly created some lingering doubts. I felt confident that we'd gathered all the evidence necessary to gain a conviction, but I'd been there before, only to have the jury decide to leave their brains at home.

The days passed, and just before the scheduled date for the initial court appearance, I realised there was one more hugely important thing I needed to do. I called a debriefing, and assembled the young team of detectives and all the other officers who had assisted in the investigation. I told them they'd done a fantastic job in following up all the leads, and without their dedication we wouldn't have made two arrests. I told them that this was an experience they'd take with them throughout their careers, and finished by saying, 'I want to personally thank you all for the hard work you have put into this investigation. It was a real team effort, and you can all be proud of the fact that you have contributed to a great result, not only for us, but also for the Hanes family.'

I meant every word, especially what I'd said about their future careers. Not too many young detectives ever got to experience being part of a murder investigation, in fact a lot of general detectives never got to be involved in a murder investigation in their entire careers. Experiences like dealing with the victim's family, following up the numerous leads and feeling the adrenalin of being part of such a big investigation were things you never forget. They'd learn from their experiences, and draw on them when required.

I watched the young officers filing out of the office, and allowed myself a wee smile. Upon reflection, it was their enthusiasm that had helped carry me through this investigation, along with the support and love of my wife and daughters. It was hard enough enduring the frustrations, pressure and stress of a murder investigation, but if you didn't have the love, understanding and support of your family, things would have been so much harder.

Coppers, especially old-school ones, don't often talk about their work, except perhaps with their nearest and dearest or with their colleagues. I was lucky to have Susie to share my pain with, but other coppers weren't so lucky, and their job could consume them entirely. When I'd started out, with the confidence of youth on my side, I'd thought I was immune. I'd thought that I was somehow above it all, untouchable, but as my career progressed, and I saw more and more horrific things, it began to take its toll. I saw the worst of what human beings can do to one another, I carried all the victims' faces around in my mind, and not once did I ever begin to understand where this evil came from.

What makes a man bash and murder his wife? What makes a mother kill her child? What makes two guys bash and murder a defenceless man? After more than twenty years of seeing this sort of thing, and pushing it deep down inside me, I was starting to struggle with my demons, but always pushed on. I stayed strong for the victims, for other people's families and for mine. However, no matter how hard I tried to convince myself that I could go it alone, I sometimes had to admit to myself that I couldn't.

Throughout my career, I'd kept myself aloof from a lot of what was going on, but there were plenty of blokes I knew who'd become chronic alcoholics, ended up in St John of God psychiatric hospital, or worse, killed themselves.

I hadn't thought much about it when I was younger, but as I got older and it started to happen to more and more guys I knew, it started to play on my mind, and I became acutely aware of the fact that I didn't want the same fate to befall me.

Yeah, I would go and have a drink with the boys after work, but we never had too many, because most of us had to get home to our families. We joked around as we debriefed on things, and chatted about what was going on. We felt comfortable talking to each other, and felt that we had someone with whom we could share our pain. We were the lucky ones, but I'd known many who hadn't been so lucky.

Chapter 14:

Where There's Harmony, There's Chaos

The investigation brief I'd put together ended up with the Crown Prosecutors at the DPP office. The DPP solicitor looking after the case was a bloke called Bryan Royce. He was based at the Penrith office, and was a very smart operator. He'd represented me in other matters before the court, and when I found out that he'd been allocated to the Hanes case, I was extremely pleased to have a top-notch solicitor on the job.

Everything seemed to be going to plan at work, and things were getting better at home, but if there was one lesson I should have learned from my time in the force, it was that life is always a balancing act; where there's harmony, there's chaos.

It was 29 September 2000, and Susie and I had been invited by some friends of ours, Tom and Lea, to join them on a weekend trip to the south coast. The girls were planning on going to the Berry town markets, and while they were off doing the girly thing, us boys were going to enjoy a round of golf.

Our daughters were really excited as we made our way down the coast, arriving at the motel at Bomaderry around mid-afternoon. We picked up our room keys, and while the girls unpacked our bags, Tom and I took the kids and went to check out the pool. It was a warm afternoon, and the kids were in the pool almost before we'd even walked through the gate. Meanwhile, Tom and I kicked back on the adjacent banana lounges. 'Bloody nice pool area,' I said to Tom.

'Yeah, there's a barbie over there too. What do you reckon we have a barbie for dinner?'

'Sounds like a plan, mate.'

Tom and I were pretty knackered from the drive down, and were content to just relax while we watched all the kids swimming in the pool. They seemed fine, so Tom and I closed our eyes and laid back on our lounges, but no sooner had we done so than we heard an ear-piercing scream.

We hurriedly scanned the pool area, and soon located the source of the scream; Tayla. She was sitting in the skimmer box, which had been built into the wall in the centre of the pool. She had her arms extended on either side of her and was desperately struggling to lift herself up out of the box. Tom and I jumped up and sprinted over to see what was going on. When we reached her, we realised that the skimmer box was turned on, and was sucking Tayla downwards! We rushed up and down the pool searching for the off button, but we couldn't find it, and when we looked back at Tayla, we realised that she was being sucked further and further down into the box. 'There's no time, Tom!' I yelled. 'We'll have to wedge our hands under her bum and try to break the suction!'

Tom nodded, and knelt down on one side of Tayla while I knelt on the other. We manoeuvred our hands underneath her butt as best we could, utterly shocked by the strength of the suction on our forearms. 'Shit, it's pretty strong!' Tom said.

'We do this on the count of three. You ready?'

Tom nodded again.

'Right! One, two, three!'

With one almighty heave, we broke the suction and Tayla was free. I scooped her up in my arms and carried her away from the pool, while Tom rushed to grab a towel, which we wrapped around her. My mind was running at a hundred miles a minute, but luckily I still had the presence of mind to search the pool and make sure the other kids were safe. Sure enough, there they were, still happily playing, oblivious to the drama that was unfolding around them.

As I held Tayla in my arms, I quickly checked her over. She seemed to be okay, but then I noticed a large bulge in her one-piece swimmers. *Whoa! She's literally shit herself. Better take her to the toilet and fix her up,* I thought. 'Sweetheart, I'm just gonna take you to the toilet and take care of you, okay,' I said as I put her down.

She took a couple of steps before she squatted down and grabbed between her legs. 'Daddy, I can't walk! It hurts!' she bawled. I picked her up and carried her to the public toilets near the reception office, while Tom went to get Susie and Leanne. I took Tayla into the toilet, pulled her swimmers down and grabbed some toilet paper to clean up the mess. It was then that I saw, to my sheer horror, that there was blood in her swimmers, and a large purplish mass protruding from her backside.

At that point, Susie rushed into the toilet. 'Oh, my God! What's happened?' she cried.

'Susie, get to the office and ask them where the nearest hospital is!' I yelled.

She rushed off towards the reception while I fixed up Tayla's costume, wrapped her in the towel again, bundled her up in my arms and set off at breakneck speed towards the car. I carefully placed her in the front seat just as Sue came rushing back from reception with the address for the Shoalhaven Hospital in her hand. She gave me the address, and then jumped in the back seat behind Tayla. 'You right to look after the kids?' I called out to Tom and Leanne, who had come to see if there was anything they could do.

'Yeah, mate!' Tom yelled back. 'We've got it! You just make sure Tayla's okay!'

The hospital was about a five-minute drive away, but I probably covered it in two. Thinking back on it now, it was bloody lucky I didn't pass any coppers! My trusty old Ford Falcon copped a flogging as I drove like a man trying to evade a highway pursuit. I have never been so focused in my life as I swerved this way and that, my concentration only broken when I heard a little voice coming from the front seat alongside me. 'Daddy!'

'Tayla, it's alright, sweetheart. We're almost at the hospital. You'll be okay,' I said as I reached over and lovingly stroked her head, realising she was shivering feverishly.

'Daddy,' she pleaded, 'I don't want to die.' I will never forget those words. More than anything I have seen in all my time in the cops, those words will haunt me until the day I die. It broke my heart to see my little girl in such pain, and the thought of losing one of my own children was tearing me apart.

This can't be happening, I thought to myself as I screeched into the driveway directly outside the Emergency Section. I tried to imagine the fear running through Tayla's mind that would cause her to say such words, but I couldn't even begin to contemplate the terror she was going through. I quickly, yet carefully, lifted Tayla out of the car and ran inside with her cradled in my arms. 'Quick! Quick! We need some help! My daughter's been in a pool accident!' I cried out.

Several staff rushed towards us from every direction and we were immediately ushered into a cubicle in front of a fairly packed waiting room. 'What happened?' said one of the nurses.

'She was sitting in the pool skimmer box and it sucked her down! There's something not right with her backside!'

The nurse carefully removed Tayla's swimmers and examined her. 'Wait here,' she said anxiously, and then ran from the cubicle. Seconds later, half a dozen doctors and assorted other staff rushed into the cubicle and surrounded the bed.

They rolled Tayla onto her right side and squirted a clear gel onto the protruding bulge. A moment later, a middle-aged man dressed in casual clothes arrived and immediately began issuing orders. Susie and

I sat alongside the bed stroking Tayla's head and holding her hand, although by that stage, a mask had already been placed over Tayla's face and she was basically out of it. Then I heard someone yell, 'Get the operating theatre ready!'

The casually dressed man, who I was later to learn was the hospital surgeon who had been off duty but only lived a few hundred metres up the road from the hospital, sat on the opposite side of the bed from us and started working on Tayla. I had no idea what he was doing, and to be honest, even if I could have seen what was happening, I don't think I would have been in any fit state to realise what was going on.

I'm sure it must have taken quite some time, but it only seemed like a few minutes had passed before the surgeon sat back and wiped the sweat from his forehead. He turned to the nursing staff and said, 'I think we might be lucky. You all did a fantastic job.' He then turned to me. 'Dad, do you want to come around here and have a look?'

I wasn't sure I did, but on the other hand I wanted a clearer understanding of exactly what was wrong with my little girl. I don't know what I was expecting to see, but I got up and walked around to the other side of the bed, and looked at where the bulge had been. There was nothing there now, but I was horrified to see that both cheeks of Tayla's backside were black with bruising. 'Is...is... she going to be alright, doctor?' I stuttered.

'Well, I've managed to manoeuvre her bowel back into her body without her appearing to have suffered any further injury, but only time will tell us the true extent of the damage. I can tell you one thing, though, we're very lucky that the staff here kept her exposed bowel moist, which made it possible for me to manoeuvre it back into position without having to take her to surgery. Time was critical, and we didn't have much of it to play with. By the way, I'm Doctor O'Shea.'

I'd lost count of how many times I'd had to talk to families about the death of loved ones, to tell them that their beloved family member would never be coming home, and throughout all those traumatic times I'd managed to hold it together, but now all I wanted to do was bawl my eyes out. I don't know if it was from relief or fear, but somehow I managed to hold it together. I think the fact that Susie held onto me so tightly as they wheeled Tayla into the children's ward kept me strong. Susie and I were standing beside Tayla's bed, holding her hands, when I heard someone say, 'We've cancelled the Careflight helicopter from Westmead.' Even though they'd cancelled the chopper, there was still the question of whether they were going to transfer her.

A moment later, Doctor O'Shea arrived. He stroked Tayla's head gently and said, 'I've just been talking to a professor at the Children's Hospital who is an expert in this kind of thing. He told me that if I hadn't been able to get the bowel back in so quickly, we would have had to move her immediately. However, because the bowel has been manipulated back inside her body, we'll keep her here for now. There's nothing they can do up there that we can't do here.'

'Thank you, Doctor,' I said as I stood up and shook his hand firmly. 'Words are not enough.'

'No thanks necessary, Mr Seymour. I'm just glad she's going to be alright.'

Now Susie and I had a heart-wrenching decision to make. We had two other kids who needed caring for, and although Tom and Leanne were there, I decided it was better that Ashleigh and Jenna had at least one parent with them, so I went back to the motel, and Susie and I took it in turns to be at Tayla's bedside over the next few days and nights.

When I arrived back at the motel, everyone was waiting expectantly. I told Tom and Leanne that Tayla was going to be okay, but when I told Ashleigh and Jenna, it was clear that they didn't comprehend the seriousness of what had happened. They knew that their baby sister had been taken to hospital, but they had no idea that she'd almost died. All I could do was explain exactly what had happened, and remind them about the dangers of pools. I told them that the doctors had said that Tayla was going to be okay, but that she would need to stay in hospital for a few days, which meant that we'd have to stay at the motel until she was allowed to come home.

The following day, I called my parents from the hospital to let them know what had happened. I walked outside into the hospital grounds so that I could be alone, and spoke to Mum first. She was pretty shocked, but after I'd calmed her down, she passed the phone over to Dad. 'Dad, Tayla had an accident at the motel pool,' I said before explaining everything again.

'Do you want us to come down, mate, to be there with you and the girls?' he said.

'Nah, Dad, I appreciate that, but there's nothing you guys can do. I'll keep you updated.'

'How are Ashleigh and Jenna?' he said.

'They're fine. I don't think they really understand what's going on. We'll stay at the motel for the time being.' I'd tried to stay strong for everyone, particularly my parents, but as those words left my lips, I broke down.

'You alright, mate?' Dad said sympathetically.

'No, Dad, not really!' I blubbered. 'I almost lost her! I don't know what I'd do without her!'

'Pete, the docs said she'd be okay. She's a tough little cookie. She'll be fine.'

'Thanks, Dad. Listen, I'm gonna have to ring you back later, okay.'

'Sure, mate. Take care, hey.'

Everything had now come to a head, and after I hung up, I went and found a bench in the hospital gardens, slumped down onto it and sobbed and sobbed until there were no more tears left. What made it worse was that the more I thought about how this wasn't helping my parents, my family, or anyone else for that matter, the more upset I became. *No, I had to be strong for everyone*, I thought as I wiped my eyes with my sleeves, took a deep breath, tried to compose myself as best I could, and headed back inside.

Tayla had the best of care over the next five days. Doctor O'Shea made a point of paying special attention to her, and he and the hospital's specialist paediatrician did a marvellous job, in fact all of the hospital staff were magnificent.

Tom and Leanne also stayed on, and provided wonderful support. The motel owners did their bit by not charging us for the extra few nights' accommodation, and visited Tayla in hospital, bringing her a gift to show how sorry they were, but my appreciation soon turned to anger when I found out that the cover to the skimmer box had been broken for some time, but they'd never bothered to replace it, instead leaving the skimmer basket exposed. When they heard this, both Doctor O'Shea and the specialist paediatrician made a point of visiting the motel to tear strips off the owners.

Despite what had happened, Tayla remained in surprisingly good spirits during her hospital stay. She got on famously with Dr O'Shea, who was a truly remarkable man. He had such a charming personality and bedside manner, and I think he took an immediate liking to Tayla, probably because she'd had such a near miss and survived a trauma that he'd only previously read about in medical journals.

It wasn't until much later, when I'd finally calmed down, that I realised why I'd completely fallen apart. I'd come so close to losing my youngest daughter, and I couldn't help but think back to the brief I'd done for the Coroner regarding the four-year-old girl who'd drowned in a pool accident. I'm not sure I'll ever get over that brief; it's just one of those things that I'm going to have to carry around with me for the rest of my days.

Having been involved in two big murder investigations, I'd started to think more and more about the fact that when something horrible happened in the blink of an eye, it completely altered your life forever, as it had done for the Haneses and the Strachans, but I'd never really considered how it would affect me personally.

The relief and joy we experienced when we were finally given the all clear to take Tayla home was indescribable, and all Susie and I wanted to do was spoil her rotten. Her recovery went well, although she would be affected for the rest of her life. Tayla had suffered permanent damage to an inner muscle, which meant that she wouldn't be able to give birth naturally, as her bowel wouldn't be able to cope with the stress. Should she ever be blessed with children, their birth would have to be via Caesarean section. Apart from that, she made a complete recovery, but I often wonder how she deals with it emotionally, even to this day.

I had only been at St Marys for three short months, but when I arrived back at work, the support I received from all the crew was unbelievable. The girls took up a collection, and one day, two of the uniformed girls turned up at home in a cop car with a board game and toys for Tayla, which completely blew me away.

Seeing the joy on Tayla's face made me think that she had been through a lot, and might need something else to lift her spirits. Suddenly, I had an idea. My family has been, and always will be, fanatical Parramatta Eels supporters, so on the off chance, I called the club, and was put through to one of their PR people. 'Hello, my name is Peter Seymour. My family and I are huge Eels supporters.'

'Well, Mr Seymour, we appreciate that.'

'Listen, my daughter had a really serious accident recently. She's only seven years old, and Brett Hodgson is her favourite player. I was wondering if you could get him to autograph a card for her?'

'Oh, really, what happened?' she asked. I quickly outlined what had happened to Tayla, and there was a brief silence. 'Um, okay then Mr Seymour, give me your number and I'll ring you back.'

I was a little surprised and annoyed, to say the least, that she had to ring me back. After all, the fans make the game, don't they? *Oh well, hopefully they'll get back to me*, I thought. A couple of hours later, the phone rang. 'Hello,' I said.

'Hello, Mr Seymour this is Erin Phillips from the Parramatta Eels club. I spoke to you earlier.'

'Hello, Erin,' I replied.

'I'm sorry it's taken me so long to get back to you.'

'That's alright.'

'Listen, we're not going to send your daughter a card.'

What on earth? I thought. *Maybe it's time to support the Panthers, Tigers, Roosters…*

'We rang Brett and told him what had happened,' she continued. 'He said a card was not nearly good enough, and he asked if he would be able to visit her at your home. Will four o'clock this afternoon be okay?'

Go you mighty Eels!

Unfortunately, I was a few minutes late getting home that afternoon, and by the time I pulled up, Brett Hodgson and Miss Phillips had already arrived. Susie told me later me that Tayla had just happened to look out the window at the exact moment they arrived. 'Mum! Mum! Brett Hodgson is here! Brett Hodgson is here!' she'd apparently squealed with delight.

I went inside and found them all sitting in the lounge room. I couldn't believe it! Brett had brought along his training jersey, which he signed and presented to Tayla, as well as a large Eels flag. I don't think Tayla could have sat any closer to him on the lounge if she'd tried! They stayed for nearly an hour, and Ashleigh and Jenna got Brett to sign their Eels jerseys as well. I got a photo of Tayla with the biggest smile on her face I'd ever seen as she sat with Brett in her Eels jersey, Eels cap and Eels shorts.

That night, I wrote two letters of gratitude; one to the staff at Shoalhaven Hospital, and one to the Parramatta Eels Football Club.

Chapter 15:
Better You Than Me

No matter how happy I was that Tayla had pulled through, I couldn't shake the image of the little girl from the Coroner's brief from my mind. I tried to forget about it, but visions of her began to creep into my thoughts more and more often, until eventually it seemed like every time I closed my eyes, there she was, her face always becoming Tayla's.

I tried to forget about her, and also to cope with what had happened to Tayla by throwing myself into my work, more determined than ever to help other people's families, but I faced several frustrations, because the Hanes investigation seemed to be taking an eternity to come to a head. We were still waiting on court dates, and it felt like they would never come. Then, in late October, we received an anonymous phone call. The caller said that near the end of July, Mark Formoza, Aaron Cooper and Ricky Mahia had travelled up to the north coast, where they'd slowed down and thrown a bag into a river as they were crossing a bridge. The caller then hung up.

It was time for me to pay Mark Formoza another visit. When I'd first interviewed him, I'd been certain that he was holding out on me. This time, I was intent on getting absolutely everything out of him. Mick and I went to his house, and his parents answered the door. 'Mr and Mrs Formoza,' I said, 'we're sorry to bother you again, but we've received further information, and we want to speak to your son about it.'

'He's not home at the moment,' Mr Formoza said tersely.

'Here are my contact details,' I said as I handed them my card. 'Mr and Mrs Formoza, may I suggest to you that your son contacts me as soon as possible. It is in his best interests to do so.'

Mark Formoza didn't call me until the following day. 'Detective Seymour?'

'Yes, is that you, Mark?'

'Yes, sir.'

'Mark, we have received some further information regarding the murder of Nick Hanes. I just want to run a few things by you, nothing major. Would it be possible for you to come in to the station?' I made a point of telling him that it was 'nothing major' because I didn't want to scare him off. I wanted him to feel comfortable about coming in, but once I had him there, I knew he'd feel more vulnerable, and that was when I would put the acid on him.

He came in later that day, and I took him into the interview room. 'Sit down, mate,' I said as I pointed to a chair. He deliberately kept eye contact to a minimum, and as soon as I sat down in front of him, I came straight out with it. 'Remember how I told you how it was an offence to withhold information from the police?'

'Yeah, so?' he replied.

'Well, guess what, old mate,' I continued, 'I've just received information that you were with Cooper and Mahia when they threw a bag off a bridge into a river up on the north coast. Let me give you some sound advice. I *will* find out the truth about this, which means you now have another decision to make. Now is the opportunity, and I assure you there won't be another one, for you to tell me what you know, otherwise you face the prospect of joining your mates behind bars. So, what's it gonna be?'

At that point, I rose from my seat, placed my hands flat on the table and leant across towards Mark to add weight to my words.

'Yeah, I remember now. I didn't think of it before,' he said.

'Oh, you didn't think of it before. It seems like a pretty big thing to simply slip your mind,' I said as I fired up the computer and readied myself to start typing up what he had to say. When I was ready, I said, 'Right, mate. Go on.'

'It was a coupla' weeks after the murder, and we were all going up the coast for the weekend. We were driving in a truck and we crossed over a large river. We slowed down and, all of a sudden, the boys threw a bag out the window.'

'Did you know what was in the bag?' I pressed.

'Nup, it was only later that Aaz told me that the bag was full of his and Ricky's blood-stained clothes.'

I left him for a moment while I went and grabbed a street directory. When I returned, I opened it up and plonked it down in front of him. 'Do you know the name of the bridge?'

'Nah, I dunno what it was called, but I know we were driving along the F3. It was just before you reach the truck weighbridge.'

I checked the index and found the Hawkesbury area, but unfortunately the maps only went as far as Brooklyn. However, after studying the maps for a few minutes, we worked out that the bridge across the Hawkesbury River was, in fact, the one he was talking about. With that confirmed, I finished typing up his statement and sent him on his way.

After he'd left, I wandered over to Mick's desk to mull things over with him. 'Mate, I just got another statement off Formoza,' I said as Mick looked up at me, 'and he confirmed the information we received about a bag being chucked off a bridge into a river up north. He said that Cooper told him that the bag contained his and Mahia's blood-stained clothes. We've worked out that it's the bridge that crosses the Hawkesbury River at Brooklyn on the F3. If they didn't weigh the bag down, those clothes could be miles away by now. However, there's a chance they weighed it down enough to make it sink. I wonder what the chances are of getting the police divers to check the western side of the bridge?' I was more talking out loud to myself rather than asking Mick the question, but his response didn't surprise me.

'I don't think you'll convince them to do that, Pete. You're gonna have to be bloody lucky to get a specialist support team to do a job like that for you. They're usually too busy.'

'Mick, you know me, mate!' I laughed. 'What's the first thing I'm gonna to do when you tell me I can't do something?'

'I know, Pete, I know. You're gonna go right ahead and do it.'

'Think I might just give them a call,' I replied as I shot him a cheesy grin. Mick just shook his head.

A few minutes later, I returned to Mick's desk. 'And?' he said.

'You don't ask, Mick, you don't get.'

'They agreed?'

'No, not exactly, but they at least agreed to consider it!'

Mick shook his head again as I made my way back to my desk to type up a request. I made sure I included absolutely everything in an attempt to convince them to do the job, and a couple of days later, I got the call I'd been hoping for; the divers had agreed to do it! I arranged to meet with them on site the following morning. After I got off the phone, I headed over to Glash's office. 'Hey, boss,' I said.

'Hey, Pete, what's up?'

'You know how we received that information about our suspects throwing a bag of clothes into the Hawkesbury?'

'Yeah, what about it?'

'Well, I thought I'd give the police divers a call on the off chance they'd have a look around the river for us.'

'Yeah, good luck with that,' Glash said sarcastically.

'Boss, I just thought I'd better let you know that they've agreed to do it, and I'm going out with them tomorrow.'

'You're unbelievable, Seymour!' he said as he too shook his head. 'Nevertheless, I'm coming with you.'

Early the next morning Glash, Mick and I jumped into an unmarked car and drove the forty-five minutes or so from St Marys to Brooklyn, where we met the divers on the north-western side of the Hawkesbury River bridge, near the old mental hospital.

It was an overcast day, which had me a bit worried that they wouldn't be able to see anything. 'Hey,' I said to one of the divers, 'it's a bit overcast. Are you guys gonna be able to see anything?'

'Yeah, the weather's not the problem,' he replied as he looked out over the water. 'The problem is that this could take us a few weeks, and that's assuming we don't get called out on any other jobs. This river's bloody wide, and tidal, which might make things more difficult.'

I looked up and down the river, back towards the mountains and then out to the islands, and then moved to the bank and looked down at the water again.

'The other reason it's gonna take time,' the diver said as he came and stood beside me and pointed to various spots in the river, 'is that it's murky down there. We won't be able to see more than a few feet in front of us, if that. We're gonna have to do the whole thing by feel.'

Better you than me, I thought to myself as I stared down into the dark and swirling depths. 'I really appreciate what you're doing for us,' I said.

'Needle in a haystack, mate, needle in a haystack,' the diver said as he pulled his diver's mask down and headed towards a nearby dinghy, where two of his mates were already waiting.

We watched them manoeuvre their boat out into the river, and as two of them disappeared over the side, I turned to Glash and said, 'Shit, boss, I've heard there's a lot of sharks in that river. I sure hope they don't come across any of them while they're down there!'

'Forget the sharks, mate, let's just hope they find what we're after,' he replied as we watched them work for a little while before jumping into the car and returning to the station. Over the next few weeks, the divers kept me updated on a daily basis. At one stage, they were called away on another job, but as soon as they could they were back into it.

About a week into the search, I decided that I wanted to get some video footage of the river so that I could demonstrate its size to a jury, and show how Cooper and Mahia had deliberately disposed of the incriminating evidence in a place where no one would ever find it, and that while their actions on the night might have been reckless, their attempts to cover up their crime were calculated and deliberate. Mick and I drove out there, and while Mick drove across the bridge, I hung out the window with the video camera, taking in as much of the river as I could. 'There, that should do it,' I said to Mick, who turned the car around as soon as we were across the bridge and headed back to St Marys.

The police divers did manage to find a few interesting items on the river bed, including a rusted old gun, but unfortunately, despite their exhaustive searching, the bag of bloodied clothing was never found. Another lead, another bust. I just hoped that what we had was enough to convict the accused.

Chapter 16:
Intention to Kill

Cooper and Mahia had their court dates set for them, and I spent my days poring over all the evidence we'd collected during the investigation. I liaised with Bryan Royce from time to time, and began putting the brief together in chronological order. I was confident that Aaron Cooper was going to plead guilty, but whether it was to the charge of murder or the lesser indictment of manslaughter was yet to be seen. Ricky Mahia was a different story altogether, because he was still maintaining his innocence, which made me decidedly angry. I couldn't believe that, even with his mate dropping him in it, he would persist and subject the family to the ordeal of living through the nightmare of a court trial.

The big day eventually came, and Cooper finally appeared in the Penrith Local Court. I sat directly behind the bar table where Bryan Royce was seated. That way, Bryan simply had to swivel around in his chair and lean over to me to whisper any questions he might have, while I, in turn, could tell him what he needed to know. Bel sat in the back of the court with the rest of her family, all of them watching on intently as they waited for proceedings to unfold.

I'd prepared as thoroughly as I possibly could, but nevertheless, I couldn't shake my lingering doubts. I'd been here before, and seen gut-wrenching miscarriages of justice first-hand, but I had to keep my faith and remain upbeat. I took a quick look around the court and realised that there was nothing more I could do now. I'd managed to bring the offenders this far; the rest was up the justice system.

As I'd expected, Cooper pleaded guilty and was remanded in custody again. The Defence and the Crown had worked out a deal whereby he was only charged with manslaughter rather than murder. Cooper redeemed himself slightly in my eyes when it emerged that the guilty plea had been entered by Cooper's legal team for no other reason than to give the Hanes family the result they were looking for as quickly as possible.

However, Mahia still maintained his innocence and entered a plea of not guilty and was remanded in custody to appear at a later date where he could lodge another bail application. Pending which, he would stand trial after that.

On the morning of Cooper's sentencing hearing, I caught the train in to Darlinghurst and met the Hanes family outside the Supreme Court. I'd barely reached the court when Bel saw me. She came rushing up, tears streaming down her cheeks, and embraced me in the same way she had when I'd gone to her house to inform her about the arrests.

'Bel,' I said as I smiled back at her reassuringly, 'everything is going to be okay. I can't give you any guarantees. I simply don't know what will happen; it's entirely up to the sentencing judge. Everyone is different, including judges, and they can all come up with different sentences based on how they see the severity of the offence,' I said as reassuringly as I could.

'Pete, it's time,' said the familiar voice of Bryan Royce from behind me. I nodded, and we all filed into the court room and sat down towards the back. Bryan Royce and the Crown Prosecutor sat at a desk to the left of the room, while Cooper and his solicitors were to the right.

'All rise,' the bailiff said as Judge Taylor walked in.

'Be seated,' Judge Taylor said.

The Defence went through all the reasons why Cooper should receive a softer sentence, such as the fact that he'd entered an early guilty plea because he wanted to save the family any more grief, he wanted to save the State of NSW a lot of money, he was still only young, and therefore had a good chance of rehabilitation, his deep remorse for what had happened, etc. The big clincher for him was agreeing to give evidence on behalf of the Crown against his co-accused, Mahia. Even though Nick Hanes was dead, there were still different degrees of culpability or maliciousness to be taken into account when sentencing his attackers. For example, Thomas Keir had been sentenced to a much higher penalty than a lot of other murderers because his actions had been cold-blooded, extremely callous and malicious, whereas Cooper hadn't *planned* to kill Hanes.

'After considering all the evidence presented to the court,' Judge Taylor said, 'including Mr Cooper's early guilty plea and the fact that Mr Cooper has formally agreed to give evidence against the co-accused, I sentence him to imprisonment for six years with a non-parole period of four years, backdated to commence on 1 September 2000.'

It was official; the sentence had been handed down, and that was when it all hit home. One half of my job was finally done. I let out a sigh of relief, and Bel and I embraced once more. I thanked Bryan Royce and the other DPP officers, and then Bel and I went outside and grabbed a coffee. 'I'm so glad that's all over,' Bel said. 'Is that the sentence you were expecting?'

'Actually, I gave up trying to work out what I thought offenders would get from the courts a long time ago, because quite often I was so wide of the mark. The fact is, you're dealing with human beings on the bench, and everyone has different views on things, but the sentence mostly reflects the fact that Cooper didn't *intend* to kill Nick. If Nick hadn't had a bad heart, he probably wouldn't have died as a result of the injuries he received, and the judge had to take that into account.'

'Still,' she said, 'it's hard to believe that my husband's life has been taken, and this person just gets a few years for it.'

'Hard to argue with your reasoning, Bel, but that's the way of the law.'

I caught the train back with the family and tried to explain, as best I could, how the trial for Mahia would unfold, the ways in which Mahia's Defence team would try to defend the charge and how the Crown would go about prosecuting the case.

With Cooper squared away, all we could do now was sit back and wait for Mahia's trial date. I'd thought that with one of the offenders sentenced, my nightmares might subside and that I would find some kind of peace for a while, but no, the same old nightmares continued to plague me.

One evening, I was sitting at my desk trying to get my head around all the investigations and cases that I was working on when I received a call from Inspector Glen Allender, who was working as the Duty Officer. 'Hey, Peter, it's Glen,' he said, his voice a little uncertain.

'G'day, Glen, what have you got for me?' I said, wondering why he was speaking so quietly. There was a brief silence. 'Glen?'

'Pete, we've just been called to a house in South Penrith.'

'Yeah?' There was another brief silence. 'Glen, what's going on, mate?'

'A three-year-old girl has gone missing.' I closed my eyes and my head dropped. Now it was my turn to be silent. 'Pete, you there?'

'Yeah, mate,' I said after taking a deep breath. I knew that the uniformed blokes thought that something serious had happened, otherwise they wouldn't be calling me. 'What are the details?'

'The family said that she was playing out the back. They went out to check on her, and she was gone. They called us, and at first we thought she might have just wandered off somewhere.'

'But you don't think that's the case now?'

'No, mate, I called in as many guys as were available, and along with the family and all the neighbours, we started searching the surrounding streets and parks. We've been searching for a while, but we haven't found a thing.'

'So, what do you think may have happened?' I asked, even though I already had my suspicions.

'Pete, we just don't know.'

'Okay, Glen, give us the address and I'll be there as quick as I can.' Glen gave me the details, and then hung up. I didn't put the receiver down immediately, but merely sat there, frozen to the seat while the phone continued to beep in my ear. I was paralysed by fear as I closed my eyes and pictured my three girls.

I soon composed myself and put the phone down, but I still couldn't drag myself up out of my chair. I closed my eyes once more, and pictured a small girl lying somewhere with nobody to help her, I pictured her parents screaming when her little body was discovered, I pictured all the neighbours, dozens of uniformed police and police dogs scouring the nearby bush and parklands, I pictured SES volunteers, dressed in their orange overalls and with sticks in hand, poking and prodding under trees and in shallow creeks, I pictured the same police divers who had checked the river for me searching for the body of the little girl, and then I began to weep.

I held my hand up to my mouth as the nauseous feelings rose from the pit of my stomach, and then buried my head in my hands and let out another deep breath. I tried to compose myself as best I could, forced myself up out of my chair, clicked into autopilot, grabbed a set of car keys and headed off to the scene. I struggled to stay focused on the road as I made my way down the highway and into the quiet suburban streets of South Penrith.

When I turned into the street that Glen had given me, I found it choked with police vehicles. There were dozens and dozens of neighbours standing around in groups, talking and waving their arms around as they discussed what had happened. I parked down the street, walked up to the house and found Glen. 'G'day, Pete, how's it going? I'll take you to meet the parents.'

'Yes, thanks, Glen.' Glen took me inside, where I found the couple sitting at their dining table as the husband did his best to comfort his inconsolable wife. 'Hello, Mr and Mrs Lewis,' I said as I offered my hand to the father. 'My name is Detective Peter Seymour. I'm here to help find your daughter.'

'Robert Lewis,' the father said as he shook my hand. 'And this is Cecilia.'

'And what is your daughter's name?'

'Cassandra.'

'Can you show me the last place you saw her?'

'Sure,' Lewis said, and stood up and headed to the back sunroom, out through a screen door and into the backyard.

I took a look around the backyard. There were a few plants and palm trees bordering the lawn, and towards the back fence there was a rectangular pool with curved corners. I walked over to the pool and examined the mesh fence, but there didn't seem to be any gaps. I opened the gate and checked the lock. It all seemed to be working fine. I moved to the edge of the pool and stared down into it. 'Gees, that water's not just green, it's the darkest green I think I've ever seen,' I said to no one in particular.

'Yeah, the filter's broken,' Lewis said. 'We haven't had the money to fix it.'

'I take it the pool's been checked?'

'Yeah,' Glen said. 'Some of the uniformed officers and other volunteers dragged the pool with the scoop, but they didn't find anything.'

'I think we'd better check it again, just to be sure.'

Glen organised for some of the uniformed officers to use the pool scoop to check the pool once more, and some of the neighbours rushed back to their houses and returned with their scoops to assist. After a solid half hour or more with half a dozen people checking, we'd found nothing. 'And no one has seen or heard from her?' I asked.

'No, mate,' Glen said as we walked out the front. 'I've checked with absolutely everybody. There's no sign of her.'

'Mr and Mrs Lewis,' I said as I took hold of Mrs Lewis's hand. 'I have three girls of my own. I promise you I will not rest until we find out what happened to your little girl.'

'Thank you, Detective,' they both replied.

I walked back to my car and returned to the station. Shortly after I arrived, I contacted everybody I could get hold of and asked them to help with the search, PolAir, the Mounted Police, the Dog Squad, everybody. As it was so late, they all told me they couldn't do anything until the next morning, so I went home picturing all the scenarios of what could have happened to the missing girl. Worst of all, my dreams that night were of those scenarios, except the little girls in them were mine.

Due to my lack of sleep, I was exhausted when I arrived at work the next day, but as soon as I walked in the door, I was on the phone to all the search parties to ensure that they would be coming out that morning. With that done, I headed out to the scene. The chopper turned up right on time, and I instructed the pilot to check around the nearby Nepean River. When the Mounted Police arrived, I told them to check any areas that the chopper pilot directed them to.

I made my way inside, greeted Mr and Mrs Lewis, and accompanied them into the dining room. 'Mr and Mrs Lewis, we are going to use every resource at our disposal to try to locate your daughter. We've got PolAir and the Mounted Police focusing on the areas around the river. The Dog Squad should be here shortly, and when they arrive, we'll organise for all the police and other volunteers to begin a doorknock and canvass the area.'

'Thank you, Detective,' Mr Lewis said. As he spoke, I looked at both his and his wife's faces and could see how red their eyes were, and I pictured both of them eventually crying each other to sleep during a night they would have spent racked with fear and uncertainty. I was about to say more about what we would do to find their daughter when one of the uniformed officers came in and told me that the Dog Squad had arrived.

We headed out the front to see two officers dressed in dark-blue overalls with German Shepherds on leashes. I asked Mr Lewis if he could give us an item of Cassandra's clothing. He ducked back inside and quickly returned with a pink dress. The Dog Squad guys passed the dress around, giving their dogs a good whiff of it as they did. The dogs immediately set off, sniffing their way around the front yard, and then headed down the side of the house and into the backyard, but although they sniffed all around the yard, they couldn't discern any particular spot where she might have been. I wasn't surprised, because the backyard would have been full of the scent of the family, and the dress would have had that scent all over it.

Having found nothing in either the front yard or the back yard, the Dog Squad guys started to work their way outwards from the property. While I watched on, I started to think more deeply about what could have happened to Cassandra. Given that all the signs were now starting to point towards a possible kidnapping, I thought it best that I return to the station and check on any known paedophiles in the area. When I got back, I found the Intelligence Officer and told him what I was looking for. He checked everything we had, including the Missing Person files to see if anyone similar to Cassandra had recently gone missing, but he came up empty-handed. Around 4 pm that afternoon, my phone rang. 'Detective Seymour, it's John from downstairs. I have a call for you.'

'Who is it?'

'It's 2UE. They want to know if they can interview you at around 8 am tomorrow morning.'

Knowing the value of the media I immediately consented. 'Sure, mate, tell them to phone me then.'

I squared away everything I could, but as evening approached, there wasn't much more I could do, so I packed up my things and called it quits for the night. As I drove home, I couldn't shake the pictures from my mind of Cassandra floating face down in the river, alternating with pictures of my own girls floating face down in our pool.

I pulled into the garage and realised that I had tears rolling down my cheeks. I reached inside the glove box and retrieved some tissues, tried to wipe away the tears as best I could, and then took a moment to compose myself before I headed inside.

When I walked into the kitchen, Sue came straight up to me and hugged me tight. 'Oh, Pete, you poor thing,' she said compassionately as she rested her head on my chest. 'I know you told me about it last night, but I saw the story of the missing little girl on the midday news today.'

When my girls came rushing up to me, I hugged each one tight and told them I loved them. 'Daddy,' Jenna said as I held her in my arms, 'have you been crying?'

'No, darling,' I lied.

'But your eyes are very red.'

I looked at her pretty little face and tight blonde ringlets, then looked at my other two girls, and began to cry again. I was willing myself not to, but the harder I tried, the harder it was to control myself. To know that all three of my girls were safe and sound warmed my heart, and I just wanted to let the tears flow.

'You have been crying, haven't you Daddy?' Jenna said.

I couldn't lie anymore. 'Yes, darling, I have.'

'Why, Daddy?'

'A little girl is missing, and it upset me.'

'Don't worry, Daddy,' Jenna said as she put her hand on my cheek. 'You'll fix everything, you wait and see.' To hear that from one of my daughters made me want to cry even more.

I sat down to dinner with my family, and Cassandra's disappearance was one of the lead stories on every channel. *Surely*, I thought to myself, *given this much media coverage, if anyone's seen her they'll come forward.*

I turned the TV off and we finished our meal. When we were done, I made a point of making time for my kids. I helped them finish their homework, played some games with them, and then read them stories before bedtime, revelling in it all, but later, when I went to bed, I lay awake for most of the night, visions of the little girl from the Coroner's brief playing over and over in my mind.

After my disturbed night's sleep, I was struggling a bit when I went in to work the next morning, and I wasn't sure I was up to doing a radio interview, but I reminded myself that there were two parents out there whose little daughter was missing. I needed to solve this case quicker than anything I'd ever done before, and the media would help me to do that.

2UE rang right on 8 am, as arranged. 'Good morning, Detective Seymour,' the announcer began.

'Good morning,' I replied.

'Can we start by asking you where you're at with the search for Cassandra Lewis?'

'We have had the Police Air Unit, the Mounted Police and the Dog Squad scouring every inch of bush and parkland in the vicinity.'

'Have you had any luck yet?'

'Not as yet.'

'Do you think that there are any prospects of finding Cassandra alive?'

'At this stage we're not giving up hope of finding her alive. We've had a few reported sightings of her, but nothing positive yet. We would urge any member of the public with even the smallest piece of information to contact St Marys police station or Crimestoppers.'

They asked me a few more questions, and then thanked me for my time. After I hung up, something inside me said that we needed to have another look at the pool. I got on the radio and told the uniformed guys that I wanted them to start from the beginning again, and in particular to have another look at the pool. About half an hour later, the phone rang. 'Detective Seymour?'

'Yes.'

'We checked the pool again.'

'And?'

'We found her.'

'What? Where was she?'

'Her body was in the middle of the pool.'

'What do you mean? We checked the pool thoroughly yesterday.'

'Yeah, it's a strange shape. The deep part is actually in the centre of the pool, rather than at one end, so every time we scooped it, the movement of the water must have moved her, and then she would roll back into the hollow.'

'Fucking hell! Thanks for letting me know,' I said. I put the phone down, rested my elbows on my knees and buried my head in my hands. I should have known she was in the pool. I should have drained it straightaway and not waited. Had I done that, I could have saved the family so much heartache. I'd given them hope when there was none. Indeed, I'd given all the police, the volunteers and the neighbours who'd joined in the search hope when there was none. I took my hands from my face and slapped my thighs. I had to see this through to the end. The best I could do now was give the family the chance to mourn.

I grabbed a set of car keys, headed downstairs, jumped into the car and headed towards Robert and Cecilia Lewis's house. The closer I got to their house, the more I could feel the tears beginning to well up, but I forced them back down. When I pulled up, it was like something out of a disaster movie. There were police cars up and down each side of the street, and the police command van was parked outside the house. The front yard, and those of the adjacent properties, were jam-packed with media crews. In between all of that, the neighbours were comforting one another as best they could. As I walked towards the house, I passed dozens of police officers, and as I looked at each one of them, I could see from their faces and body language that they were shattered. It also became painfully apparent that every pair of eyes was firmly fixed on me.

When I reached the house, I made my way inside, and finding the house empty, I continued on out into the backyard, where I was confronted by a scene that I will never forget. Mr and Mrs Lewis were sitting on the steps at the back of their house surrounded by various friends and relatives. Mr Lewis had his right arm wrapped around his wife, who was sobbing uncontrollably. 'Hello, Pete,' a uniformed officer said quietly. 'Let me show you where she is.'

I didn't even get to the pool gate before I saw her. Cassandra was still lying face-down in the pool, now in the shallows, her long, blonde hair swaying gently in the water. I wanted to leap into the pool, wrap her up in my arms and take her away, but I had to leave the body where it lay, because until the Forensic Pathologist told us otherwise, this was still considered a crime scene. 'Is the Forensic Pathologist on the way? Is the Video Unit here?' I said.

'They're both on their way,' the uniformed officer replied.

'Good. We need to get this over with as quickly as possible. It's taking a heavy toll on everyone.'

The Forensic Pathologist and the Video Unit turned up shortly afterwards. The Video Unit guys filmed everything as Cassandra's body was retrieved from the pool and the Forensic Pathologist began to conduct his initial examination. When they rolled the body over after removing it from the pool, Cassandra's face suddenly became Tayla's, and I had to momentarily turn my head to one side as I tried to compose myself. Knowing that that little girl had lain in that pool for two days haunts me to this day, in fact I don't think any of the officers who were involved in the search will ever forget it.

It was left to me, due to my experience at the Coroner's Court, to explain to the parents what would happen next. I sat them down at the table on the patio at the back of the house. They were very quiet, yet plainly shattered. 'Mr and Mrs Lewis,' I began, 'we're going to have to take your daughter to the Westmead Mortuary.'

'How long will it be before we can get her back so we can bury her?' Mr Lewis asked.

I lowered my head and rubbed my eyes before I looked back at them. 'First, I need you to formally identify your daughter's body for me. I will then make my report to the Coroner. Once that has been done, they will conduct a post-mortem to determine the exact cause of death. Only then will they release the body and you can begin to make funeral arrangements.'

Saying the word 'funeral' was one of the worst things I ever had to do, because I could see that the finality of it all had hit home. I finished explaining the process, and then gently took each of their hands in turn and said, 'I am so sorry for your loss.'

The media pressure was intense over the next day or so, and I spent most of my time fielding questions from TV and radio stations and newspapers.

That afternoon, I went home and did my best to shut it out of my mind. Sue asked me about it, and I told her everything, but when it came to my girls, I only told them what I had to. Throughout dinner, I couldn't stop thinking about Cassandra lying face-down in the pool. Several times I felt like bursting into tears, but I restrained myself and managed to finish my meal. Later, when I went upstairs and had a shower, I let the tears flow freely.

I think the reason I managed to hold out that long was because I knew that the water from the shower would wash away my tears. Over the next couple of days, I would often cry, but only in the shower. I never wanted my girls to see my tears, nor did I want them to know I wasn't coping.

Once all the formalities were completed, I had to do one of the hardest things I have ever had to do; I had to give the major debriefing at Penrith. Everyone who'd been involved in the case was there; the police officers, the SES volunteers, the neighbours, the ambos, everyone, even Mr and Mrs Lewis. As I stood at the front of the room and prepared to begin, I looked out at their faces and it was clear that not a single one of them had a dry eye, indeed some of them were sobbing openly. I felt like shit.

I should have drained the pool. I should have spared them this trauma. We, particularly me, were all highly trained in this kind of thing, and I should have known better. I scanned all the faces again, and started to speak, but nothing came out as I choked back my own tears. I took a moment to compose myself before I tried again.

'I would like to start by thanking everyone here for their efforts. If we can take anything away from this investigation, it should be that we should always learn from what we have done. If any of you ever find yourselves in a similar situation again, we will always remember to drain pools if possible, rather than make assumptions, especially if we cannot see the bottom. I will finish by saying that this is one of the most difficult things most of you will ever have to do, and to say that you have all done your duty admirably would only lessen the true value of what you have all done. It is with the most sincere and heartfelt gratitude that I thank you all.'

When I was done, Mr and Mrs Lewis came up to me, took me to one side, and asked if Mr Lewis could say a few words. They bravely stood up at the front of the room, and even before they'd started, anyone who hadn't been crying earlier was now.

'I'd like to thank each and every one of you in this room for what you have done for us,' Mr Lewis began. 'Yes, this has been the hardest thing we will ever have to face, but you have all been so supportive and wonderful. Cassandra was a beautiful little soul, and even though she is gone, her spirit will always stay with all of us.' He then sat down and comforted his wife. I looked around the room and saw that everybody had their heads bowed.

Several moments of silence passed before I stood and thanked everyone. As everyone filed out of the room, Mr and Mrs Lewis came over to me. 'Thank you for everything you have done for us, Detective. It really means a lot,' Mr Lewis said.

I didn't really know what to say, so I simply told them about the counselling services that were available and gave them my card in case they needed to contact me. I don't know if any of it really helped them, indeed I think it was probably more for my benefit than anything else. I shook their hands, gave Mrs Lewis a prolonged hug and thanked them both for coming in.

As I watched them walk out of the station, I thought about Tayla's pool accident, and began to wonder how they hell they were going to deal with all of this. I tried to put myself in their shoes. If it had been Tayla, what would I have done? I didn't know, and I didn't want to know. All I knew was that I never wanted to experience that kind of situation ever again.

Chapter 17:
A Tremendous Mentor

Cassandra's death shocked me to the core, and I wanted nothing more than for the Hanes murder investigation to come to an end so that I could hopefully go back to a quiet life as a policeman. We had one down, but there was one to go.

One afternoon, I received a call informing me that Mahia had made another application for bail to the Supreme Court after having spent fifty-four days in custody, and this time he had been granted conditional bail. That didn't exactly fill me with confidence that we would get the conviction we were so desperately seeking. I put the phone down, shut my eyes and let out a deep breath, before picking up the phone again and calling Bel Hanes. 'Hi, Bel, it's Peter Seymour here. How are you?'

'Living day to day,' she said, somewhat solemnly.

'Listen, I hate to be the bearer of bad news, but I just got word that Mahia has been granted bail in the Supreme Court. He's been released, but it's only until he faces trial, and hopefully he'll be found guilty and go straight back to jail. All we can do is let the process take its course.'

'He will be found guilty,' Bel said resolutely. 'I have a feeling.'

Mahia's trial eventually commenced in the Supreme Court in King Street, Sydney on 3 September 2001 in front of Justice Taylor. I'd been having my doubts about how we'd go, but a few weeks before the trial, Bryan Royce rang me at the Ds office. 'Hey, Pete, how are you this morning, mate?' he said.

'Not too bad. Yourself?'

'Yeah, good. Listen, I thought you might want to know that your brief was commended by the Crown Prosecutor who initially reviewed it.'

'Wow, that's good to know. Mate, listen, there's something that's been bothering me for some time. I showed the CCTV footage to Jack Dupont, who was one of the two young fellas who witnessed the murder. Consensus was that by showing him the footage of the offenders, I may have burned him as a witness. Do you know if we'll still be able to use him in court?'

'Yes, mate, there's no problem there. So, I've given you one piece of good news, but I have another one for you.'

'Yeah, what's that?'

'The brief was given to the second most senior Crown Prosecutor in New South Wales, Mr Barry Newport QC, who'll be prosecuting. I've had a briefing with him, and he actually commented on the two boys, and said there's no problem with the identification process. In fact, he even said that you made the right call as far as that's concerned.'

'You're shittin' me! Well, it's good to know that we can get Jack's evidence in. That's also great news about the Crown. How come we got someone so senior to do it?'

'Luck of the draw, mate. Pete, you have no idea how lucky we are to have Barry Newport prosecuting,' Bryan said.

'If you rate him, Bryan, that's good enough for me. I'll see you in court.' And so I did, on 3 September 2001. It was a special day, not only because I felt confident we were going to get justice for the Hanes family, but also because there was another special person who would be present in court that morning to watch the trial unfold; my dad. I was so proud to have him there.

Dad had retired as a director at Johnnie Walker Scotch in Sydney, but throughout his career he'd always taken an interest in my police work, and apart from Susie, he was probably my number one supporter when times were at their toughest. I think Dad's keen interest in my work stemmed from the fact that he'd associated with a lot of cops over the years, and a couple of his close mates were coppers too. Dad had often asked me how I collected evidence, or general questions about particular jobs I'd been on. If he saw something on the news, he'd ring me up and ask questions about how the cops might do things. For example, he might have heard about a drug bust, and he would ask me what happened when we did jobs like that, whereupon I'd tell him about my experiences, as well as a few other war stories.

I was so happy that both my parents were genuinely interested in what I did. I was really close to Mum, but I'd only tell her about the good things that happened, because I knew the bad things would only upset her, and I never wanted her to worry. Dad was a different story. I could tell him anything, and he always had a way of making me feel good about myself and the job I was doing. Dad was from the bush, a real old-school Aussie who respected others and was, in turn, deeply respected himself.

When we were kids, Dad used to take us up to our uncle and aunt's farm at Gloucester, and he'd teach us how to shoot, using shotguns, .303 rifles and the normal .22 rifles. We'd go swimming in the Barrington River, milk the cows, work on the farm and generally live the good country life. I also played soccer as a little kid, and because we didn't have a car, Dad would walk me to our home ground, and then if we were playing away, I'd get a lift from there. Dad always watched our home games, and sometimes Mum and my grandparents would come and watch too. I was always so proud to have Dad and Mum come and watch me play, and it really set the seal on the deep bond I had with my father. He always called a spade a spade, and was always straight down the middle with his three boys. He'd been a tremendous mentor to all of us, and the fact that he'd made the effort to come all the way down to Sydney just to sit in court and listen was so heart-warming.

Having Dad in court convinced me that we were going to get the right result, and as everyone filed into the courtroom and sat down, I took a brief glance around at Dad. He smiled and nodded as Judge Taylor entered the courtroom, whereupon we all rose, and then sat down again. 'The selection of the jury will now begin,' Judge Taylor said.

The prospective jurors, who were seated at the front of the court, were called forward one by one. The Defence objected to some, who were duly dismissed, but eventually twelve jurors were selected, an even mix of men and women covering a broad age range.

Trials are strange things, I thought to myself as I looked around the court. *You take the Crown and the Defence, a mix of maybe six legal representatives and the accused. You throw in the twelve members of the jury, the bailiff, the judge and any witnesses you have, and all together, you've got more than twenty different people and different personalities taking part.*

The Crown made their opening statements, and as I watched Barry Newport, he immediately struck me as an imposing character, even though he was only about five feet eight inches tall and of medium build, with short brown hair and a neatly trimmed moustache. He wore glasses, and was a very dapper dresser. He had a quiet yet confident manner, and his presence in the court was undeniable. Everybody sat on the edge of their seats, most importantly the jury, and when he spoke, his voice and demeanour commanded absolute attention. The Defence Barrister was a guy called Ainsworth, who was a very loud, animated man. Throughout the course of the trial, he would often raise his voice and wave his arms around. I watched the jurors intently, and got the distinct impression that they were quickly becoming tired of his antics, and just wanted to concentrate on the factual evidence.

As the trial proceeded, I would have lunch with the Hanes family each day, and at the end of the day's proceedings I would take them aside outside the court and try to explain, as best I could, where we were at with the evidence, and how I thought things were going. Some days I'd catch the train back to St Marys with them and try to keep them as calm as possible, but as the trial progressed they became increasingly nervous, even though I did my best to reassure them that things were going well.

I was one of the first people to take the stand, followed by Dukesy, and the evidence that we gave was relatively brief and uncontested, certainly not the centrepiece of the trial.

Dr Little was the next witness called, and as always, she was absolutely brilliant as she outlined everything she had told me previously, and her findings from the post-mortem. She confirmed that Nick Hanes's death was a result of a combination of things; his enlarged heart, the level of intoxication and the stress he had been placed under as a result of the assault. As she spoke, I watched the jurors, and I could see they were hanging on her every word. Her testimony was so good that Ainsworth didn't even bother to cross-examine her to any great degree.

Barry Newport had done a fantastic job thus far, but his real gift as a barrister was his ability to extract absolutely everything he needed from the Crown witnesses with poise and dignity, something that came to light as soon as he called Ben Schmidt and Jack Dupont to the stand. Now I truly understood Bryan Royce's excitement when he'd learned that Barry Newport would be prosecuting.

Newport submitted the photographic evidence and the CCTV footage, and then used them to adeptly question the boys as he walked them through their evidence, which was almost identical to what they'd told us when they'd first come in to the station.

The boys came across as outstanding Crown witnesses, but I wasn't sure how they'd hold up when the Defence had their turn. Much to their credit, even though Ainsworth threw his arms around and carried on, the boys were unshakeable throughout his cross-examination. Ainsworth did his best to suggest that the boys hadn't heard his client, or his co-accused, demand the wallet, but both boys swore blindly that they had. He also suggested that there was no way they could have gotten a clear view of the incident, as they were on the other side of the road, and the fact that it was dark would have hampered their vision even further, but the boys stayed firm. They were adamant that they'd seen it clearly, because the street lights were bright. They were very impressive witnesses, and I began to feel more and more confident. Things were going exactly how we'd all hoped they would. Then came the big moment, the make or break.

All things considered, the Crown was well on top, but depending on the quality of Aaron Cooper's evidence, the whole thing could yet come toppling down. If he came across as believable and reliable, it would all but seal the Crown's case. However, if the opposite occurred, we would be right back behind the eight ball.

The Crown called Cooper to the stand, and he was brought up from the cells dressed in his prison greens. I looked over at Mahia to gauge his reaction, but his face was deadpan. He didn't even look at his so-called mate, and it seemed to me that the whole trial process might be getting to Mahia, and now, with Cooper taking the stand, he was totally shitting himself.

Cooper was escorted to the witness box by a couple of corrective services staff, but before he could commence giving his evidence, Judge Taylor made a point to the jury on how they should consider Cooper's evidence. 'The jury must remember that it is dangerous to convict a person solely on the evidence of a co-accused, because sometimes a co-accused might want to make out that the other person was more responsible for what happened, or to try to get a lesser sentence by appearing to be helping the prosecution to gain a conviction. Given that Mr Cooper is a co-accused, you must be very careful when considering his evidence.'

Once Judge Taylor was finished, Newport began to question Cooper in a calm voice. 'Mr Cooper, can you please tell us, in your own words, what happened on the night in question?' he began.

'Ricky and I had been at the RSL, and we'd had a fair few drinks. I had an argument with this girl, and so we decided to go to the Band Club instead.'

'And when you say you'd had a fair few drinks, do you remember exactly how many you had?'

'No, but it was a lot. Ricky and I were blind drunk.'

'Do you remember much of what happened after you left the RSL? Do you remember coming across Mr Hanes?'

'Vaguely. I think he threw several insults at us.'

'And do you remember much of what happened next?'

'No, I think I might have punched him a coupla' times.'

'And what was Mr Mahia doing during all of this?'

'Well, we were so drunk, we didn't even know what was going on.'

'Did you see Mr Mahia kick Mr Hanes while he was on the ground?'

'I'm not sure if he kicked him. If he did, he must have kicked him while I wasn't looking. To be honest, I wasn't really watching.'

Shit! I thought to myself. *This can't be happening!* My jaw literally dropped in disbelief. I couldn't fathom it; Cooper had turned on us! This was going to severely damage our chances of gaining a conviction. Ainsworth stood up to take his turn at questioning Cooper, and now my initial dislike for him only intensified. He was oddly calm as he paced back and forth at the bar table several times. Meanwhile, Cooper looked from Ainsworth to Mahia and then back to Ainsworth several times, and as I watched the uncertainty on his face, I began to get very nervous.

'Mr Cooper, you have just said that you weren't really watching, and yet in your Record of Interview with the police, you said that my client had participated in the assault. Which one is it? I put it to you that Mr Mahia played absolutely no part in the assault at all.'

Spurred on by Ainsworth, Cooper started to go along with it.

'To be honest I don't really remember what happened.'

'You were too drunk to remember what happened, weren't you, Mr Cooper?'

'Yes.'

'You were too drunk to know, for certain, whether my client assaulted Mr Hanes. Correct?'

'Yes.'

'Can you say for sure that Mr Mahia actually kicked Mr Hanes?'

'No, I can't say that for sure.'

I looked at Barry Newport. He was holding a pen in his hand, and when he heard this, the fingers on his right hand slowly wrapped around the pen. As Ainsworth went on, Newport's fingers gradually clenched into a fist. Newport was pissed off, as was everyone else other than the Defence, but he kept his cool, and when Ainsworth had finished and Judge Taylor asked Newport if he had anything further, he stood up and looked directly at Cooper. 'Mr Cooper,' he began, 'in your initial interview on 1 September at Mt Druitt police station, you told Detective Seymour that you were not very intoxicated at the time. Now you're telling this court that you were blind drunk?'

'I didn't want to admit to being really drunk. I thought it might make things worse for me. Pretty much most of what I said wasn't really true.'

'You lied to police?'

'I didn't want to be the only one that got blamed for everything.'

'But you've already given evidence to the contrary. You've changed your evidence.'

'Yeah, I suppose I have.'

'Can you offer the court any reason as to why you may have done this?'

'No, not really.'

'Isn't it just possible that you are changing your evidence just so you can help your friend?'

'No, that's not right at all.'

Bullshit! I thought to myself. *Someone has got to him and made him change his evidence!*

It crossed my mind that he had played us when it came to his sentencing, and had never had any intention of helping us out. It infuriated me that he had received a bloody discount on his sentence on the basis of assisting the Crown with their case against the co-accused, and now he was doing this. I was going to make bloody certain that we appealed his sentence, but first we had to get through this trial.

Formoza was the last witness to take the stand, and as I'd expected, he said the bare minimum, only telling the court what he'd told us; that Cooper had admitted his involvement, and that he'd helped them dispose of the clothing. When asked about Mahia's involvement, he kept repeating that the only thing he knew about that was what Cooper had told him, and that Mahia had never made any admissions to him.

Suddenly, getting a conviction against Mahia wasn't looking so assured. All I could hope was that the jurors would see Aaron Cooper for the discredited liar that he was, and form their own conclusions as to what had happened to Nick Hanes.

Chapter 18:
A Decade or So

The Defence only had a few witnesses they could call. First up was Mahia's girlfriend, who gave evidence as to what a nice person her boyfriend was, and finally, Mahia himself took the stand. He was adamant, with the weight of Cooper's flawed testimony to help him, that he was nothing more than a bystander who'd had no involvement whatsoever in the assault. He claimed he was too drunk to remember anything, and in particular, he didn't recall ever demanding *poor* Mr Hanes's wallet.

I couldn't believe what I was hearing! In his Record of Interview, he'd clearly stated that he wasn't there at all, and they hadn't come across Nick Hanes that night. Whether it was just wishful thinking on my part or not, it seemed like the jury weren't buying his testimony, especially when he told them that he could never do anything like this, and was just an innocent man accused of a horrendous crime. Mahia eventually stepped down, and all that was left was for the Crown and the Defence to do their summing up to the jury.

Barry Newport was the total professional, and had the jurors hanging on every word. 'The defendant's version of events,' he began, 'is convoluted, to say the least. There are numerous inconsistencies between what he said in his Record of Interview that he gave to police and what he has told you in this court. Given this, there can be little doubt that Mr Mahia is a liar, and is merely saying whatever he thinks you want to hear. Therefore, this casts suspicion on anything Mr Mahia has said to you. There is no doubt he was at the scene of this horrendous assault, as he himself has described it. His accomplice in this crime has even stated in his interview with police that Mr Mahia was not only there, but also took part in the assault, despite the fact that he has since decided to alter his testimony. You have also had two eyewitnesses testify that the assault did take place, and that Mr Mahia was present. Further, these two young men were strong and unshaken in their account of what they saw and what they heard. The last thing you must consider is the medical evidence that has been presented to you. Yes, Mr Hanes had a bad heart, but you cannot take this as the sole cause of death. The medical evidence clearly demonstrates that were it not for the fact that he was brutally assaulted, Mr Hanes may well be here with us today.'

Ainsworth stood up and, animated as ever, began his address. 'The Crown has tried to convince you that the word of the two young witnesses is beyond question, and that this is clear proof that my client was involved in this assault, but I will remind you all that Mr Hanes passed away in the early hours of the morning. It was dark, and these witnesses were on the other side of the road, and some distance away. By their own admission, they were scared, and they didn't stay around. The other person who was there that night was Mr Cooper, and he has testified that my client had absolutely nothing to do with this crime. The Crown has tried to cast doubt on my client's testimony, particularly on the variations in my client's versions of events. You must remember, however, that my client was rather scared at the time he was interviewed, and as you can imagine, felt like he was under a great amount of pressure. It is quite understandable that he might have got a few things wrong.'

I don't really remember much else of what Ainsworth said. I was too angry and too frustrated by the whole thing, so I just switched off and watched the jury to see how they were reacting. Some of them paid lip service to Ainsworth, but many of them were beginning to lose focus, and several were even looking around the courtroom. Eventually, Ainsworth finished and sat down.

Judge Taylor then gave his final directions. 'The jury is instructed that they will only consider the evidence that has been placed before them. I will warn you all, in no uncertain terms, that you must be extremely careful when considering the evidence given by Mr Cooper. It is also very important that you, the jury, carefully consider the testimony given by the defendant. It is clear that Mr Mahia's version of events that he related to police when he was first interviewed is different to the version of events he has given in this court, but you must decide whether this was simply because the defendant was under pressure at the time of the police interview or if his changing his story equates to something else.'

Judge Taylor continued on with several other legal points, and finished by saying that the case came down to a fairly simple decision; who did the jury believe? Was Mahia simply a bystander who had taken no part in the assault, as he claimed, or was he, as Cooper and the other witnesses had said, far more involved. The jury now retired to consider their verdict.

As they disappeared into the jury room, the Hanes family and I made our way outside to await the verdict. Given that some doubts had been raised and that Cooper had turned, I fully expected a long, drawn-out deliberation, but it was just one of those things; you never could tell. Sometimes juries took days, other times less than an hour. I just prayed it would be the latter.

We'd barely set foot outside the court when Bel looked up at me, her eyes again reddened and watery. 'What do you think, Pete?' she asked, her voice shaky and broken.

'Bel, I have to be honest with you, I'm just not sure. I think the Crown case was more convincing, but when Cooper changed his mind, that really put the cat amongst the pigeons. It's up to the jury now. We're in their hands.' I gave her a hug, and then she went over to be comforted by her family.

There was a lady from the Homicide Victims Support Group with them who'd been there every day, and it was clear that she'd provided great support for the family. The word 'hero' is often tossed around, and perhaps not always used in the right context, but the people from Homicide Support certainly fit that bill. Initially, I'd thought this lady was just a family member or friend, but when Bel introduced me to her, it made perfect sense.

Eventually, we got the message that the jury had reached a verdict. We filed back into the courtroom, and I took a seat with the family at the rear of the court, in the same way as I had done for Christine Strachan throughout the Keir trials. My heart was beating so fast I thought it would burst out of my chest as I watched the twelve jurors filing back into the courtroom.

Mahia stood in the dock and watched them intently. His body was rigid, the only movement some nervous twitching in his hands. Beads of sweat were beginning to form on his forehead as the jurors took their seats.

Judge Taylor turned to the jury foreman. 'Has the jury reached a decision?'

The foreman, a middle-aged male, rose to his feet, his arms held stiffly at his side. 'Yes, Your Honour, we have. We find the accused guilty.'

My head turned skywards, and I let out a deep sigh of relief. Bel turned to her daughter-in-law and embraced her. She was in tears again, but these were different tears to the ones I had seen from her previously; these were tears of pure and absolute joy.

'The jury is to be thanked for their fine service in this trial. They are dismissed,' said Judge Taylor. With that, the members of the jury stood and filed out of the courtroom.

When I recovered my senses, I realised the courtroom was abuzz. The first place I looked was to the Defence team. Ainsworth leant over and spoke to Mahia, who sat stunned in the dock. Judge Taylor then turned to the Crown and the Defence and went through the formalities. 'I would ask both the Crown and the Defence to provide a suitable sentencing date, and for the Defence to provide any documentation that you may wish to put forward.' Judge Taylor then turned to face the still stunned Mahia. 'Mr Mahia, you have been found guilty by a jury of your peers. You will be formally remanded into custody to appear again in this court for sentencing on 4 October.'

The Hanes family then stood and made their way outside, while I headed over to the Crown lawyers and feverishly shook both Bryan Royce's and Barry Newport's hands. 'Thanks for everything,' I said to them both.

'It was a pleasure, Detective Seymour,' Newport replied.

Bryan Royce smiled back at me. 'You did a great job with this investigation, Peter. Congratulations.'

'Thank you, Bryan,' I said, and then excused myself and headed outside to where I knew the Hanes family would be waiting. As I emerged from the courtroom, I saw Dad standing to the right of the exit, and walked over to him.

'Congratulations, mate,' he said as we shook hands.

'Thanks, Dad,' I replied. 'It was a tough one. I honestly had no idea which way the jury was going to go.'

Just then, Bel came over to us. 'Bel, let me introduce you to my dad.'

'Hi, nice to meet you,' Dad said politely as they shook hands warmly.

'Nice to meet you too,' Bel replied. 'Wow, I can see where you get your good looks from, Peter. You know, Mr Seymour, you have a really wonderful son here. I cannot begin to explain just how much he has done for me and my family.'

Dad smiled and looked at me. 'I sure do, but thank you for saying so. Well, mate, I'm going to head off home and leave you to look after things here. Give me a call later to let me know how things go.'

'Okay, I'll give you a call tonight, Dad.' As he turned to leave, I said, 'Dad, wait.'

He paused and turned to look at me again. 'Yes, mate?'

'Dad, it really meant a lot having you here. Thanks so much for coming.'

'No worries, bud. It was very interesting. For what it's worth, I think the jury got it right,' he said with a smile.

I watched Dad walk off towards the railway station until he turned a corner and left my sight. I remember feeling so proud that Dad had been there with me to the end of the trial, and that somehow I had shown him that I had done a good job with the case. It wasn't that I felt I had to prove anything to him, it just meant a lot that he'd seen me successful in my work. Unfortunately, Dad has since walked out of sight again, at least in the physical sense, having lost his battle with cancer in 2011, but my memories of him will never fade.

Once Dad had left, I walked over to Bel Hanes and her family who were all talking to Dukesy. I hugged her more tightly than I ever had before, and as I did, I could feel her body trembling. 'Thank you so much!' she said, her voice thick with emotion.

'It was my pleasure,' I replied. 'Now all that's left is for him to be sentenced on 4 October.'

Her voice immediately lost its shakiness and took on a tone of determination and resolve. 'We'll be here for that!' she replied.

I explained the sentencing process to the family, and then they all headed off, eager to make their way home. Dukesy and I watched them until they were out of sight. 'Fancy a beer to celebrate?' Dukesy said.

'Reckon that's a great idea, mate.' We walked to the nearest pub, where we enjoyed a few well-earned beers and discussed everything that had happened before we headed back to St Marys to join in the celebrations with the rest of the crew.

On 4 October 2001, we all returned to the Supreme Court for Mahia's sentencing. All the same people that had been there for the trial were present once again. Judge Taylor walked into the courtroom, sat down at the judge's bench and began. 'The defendant is still quite young, at twenty-three years of age. In considering your sentencing, I have taken into account the fact that you have no criminal history, and you do not appear to have a social history of violence. You come from a stable family situation, but what is of most concern is the psychological report, which indicates that you have a drinking problem. In that report, the psychologist concluded that the defendant would, under the influence of alcohol, be more disinhibited and likely to act more impulsively. Having taken all things into consideration, I sentence you to six years imprisonment with a non-parole period of four years. Given that the defendant has already served fifty-four days in custody, his sentence is to be backdated to 13 July 2001, to conclude on 12 July 2005, when he will be eligible for parole.'

Mahia was then led from the court, and we all shook hands and hugged and congratulated each other. 'Fancy a coffee?' I said to Bel when we got outside and things had calmed down.

'Yes, that would be lovely,' she said, so we headed to a nearby café, where I bought two coffees and we sat down at an outside table.

'Well, at least that's all over,' I said.

'Yes, true,' she said as she sipped her coffee.

'You don't sound overly pleased.'

'Pete, I am glad it's finished, but I can't help but be disappointed.'

'Disappointed about what?' I knew the answer, but I asked anyway.

'Well, taken altogether, it seems that Nick's life is only worth a decade or so.'

'At least we got the result we were after,' I said, trying to sound as reassuring as I could.

'Yeah, I guess.'

We finished our coffees, and I spent the train trip back to St Marys listening to Bel reminisce about Nick's life.

I'd finally done it. I'd obtained justice for the family, and now it was time to return to some form of normality. It was time to return to my family. I'd sacrificed their welfare for the sake of another investigation, just like I'd done throughout the Keir case, and I didn't want to do it anymore. I couldn't believe that, bookending my time in the Prosecutors, I had been involved in two huge murder cases and, best of all, I'd managed to gain justice for both families involved.

The next day at work, Mick and I shared a coffee and discussed the sentencing. 'Are you glad it's all over?' Mick asked.

'Mick, next time I open my big mouth and say I need another murder investigation, tell me to shut up!'

'No worries there, mate!' Mick laughed.

St Marys is one of those places where everyone knows everyone else, and word of the convictions and sentencing soon got around the community. A few days after the verdict, I received a phone call late in the afternoon. 'Detective Seymour?' a voice said.

'Yes.'

'It's Wazza here, mate.'

'G'day, Wazza, so I take it you've heard the news?'

'Yeah, glad to know you got both those bastards.'

'Thanks, mate. I'm just happy we got the right result for the family.'

'I don't normally say this to a copper, but Pete, you're a bloody diamond, mate.'

'Thanks, Wazza, that means a lot.'

'Listen, are you busy this arvo?'

'No, mate, I was just about to head home actually.'

'Do you reckon you might want to come down to the Parkview Hotel and have a beer to celebrate?'

'You know what, Wazza, I reckon I just might.'

'Great, mate, see you in a bit then.'

I rang Susie and organised for her to pick me up later, then finished up for the day and headed down to the hotel, arriving at about 5 pm. I walked inside and found Wazza already standing at the bar with a beer in his hand. He spotted me straight away. 'Hey, boys!' he called out, loud enough so that the whole pub could hear, 'here's the detective who locked up those two bastards who killed our mate!'

I glanced around the pub and saw about a dozen blokes converging on me. They were a pretty rough bunch, labourers and tradies mostly, some of whom looked like they'd been on the wrong side of the law on more than a few occasions, certainly not the type of blokes who would normally drink with a copper. *Shit*, I thought to myself, *maybe it wasn't such a good idea to come down here for a drink after all!* Too late. I was committed now, so I did the only thing I could that might protect me, and that was to walk straight over to Wazza. 'G'day, mate,' I said uneasily.

'Glad you made it down here, Detective Seymour!' he said with a huge smile on his face. 'What do you want to drink? It's my shout.'

'Thanks, mate, I'll have a Tooheys New,' I replied, just happy to be viewed as a friend amongst the boys in the pub, as I sure wouldn't want to be their enemy.

Wazza bought me a schooner and handed it to me. 'To Nick,' he said as he raised his glass.

'To Nick,' I echoed, and sipped on my beer while Wazza reminisced about the times he'd spent with Nick. He was midway through his story when a particularly large Islander bloke came up to the bar and looked me squarely in the eye. *Shit, this bloke might be one of Mahia's relos*, I thought to myself as I prepared myself for what might be coming.

He skulled his beer and slammed the glass down on the bar. *Here it comes*, I thought. He suddenly extended his humungous right hand, wrapped it around mine and started shaking it furiously. 'Nick was my friend. Thank you, bro!' he said, and then slapped me on the back and turned and walked away.

I turned to Wazza. 'Nick sure did have a lot of mates around here,' I said. 'It doesn't really surprise me, from what I learned about him during the investigation.'

'Yeah, but tell me something,' Wazza said. 'How did you end up catching those two pricks?'

'It wasn't a one-person job, mate. I had a good team of cops working with me. If I hadn't had such a good team, I doubt we would have got the result we wanted. You know what though.'

'Yeah, what's that?' Wazza asked.

'I probably would have got this done a lot quicker if you hadn't of given me a bum steer!'

'Whaddya mean, a "bum steer"?'

'Your info about Smith, it turned out to be a complete waste of time!'

'Hey, I was just tryin' to help, besides, gotta keep you on your toes, Detective!'

We both had a good laugh before Wazza finished another beer and said, 'Well, mate, the main thing is you caught them, and to all these blokes here at the pub, you're a bloody legend!'

I wasn't allowed to buy a beer that afternoon, in fact there were always at least two beers sitting on the bar waiting for me, as every one of Nick's mates were desperate to buy me one. It was about 8 pm before we finished up and I was able to call Susie to come and get me. 'Had a good night,' she laughed as I got into the car, my legs a little unsteady beneath me.

'Yeah,' I replied as I looked into the back seat to see our three girls, all in their dressing gowns and all looking up at me with their puppy-dog eyes.

'Have you been drinking too much beer?' Jenna finally said.

Bloody hell! I thought as I pondered the best way to respond. 'Oh, Daddy's just had a couple of beers with some friends, sweetheart,' I said.

'I really didn't have that many,' I said to Susie. 'Mind you, I didn't have to pay for any of them, because I wasn't allowed too.'

'Oh, well,' she said, 'it just goes to show how much they appreciated the job you did. You should be proud of that.'

'Yeah, I guess,' I replied as we headed home.

Even though I'd had a few beers, I still couldn't help thinking that this was it; my job was done. I'd set myself a goal, to obtain justice for the Hanes family, and now I'd achieved it. I'd returned to the detectives because I wanted to spice things up again, and I'd barely been back a few weeks before I'd been thrust back into an intense investigation. I wasn't sure I could do it again. I knew deep down that should there be another murder, I would do the same as I had on the last two; sacrifice my own family's happiness while I strove to gain justice for someone else's.

As we drove home, I looked at Sue, and then at my girls, and thought to myself, *No, I'm not going to do it to them anymore.* I'd gotten into the cops to make a difference, and I would have to be satisfied with what I'd done. I may not have climbed to the top, I may not have solved every case I'd ever worked on, or even gotten the right result every time, but I had done the best I could. I had given all of myself to every investigation I'd ever been involved with, often to the detriment of my family. The time had come to focus on the one place where I could make a massive difference; at home with my girls. I would be there for them no matter what. I would guide them as best I could, and make sure they grew up to be happy and healthy. It was time to commit myself wholeheartedly to something again. It was time to be a daddy.

Epilogue

Even though my priorities had changed I was still a cop, and late in 2001 I was called to a fatal accident on the M4 motorway in western Sydney. Four young students, two boys and two girls, had been heading out to their lectures at the University of Western Sydney Nepean campus. They were sitting in heavy traffic and the driver was getting impatient, but he couldn't go anywhere because there was a cop car sitting in the traffic with them. The copper eventually turned off at Wallgrove Road, and the young fellow gunned it into the breakdown lane, however he failed to notice a truck stopped in the breakdown lane up ahead. He was pushing 120 km/h, and when he finally saw the truck, he tried to scoot back into the normal lanes, but he didn't make it.

They'd ploughed into the truck, and the left-hand front of the car had gone under the right-hand rear side of truck, peeling the roof off as though someone had opened a can. The male driver and the other young man in the front passenger seat had seen what was about to happen and had enough time to duck, as had the girl sitting in the back seat behind the driver, but the other girl hadn't been so lucky.

She'd been instantly decapitated, and the rest of her body all but ripped to shreds.

I was relieving as the Duty Officer Inspector at St Marys at the time, and was out with Glash doing an inspection of a small station prior to deciding whether it should stay open or not. Glash and I duly arrived at the scene to find the poor girl's body parts spread across the three lanes of the M4, as well as the breakdown lanes on either side. 'You're a bloody shit-magnet, Seymour!' Glash said as he surveyed the carnage. 'I am never going out in the car with you again.'

'I think you might be right, mate,' I said as I circled the scene, trying to take everything in. 'I reckon it's gonna be one of those days.'

I'd never given much thought to how having to attend scenes like that affected me. I'd been to dozens before, and I'd always tried to push it to the back of my mind, forget about it and move on. Throughout my career, coppers had never received much help when it came to the mental side of things. We were all expected to just toughen up and take it on the chin. There was a culture whereby the only unloading you did was through having a chat with your mates over a few beers. It wasn't just the police force, though. I don't think people really knew about psychological damage back then. However, by 2001, a lot more research had been done, and people had started to realise that seeing such horrendous things did have an effect on your everyday copper, and counselling sessions and psychological debriefings were always strongly recommended.

Given the prevailing culture in the force, these debriefings were often considered a necessary evil, rather than something that might actually help you. After this particular incident, it was suggested that I should do a debrief with the psychologist, Mark Basedow, who was an ex-cop I had worked with at the On The Job Training Unit in 1988. I don't think Mark had seen the kind of stuff that I'd seen in my time in the cops, but nevertheless he'd decided that being in the cops was not for him, and that psychology was his thing. Because he'd been a cop himself, I think any copper who went and saw him trusted him more than they normally would, because his counselling sessions often incorporated discussions about things the average copper was familiar with. At least he had first-hand experience and knowledge of what cops went through.

When you sat down with him, he would discuss what had happened, ask you how you felt about it, and how you were coping. Whenever I went to him, he would let me do most of the talking, getting me to answer my own questions so that I was actively dealing with my issues rather than waiting for him to give me some kind of magical solution. He would ask me how I was coping, or more to the point, whether I was actually coping. After the pool incident, and again after the M4 fatal, he contacted me privately and said, 'Mate, what the hell are you still doing in that job after all these years? Perhaps it's time to give it away. Come and see me for a chat.'

'Nah, I'm okay, mate, but thanks for the offer,' I said, still thinking I could deal with everything on my own. I had now been involved in two huge murder investigations and I'd been commended for my work on both occasions. Given that, I reminded myself why I had gone back to the Ds, and that was to get promoted in order to make more money for the benefit of my family, so I decided to apply for promotion.

I was duly successful, and was elevated to the rank of Senior Sergeant in charge of the Crime Management Unit at Green Valley Police Station in the south-western suburbs of Sydney. For most people, a promotion would have been just the shot in the arm needed to get your career started again, but as soon as I got promoted, my world started to cave in around me.

To be honest, I believed in myself, and was confident that I was the right candidate for the job, and I sailed through the interview due to my ability to answer questions based on my time in the Prosecutors. What I hadn't considered was that with promotion came more stress. I was now the Crime Coordinator, which meant that I didn't go out on investigations anymore, but allocated jobs to the cops out in the field. A lot fell on me, not just in relation to one investigation, but for all of them, and I often liaised with the Detective Senior Sergeant about the various investigations that were in progress.

I soon began to question everything I was doing. Whenever a new job came in, I would think long and hard about who to put on the case. Was I giving this job to someone who could handle it, or was I setting them up for failure?

One of my jobs was to coordinate various operations such as surveillance. One particular job involved some suspected robbers whose *modus operandi* was to loiter around the local shopping centre car park and wait for women to go to their cars. When they did, these guys would assault and then rob them.

I decided we should set a trap for them using a policewoman as a decoy. I called in PolAir, and told them to hover nearby, but not so close as to spook our targets. I also arranged for the Dog Squad to position themselves near the shopping centre, as well as sending undercover operatives into the centre itself to keep an eye on the policewoman, just in case she got into trouble and needed assistance. There was a lot of pressure involved in ensuring her safety to start with, and in choosing the right policewoman for the job. If anything went wrong and she got hurt, it would fall on my head. We set the plan in motion, and there was one guy who came out into the car park and looked promising, but despite having mounted a huge operation, nothing came of it.

Putting a colleague in potential danger like that was something I'd never had to deal with before, and it didn't sit well with me, in fact I was deeply troubled by it. Throughout the entire operation, I couldn't shake the feeling that I might have signed someone's death warrant. That was when I started to realise that maybe I wasn't right in the head.

Every morning, during the drive to work, I would approach the set of traffic lights where I would make a right-hand turn and head towards the station, and every morning I would contemplate whether I should just keep on driving straight ahead and never return to work again. I always made that right-hand turn, but I desperately wanted to be anywhere other than at work, and with every passing day the desire to just keep on driving intensified.

At home, I got worse. The slightest thing would make me snap, and whenever it happened, I would be painfully aware of what was happening and how I was reacting. I honestly don't know how Susie put up with me, and sometimes I wonder how it is that we're still married.

In addition to my psychological issues, I started to experience severe chest pains, so I took myself off to my local doctor, who checked me out and told me he believed it was stress related. 'Any chest pain is a warning sign,' he said. 'Do you have any very stressful things going on in your life at the moment?'

'Doc, everything at home is okay, apart from me snapping at my kids and wife a bit more.'

'And what about work?'

I paused and looked down for several moments before I looked back up at him. 'In all honesty, Doc, work is really starting to get to me. I don't feel like I want to go back.'

'I think it's best you take a few days off, and see how you go,' he said.

'Nah, Doc, she'll be right,' I said, and got up and left.

As I drove home, I knew I was struggling, and I remembered Mark's offer to come and talk to him. At work the next day, I was sitting in my office when my hand instinctively made its way towards my back pocket. I pulled out my wallet and flipped through all the cards until I found Mark's business card. I rang the number and left a message for Mark to ring me. He called back later that afternoon, and I made an appointment to see him for a thirty minute 'chat'.

When I walked up to his office, which was in his house in Penrith, I felt totally numb. I paused at the front entrance, then turned on my heels and walked back towards the gate, then stopped, turned around and walked back to the front entrance. Eventually, I worked up enough courage to knock. Mark answered the door a few moments later. 'Hey, Pete! How are you, mate?' he said with a tremendous smile. 'Great to see you. Come inside.'

I followed him inside and he led me through to his office, where I sat down in a comfortable chair and looked down into my lap, fidgeting with my hands. Meanwhile Mark moved over to his stereo system and turned on some soft music. It all felt a little freaky, but I thought, *Well, now I've come this far, I might as well go through with it and see how we go.*

'So, Pete, how have you been feeling over the last couple of months?' Mark said.

Normally, my defence mechanisms would have come straight out and said, 'All good, mate,' but I knew I wasn't right, so I decided to be truthful. 'Mark, I've been struggling.'

'What exactly have you been struggling with?' he said.

'Well, I dread getting up and going to work, and when I get home, I'm angry with my wife and kids. I've been replaying cases I've worked on over and over again in my mind, and I've also been having a lot of nightmares. I'm waking up at around 3 am nearly every morning. It's like a switch goes off in my head.'

'Pete, do you think you could tell me about some of the cases that you've worked on?' Mark said.

I told him about all the scenes involving fatalities that I had visited, as well as the foiled bank robbery at Marrickville and the knife-wielding robber.

'And why do you think these incidents made you feel the way they did?'

I didn't even ponder my answer, but just came straight out with, 'Because if I was killed, I don't know how my family would have been able to deal with it.' With that, I broke down and sobbed uncontrollably. Everything that I had been bottling up spilled out, and I finished by telling Mark about the chest pains.

'Pete, I think the most important thing for you right now is to look after yourself and think about the people who depend on you most, especially your wife and children. I'm recommending that you take some sick leave for the time being.'

What was supposed to have been a thirty-minute chat eventually ended two hours later. I saw Mark a few more times after that, and with each subsequent session, the realisation intensified; the end had come. I was done as a police officer. I just couldn't do it anymore. If I'd stayed in the force, there's no doubt I wouldn't be alive today.

Mark referred me to a specialist psychiatrist, and once again I went through everything I'd said during the sessions with Mark.

'Peter, what you have is Post Traumatic Stress Disorder,' the specialist finally said.

'What?' I said, somewhat confused.

'What you have is similar to what I have seen in Vietnam Vets. Think about it. They see death and destruction of all kinds, and then they have to try to go back and live a "normal" life with their families. It's not much different to what you have experienced, is it?'

'No, I guess not,' I replied.

'I'm sorry to say this, and I'm sure this must be hard for you, but I cannot allow you to return to work, due to your Post Traumatic Stress Disorder. I'm sorry, but you won't be able to work as a police officer ever again. You can't go back to work in the police force.'

I'd heard what he said, but hadn't really taken it in, certainly not the magnitude of what he was saying. The whole thing seemed surreal. All I'd ever wanted was to be a cop, and *bang*, all of a sudden it had been taken away from me. I'd never given any thought to what I would do with my life outside of the cops. He also put me on antidepressants, but they made me feel even worse, so I eventually took myself off them.

Everything else that happened around that time is still a blur. Someone phoned Green Valley Command and told them that I was not well. Over the next few weeks, all my mates from the cops visited me regularly, or at least phoned to check how I was.

A mate of mine, John McGee, who I'd worked with for many years and who was now the Detective Senior Sergeant in charge of Green Valley Detectives, came out to see me one day, along with Sergeant Gary Phillpot, who was my Intelligence Officer at Green Valley. 'How are you travelling, Pete?' John asked as he sipped on his cuppa.

I paused for a moment before I looked up at him and said, 'John, to be honest, I'm fucking finished!'

John just nodded, as though what I'd just told him was nothing out of the ordinary. 'Don't worry about it, mate. We'll take care of everything.'

It wasn't like I was in the cops one day and out the next. It took more than twelve months before I was eventually discharged, but that year was the loneliest of my life. I revelled in the times when my girls were home, but Susie would go off to work and the kids would go off to school and I would be left in a big, empty house with nothing else to do but think. At first, I would simply sit on the lounge at home and stare into space, begging and pleading for the pain to stop, wondering if and when I was going to feel like my old self again.

When I'd had enough of sitting on the couch, I'd wander around the house, and then all of a sudden I would break down for no apparent reason. Then I'd go and look at our family photos of me and Susie and the girls, and it would remind me that I had something very special to live for. As I gazed upon their beautiful faces, I would wipe the tears away and tell myself I was being a bloody idiot, and to get over it.

I couldn't figure out what I wanted to do or what my new form of employment should be, so I immersed myself in activities at the kids' school, like volunteering to help out with fundraising for walkathons and doing my bit at sports days. I drove the girls to school in the morning and picked them up in the afternoon, but in between that, I had to make sure I kept myself busy, otherwise I would have gone insane. Throughout this difficult time, Susie and the girls were brilliant. They knew I was struggling, but they just kept the hugs and smiles coming. I was eventually discharged from the NSW Police Force on 6 February 2004 on the grounds of being medically unfit.

A couple of weeks after I'd finally been discharged, Mick Lyons put on a do at the Penrith RSL for me, nothing much, just dinner and a few beers. People like Muzza, Clarkey and a few other guys I'd worked with at St Marys were there.

I got up and made a brief speech, and when the other guys spoke, they talked about how hard the job was, and told me that I should enjoy the next part of my life, that I should be happy that I had made a difference to people's lives and that I deserved my break.

Mick Lyons then got up and presented me with a framed certificate signed by the Police Commissioner, Ken Moroney, for my twenty-four years of service in the NSW Police Force. When I took the certificate from him, I wasn't sure how to feel. I was proud of what I had done, I was pleased I had helped as many people as I possibly could, and I felt comfortable that I had done everything to the best of my ability, but this was all I had ever known, and I was apprehensive about what the next chapters of my life held.

However, I knew I was one of the lucky ones. I had good people around me giving me the support I needed, and I'd been fortunate enough to realise that I needed help, and to then go and seek it out. The moment when I realised I had made the right decision was when I was out playing golf with my social club one day.

Back in 1996, I'd had an idea to start the club to raise money for the girls' physical culture club at St Clair. In the beginning, I'd asked a couple of mates around to have a chat about it, and the NAGA social golf club had been formed. NAGA stood for Not A Golfer's Arsehole, but our wives thought it meant the Nepean Amateur Golf Association!

We played once a month on a Sunday morning at various golf courses, mainly in the western suburbs of Sydney, and once a year we would have a trip away to a golf course in the country. We'd take our wives with us and stay in a motel adjacent to the golf club so we could have a few beers and a meal without having to worry about driving. The next day, the blokes would head off for a hit, while the wives would go shopping at the local markets or craft fairs. When we were done, we'd all meet up for lunch and then head home.

Looking back, I think it was golf that kept my head together. I was missing the sense of camaraderie that came with the cops, and I think golf filled the void. Additionally, I loved that we were helping others out, because our golf days would raise almost $600 each year for the kids' Physie. Nearly seventeen years have passed since that initial chat, and NAGA is still going strong.

One Sunday in 2004, I headed out early in the morning feeling pretty good about myself. Life had changed for the better. I was starting to come to terms with what had happened, the chest pains had disappeared and my nightmares were becoming less frequent.

Sometimes I would still wake up in the middle of the night, but I now found it easier to get back to sleep. I was standing near the first tee, handing out the scorecards to all the guys, when one of my best mates in the club, John Dallis, came up to me, looked me in the eye, and with a huge smile said, 'Glad to have you back, mate,' and shook my hand.

I shot him a strange look. 'What are you talking about, mate? I haven't been anywhere. I've played every game this year.'

'Pete, what I mean is that you're finally back to the bloke you used to be, to the Pete we all know and love. You haven't been the same for the last eighteen months, and some of the boys were a bit worried about you. Looks like everything is starting to sort itself out for you now.'

'Yeah, JD,' I replied. 'Things are going well. Thanks mate.'

When my discharge finally came through, I thought it would be a good idea for the family to go on a holiday to help us reconnect and put all the bad times behind us, so I decided to use my long-service money to take Susie and the girls to America. We flew to Los Angeles, where we went to Disneyland and Universal Studios, then spent a day at the Grand Canyon before travelling on to Las Vegas, where we stayed at the Luxor Hotel. After all the emotional upheaval I had experienced over the previous couple of years, this was one of the best times of my life, and the kids had a ball. It was the holiday of a lifetime, but it was more than that for me. It was a time to really get myself together, and realise how lucky I was to have come through some of the darkest moments anyone could experience in their life.

I'd be lying if I said I'd never thought about doing myself in. There were times, the blackest of them, when I felt completely and totally hopeless. Those times when I was in the house on my own, I often wondered what it would be like if I just left it all behind and didn't have to deal with life anymore. How could I even have contemplated doing that to my wife and kids? After all, if it wasn't for them, I wouldn't be here today, and I certainly wouldn't be the man I am.

Afterword

Pete is my life, my world. When I first met him, I was completely taken. I knew he was a cop, but all the baggage that came with that never really occurred to me. As time went on, being married to a cop was like being part of a large family in which you knew someone always had your back.

I think the time when this was most apparent was when Tayla had her accident in the motel pool. We'd returned home after her hospital stay, and one morning I made myself a cuppa and went outside to sit on the bench on the front veranda. I was sitting there thinking about how lucky we had been when a paddy wagon pulled up. Out stepped two female officers with a giant teddy, which to this day Tayla still won't part with. It was a small gesture, but it made me realise that we were part of a family, and at that moment, it felt like Pete and I really mattered, as though no matter what happened, we always had someone who would look after us.

There were so many nights when Pete was out late, and I always worried that he wouldn't be coming home. I used to lie in bed when he was on night shift, or working late on an investigation, and envisage terrible things happening to him. I used to picture his police funeral, and the Australian flag draped over his coffin. Sometimes I'd pretend to be angry at him when he finally came home, but mostly, it was all just for show. The reality was, I was just glad to have him home.

Pete was an honest, loyal cop who genuinely cared for people. He would have endless sleepless nights when he would toss and turn, or wake suddenly after having one of his many nightmares. This was probably the hardest thing to have to deal with as his wife. I never knew what to do. I desperately wanted to help him, to fix it all, to make it all better, but I didn't know what I could do for him apart from just being there. Paul Garland, a very close friend of ours, once said to me, 'You know, Sue, I can always tell when Pete has had a rough day or has dealt with a tragedy involving kids.'

'What do you mean, Paul?' I asked.

'Well, whenever Pete is involved with something like that, he's always very quiet. You can tell by looking at him that he's trying to deal with things himself, and doesn't want to talk about it.' That was the main thing I had to learn as a cop's wife; knowing when to say something, and when to remain silent and simply let Pete be.

There were many times when I felt utterly alone, especially as a young bride. I went to so many parties on my own, and I was lucky I had a good friend, Dimi, who would accompany me whenever Pete was on a shift. When he was on night shift, I hardly slept, and to have him in my arms when the two weeks' of night shift was over was so comforting that I would hold onto him like I was never going to let him go.

I often wished we could be like normal families and spend weekends and nights together, but Pete would often be absent for days on end during the murder investigations. When the children came along, I sometimes felt like a single parent, as Pete was often on call or working long hours. I would get a sick feeling in my stomach whenever the phone rang late at night, knowing that he would be called in to work. However, it was his passion, and what he had always wanted to do. I loved him for it, and knew that not only did he want to make a difference, he *was* making a difference to many families, just like all the other hard-working police and emergency services people.

I always reminded myself that if my family ever needed help and Pete was gone, there would be someone just like him ready to help us out at a moment's notice. Coppers are straight out good people. People like Mick Lyons, Carl Clarke, Steve Adams and Col 'Pussa' Kelson are true gems, and as a police wife, I can honestly say I am so proud of my husband, and I am sure every other woman who is married to a copper feels the same way.

End Note

Ricky Mahia's appeal was heard by the NSW Court of Criminal Appeal on 2 August 2002 and his guilty verdict was overturned on 12 December 2002. Three Appeal Court Judges determined that there was sufficient doubt as to the credibility of the evidence of Aaron Cooper and Mark Formoza, and that the decision of the jury was unsafe. Mahia was immediately released from custody. Aaron Cooper served his sentence and was subsequently released from jail.

About the Authors

Peter Seymour, joined the NSW police force in 1980 as a general duties officer before gaining the rank of Detective and then moving into the Police Prosecutor's Branch. He has worked on many investigations, including a number of high profile cases. He is the successful author of the best-selling true-crime book *Seven Bones: Two Wives. Two Violent Murders. A Fight for Justice* written in collaboration with author Jason K. Foster and published in 2011.

Jason Foster is an author with an interest in true crime and Australian history. A poet, journalist and history teacher, he holds a Masters Degree in History. He has taught in Australia, the United Kingdom, Spain and Argentina. In addition to a number of non-fiction books, he has been published in American History magazines, Australian travel magazines and poetry anthologies in the United Kingdom.

SEVEN BONES

TWO WIVES, TWO VIOLENT MURDERS, A FIGHT FOR JUSTICE...

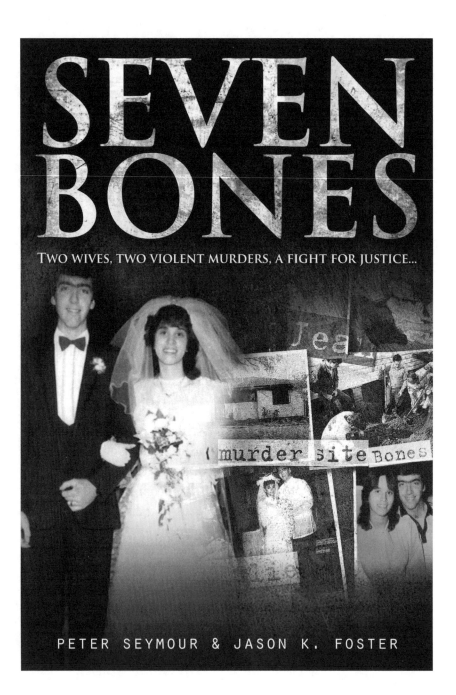

PETER SEYMOUR & JASON K. FOSTER

Seven Bones, Two wives. Two violent murders. A fight for justice...
Also by Peter Seymour with Jason K. Foster

**'We have a dead second wife and a missing first wife...
we've got a huge problem here.'**
Detective Peter Seymour

Seven Bones tells the story of one of the most bizarre murder investigations in Australia's criminal history. Two wives die in suspicious circumstances: is it just a co-incidence or, as husband Thomas Keir describes it, 'sheer bad luck'?

In April 1991, Detective Peter Seymour is called to a house in the west of Sydney where police have discovered the remains of Keir's second wife, Rosalina. She was set alight and brutally strangled. Three years earlier, Seymour had been to the same residence to investigate the sudden disappearance of Keir's first wife, Jean – who was Rosalina's cousin and alleged by Keir to have run off with a lover.

A hard-working family man and a policeman in one of the toughest and poorest parts of Sydney, Seymour thought he'd seen and done it all – but nothing could prepare him for the investigation that would unfold. The more he delves into the case, the more Keir's 'unlucky in love' story begins to unravel.

Written through Seymour's eyes, *Seven Bones* tells of his dogged quest to find answers for a family torn apart by a violent and pathologically jealous husband. It follows his relentless pursuit of justice through the dramas and revelations of the investigation and an obstacle course of trials and appeals that would take 15 years to reach a conclusion.

Available at all good bookstores, and at www.bigskypublishing.com.au

THE
DARK MAN

Australia's first serial killer

JASON K. FOSTER

The Dark Man, Australia's First Serial Killer
By Jason K. Foster

The Dark Man is the amazing true story of one of Australia's first serial killers, who kept the colony of New South Wales in the grip of fear as the police ruthlessly hunted their man.

In late 1896, three men go missing in the Blue Mountains, west of Sydney.

Each man has answered a newspaper advertisement posted by charismatic conman and notorious criminal, Frank Butler. Lured to the western goldfields by stories of the untold wealth that awaits them, the men find themselves at the mercy of the psychopathic Butler in some of Australia's most isolated and inhospitable terrain.

This compelling account of a cold and calculating killer is told in a gripping historical narrative that brings Australia's Gold Rush period vividly to life.

Available at all good book stores, and www.bigskypublishing.com.au